The Afterlife
of Adam Smith

ALSO BY WILLIAM FARINA
AND FROM MCFARLAND

*Man Writes Dog: Canine Themes
in Literature, Law and Folklore* (2014)

The German Cabaret Legacy in American Popular Music (2013)

*Eliot Asinof and the Truth of the Game:
A Critical Study of the Baseball Writings* (2012)

Chrétien de Troyes and the Dawn of Arthurian Romance (2010)

*Perpetua of Carthage:
Portrait of a Third-Century Martyr* (2009)

*Ulysses S. Grant, 1861–1864: His Rise
from Obscurity to Military Greatness* (2007)

*De Vere as Shakespeare:
An Oxfordian Reading of the Canon* (2006)

The Afterlife of Adam Smith

The Influence, Interpretation and Misinterpretation of His Economic Philosophy, 1760s–2010s

WILLIAM FARINA

McFarland & Company, Inc., Publishers
Jefferson, North Carolina

LIBRARY OF CONGRESS CATALOGUING-IN-PUBLICATION DATA

Farina, William, 1955–
 The afterlife of Adam Smith : the influence, interpretation and misinterpretation of his economic philosophy, 1760s-2010s / William Farina.
  p. cm.
 Includes bibliographical references and index.

 ISBN 978-0-7864-9484-2 (softcover : acid free paper) ∞
 ISBN 978-1-4766-2360-3 (ebook)

 1. United States—Foreign economic relations—Great Britain—History. 2. Great Britain—Foreign economic relations—United States—History. 3. United States—Economic policy. 4. Great Britain—Economic policy. 5. Smith, Adam, 1723–1790. I. Title.
 HF1456.5.G7F37 2015
 330.15'3—dc23   2015022490

BRITISH LIBRARY CATALOGUING DATA ARE AVAILABLE

© 2015 William Farina. All rights reserved

No part of this book may be reproduced or transmitted in any form or by any means, electronic or mechanical, including photocopying or recording, or by any information storage and retrieval system, without permission in writing from the publisher.

On the cover: *The Bostonian's Paying the Excise-man, or Tarring and Feathering*, mezzotint and etching attributed to Philip Dawe for R. Sayer & J. Bennett (London), Publishers, October 31, 1774 (Library of Congress)

Printed in the United States of America

McFarland & Company, Inc., Publishers
 Box 611, Jefferson, North Carolina 28640
  www.mcfarlandpub.com

To the memory of
Joseph Anthony Farina (1916–1990) and
Frances Jane Cox Farina (1923–1986)

Acknowledgments

Many thanks (yet again) to Philip and Kathleen Farina for their unending support, encouragement, and feedback. Special thanks to Young Kim (a genuine LSE graduate) for his perceptive reading and informed comments. Thanks to Chuck Egle and Joan Oullette for their continuing interest, good humor, and infectious enthusiasm. Thanks to the University of Wisconsin library staff for their cheerful and dedicated assistance. And last but not least, thanks to my better half, Marion Buckley, for being a patient listener and making many a helpful suggestion.

Table of Contents

Acknowledgments vi
Introduction 1

1. Businessmen Become Revolutionaries (1764–1777) 11
2. A New Republic Grapples with Old Issues (1778–1790) 22
3. The British Empire Makes War Against Its Offspring (1791–1815) 33
4. Almost Free Labor (1816–1837) 45
5. Might Makes Right (1838–1850) 57
6. Northern Industry Tames Southern Agriculture (1851–1865) 67
7. More Competition, More Oppression (1866–1877) 78
8. The Great American Relocation (1878–1890) 89
9. A Clumsy Foray into Colonialism (1891–1901) 100
10. Trustbuster (1901–1913) 111
11. Anglo-American Power Shift (1914–1921) 121
12. Ascendant Consumerism (1922–1928) 130
13. The Implosion of Laissez-Faire (1929–1939) 140
14. An Unprecedented Middle Class (1941–1959) 152
15. Military-Industrial Complex (1960–1975) 164
16. Tax Credit Utopia (1976–1988) 175
17. A Kinder and Gentler Corporate Mandate (1989–2000) 185
18. Post 9-11 (2001–2015) 196

Summary 206
Chapter Notes 213
Selected Bibliography 231
Index 233

Introduction

"It's a classic ... something that everybody wants to have read and nobody wants to read." —Mark Twain[1]

On March 9, 1776, less than four months before the American Declaration of Independence was signed, a lengthy two-volume treatise was published in England, sweepingly titled *An Inquiry into the Nature and Causes of the Wealth of Nations*. The author was an eccentric 52-year-old bachelor Scotsman and former professor of moral philosophy from the University of Glasgow, then living modestly as a pensioner in London. Despite unswerving loyalty to king and country, Adam Smith, like many British-sponsored intelligentsia of the time, was surprisingly sympathetic to the pressing grievances of the American colonies. Late 18th-century Anglo-American opinion was hardly uniform or monolithic in this regard; many respected voices on both sides of the Atlantic favored parliamentary representation of the colonies or, more shockingly, total separation as being in the best interests of everyone.[2] In fact, it would not be overstatement to say that those arguing for continued unity at all costs were powerful special interests, both British and American colonial, who stood to lose financially from any change in the status quo. Unfortunately for everyone involved, these same mercantile combinations held considerable sway over both British Crown and Parliament, and their short-sighted views would prevail for a little while longer until the Battle of Yorktown put a temporary stop to them. Moreover, in no sense of the word could anyone have ever described the unassuming Adam Smith as revolutionary in personal character or political opinion, although many of his then-new and often unorthodox economic ideas now come across that way in hindsight.

It should therefore not be surprising that Smith's *The Wealth of Nations* (*WN*) has since its publication found continual favor in the United States, as well as in Great Britain, whose colonial empire experienced a great resurgence in the century following the American Revolution. Economic policies of both nations were partly guided by Smith's new theories in the wake of *WN*'s publication. Likewise, *WN* has been quoted, filtered, interpreted, misrepresented, and cited for policy justification over the last three centuries wherever English-speaking capitalism has traveled, including (more crucially of late) Asia, Africa and Latin America. Smith himself would have been likely surprised by this alleged near universal acceptance of his ideas, as well as by his current status as a founding father of modern economic thought. A supremely well-educated product of the 18th-century Scottish Enlightenment, as well as a younger contemporary and friend of David Hume, Smith is best described as a complex, contradictory, oftentimes enigmatic figure espousing unconventional theories, after having maintained a long, professional academic career within a highly conservative political atmosphere.[3] While Smith was severely critical of British economic policies towards the American colonies, he nevertheless emphasized that political union between the two might be maintained (hypothetically at least) via parliamentary representation for the colonies in tandem with more realistic attitudes by the colonists in regards to shouldering a fair share of past and ongoing expenses for military protection.[4]

Touring pre-revolutionary France in the entourage of his English patrons during the 1760s, Smith was on friendly conversational terms with the leading French freethinkers of the day, including the acknowledged champion of *laissez-faire* free trade, Dr. François Quesnay. Later, instead of being detained or condemned for "the very violent attack I had made upon the whole commercial system of Great Britain" (as he himself described *WN*), Smith found himself celebrated and feted by numerous leading British intellectuals of the era.[5] Many American Founding Fathers, beginning with George Washington, owned personal copies of Smith's magnum opus, while one, Benjamin Franklin, had previously met with Smith while traveling through England. Today, in the wake of our recent Great Recession, there appears to be another wave of renewed interest in Smith's work. The debate over establishing a correct balance between private enterprise and government control seems more heated than ever, particularly as western capitalist societies confront burgeoning economic challenges from Asia. Whereas English has become (at least for the time being) the undisputed international language of commerce, Adam Smith has become the patron saint of sorts for international capitalism. In spite of this, or perhaps because of it, finding any interpretive consensus for his writings can prove to be an exercise in futility, depending on the specific time and place in Anglo-American history being examined. As John Kenneth Galbraith once observed with considerable understatement, "There were many contradictions and ambiguities in Adam Smith."[6] Recent biographer

James Buchan put it more succinctly: "Adam Smith is a much fought-over philosopher."[7]

A significant part of this interpretive problem is that *WN* had strong philosophical underpinnings stemming from Smith's earlier work, foundations in turn deeply influenced by ancient Greco-Roman ideas on morality and ethics—ideas rarely examined by contemporary students of "the dismal science."[8] For that matter, Smith seems to have considered his greatest book not *WN*, but rather his earlier, rarely read philosophical treatise from 1759, *The Theory of Moral Sentiments* (*TMS*), an elegant attempt to condense all of the world's great ethical teachings into a universal, non-denominational handbook. This was a common enough intellectual exercise during the Enlightenment, not unlike Thomas Jefferson's de–Christianized Bible from roughly the same epoch. Even a contemporary conservative interpreter like P.J. O'Rourke has insisted that "*Wealth [of Nations]* cannot be understood without understanding *The Theory of Moral Sentiments*."[9] The very title of *TMS* suggests a reverence for the cooperative human spirit, one quite at odds with the all-too-common modern image of Smith as strictly a promoter of self-interest, if not outright selfish behavior. In one extraordinary concluding section of *TMS*, Smith even goes so far as to inseparably link our own personal happiness with the happiness of others.[10] American Founding Father John Adams, among many others, was particularly impressed with Smith's observations on human vanity and pride in *TMS* (see Chapter 3).

Smith's classical education is on full display throughout the text of *TMS*, as is his enthusiasm for the humanities, especially theater. In many respects, *TMS* is a startling reminder to the modern reader just how much academic training itself has changed over the last three centuries. To write the definitive work on 18th century European economics, it would seem necessary that the author would have been first thoroughly familiar with ancient writers such as Sophocles, Euripides, and Plutarch (see Chapter 9).[11] *TMS* also contains the early seeds of Smith's later and more fully developed economic theories, including his first published use of the phrase "invisible hand" (see Chapter 7), though in a somewhat different sense than one he later used in *WN*. Following the earlier usage, Smith makes allusion to the legendary encounter between Alexander the Great and "the beggar" Diogenes the Cynic, who despite their vast differences in class and rank, are viewed by Smith as being "nearly upon a level" because of an "invisible hand" ceaselessly working to distribute "the necessities of life."[12] Even "kings" find it convenient or necessary to maintain their subjects and followers, observes Smith, if for no other reason than they are physically incapable of consuming absolutely everything within their dominions, no matter how otherwise "vain and insatiable" they may be.[13] Spoken like a true Scottish philosopher of modest means.

Another common misconception about Smith is that he supposedly held himself out as a theoretician or advocate of state policy, when he in fact was primarily an observer and explainer of economic phenomena, although his favorable attitudes towards free trade and state-supported public education are hard to miss by any reader taking trouble to closely examine his works. Both *WN* and *TMS* had been conceived and written by Smith as the first two installments of a grand philosophical tetralogy, which he spent most of his life planning but, to his later frustration and disappointment, was never able to complete. Smith intended to produce at least two other major works: one on the philosophical history of all the different branches of literature, of philosophy, and poetry; the other, a theory and history of law and government.[14] His earlier writings, beginning with *TMS* and later published lectures and essays, are infused with a great awareness of and concern over these diverse matters. Advancing age, poor health, and a full-time government day job at the Edinburgh customs house, however, combined to thwart Smith's ambitious plan. After his death, his unpublished papers, with a few select exceptions, were destroyed at his express direction. An inventory of his personal library, however, was thankfully preserved.

Interpretive Problems

Arguably the biggest problem with interpreting Smith over the last half century is that his actual readership, never extensive to begin with, appears to be slipping to all-time lows even (somehow) as his modern academic reputation continues to grow apace. American political commentator Noam Chomsky hit the nail on the head when he recently characterized Smith as "a dangerous radical ... whom people worship but don't read."[15] At the opposite end of the political spectrum, P.J. O'Rourke agrees with Chomsky on this particular point: "Some acolytes of Smith might be surprised if they ever read him."[16] Bear in mind that *WN* is considered a masterpiece of western literature by almost any standard, a work written in eloquent English less than 250 years ago, easily found on the shelves of almost any public library and readily accessible online. One prominent British historian of the Victorian era, Henry Thomas Buckle (1821–1862), hyperbolically characterized *WN* as "probably the most important book that has ever been written."[17] Nevertheless, while most literate people have certainly heard of *WN*, as well as its author, few have ever opened its pages outside the realm of specialized academia, and only then (it would seem), when the reader has an axe to grind. More incongruously, any casual quick search on World Cat reveals hundreds upon hundreds of detailed studies on Adam Smith, but relatively few offering any analysis going against the then-dominant grain of fashion. For example, in the celebrated opening pages of *WN*, Smith praises the division of labor as a tremendous engine of progress, but much later in the same text warns against its inherent and dangerous consequences to any society not properly emphasizing or funding public education (see Chapter 14). In more recent years, the first passage is frequently quoted, but (as one might well expect) the second is not.

As for Smith's ubiquitous "invisible hand" (of the market place, as it is too often typically assumed), the phrase appears a grand total of three times in his writings (only once in *WN*), each in a notably different context than generally used nowadays.[18] James Buchan mischievously points out that the same phrase had been recently used in English literature by Daniel Defoe's fictional anti-heroine Moll Flanders (from 1722), but in a somewhat more sordid context. Even earlier in 1702, Jonathan Swift, of whom Smith was an express admirer, used the expression in his poetry.[19] Its original usage in English, however, is properly credited to William Shakespeare in *Macbeth*, a play first published in 1623, another work with which Smith was surely familiar (see Chapter 18). Rarely quoted from *WN* is Smith's stern, emphatic warning against what he termed the "the vile maxim of the masters of mankind"—specifically, "all for ourselves, and nothing for other people" (see Chapter 4), more or less the opposite of "greed is good" (see Chapter 16).[20] If today's academia has too often persuaded that, say, a relatively esoteric topic like the Shakespeare Authorship Question is not in fact a real issue, then its frequently accepted misinterpretations of Adam Smith's economic theories represent an even more disturbing development. The problem becomes more frustrating when one ponders that Smith was a firm advocate in *WN* for taxpayer-supported public education in order to prevent this kind of misinformation from being too widely accepted.

In Book IV, Chapter II, of *WN* ("Of Restraints upon the Importation from foreign Countries of such Goods as can be produced at Home"), Smith elaborates on his two most celebrated ideas: that import restraints are generally bad things; and that freedom of trade is generally a good thing. While contrasting the relentless self-interest of merchants and traders with that of the higher "public interest," Smith makes the timeless observation that business people are mainly, if not exclusively, concerned with maximizing profit, as opposed to being do-gooders. Whether that entails trading in foreign imports or domestic products is merely a mathematical calculation to them. If they happen to opt in favor of domestic-made, then this choice is guided strictly by a cold, rational cost-benefit analysis, not by any desire to keep domestic workers employed. It just so happens that, in this particular scenario, domestic workers are also kept on the job by another agent's commercial decision—someone who could really not care less whether those domestic workers are employed. As Smith famously explained:

> By preferring the support of domestic to that of foreign industry, he [the merchant] intends only his own security; and by directing that industry in such a manner as its produce may be of the greatest value, he (the individual) intends only his own gain, and he is in this, as in many other cases, led by an invisible hand to promote an end (the public interest) which was no part of his intention.[21]

Tartly, Smith adds: "I have never known much good done by those who affected to trade for the public good."[22] In recent years, some scholars have suggested, not without reason, that Smith's invisible hand reference from *WN* may have been ironic (see Chapter 18). At the very least, the most neutral (and possibly most appropriate) interpretation might be to view the invisible had as an instrument of desirable unintended results or consequences—not all bad and some good, at least in the long term. That is all; no thing more than that, and certainly not the grandiose system of macroeconomics or legislative policy that many later commentators have attempted to build upon what may well have been simply a humorous aside by an engaging and witty Scottish writer.

Structure and Format

Generally, each chapter in this study will follow a similar pattern of organization. A brief overview of a chronological historical period (from an Anglo-American perspective) will be presented. Next, Smith's biography, work and later reputation within the specific context of that historical period will be examined, including his less frequently quoted writings on similar pertinent issues. Lastly, a short detour will be made into the corresponding worlds of art, music, or film from the same era delving into commercial themes or commentary, of which there are a surprisingly large number. Charts, metrics, and graphs, too often employed in economic studies, are avoided for the sake of keeping the material accessible. The so-called "dismal science" need never come across as such, and by contrast can prove quite provocative if properly discussed within the framework of real world politics. No attempt has been made to thoroughly analyze Smith's economic theories in relation to the development of Anglo-American capitalism over the last three centuries; I leave that task to abler hands—an ongoing deluge of works on this topic is on one hand encouraging; on the other, we wish to promote a broader discussion of these complex issues by a wider group of critics than those confined to universities. Those looking for careful delineation of the many profound subtleties in Smith's philosophic thought, however, will have to look elsewhere. Above all, more general readers will hopefully be encouraged to explore Smith's rich legacy for themselves, well beyond the media sound-bites and critical distortions so commonplace in recent years. They will surely find (as have I) that Smith cannot be pigeonholed, trivialized, or reduced to a mundane level by anyone spending quality time perusing his multi-dimensional texts.

Critical Sources

Beginning with the *Life of Adam Smith* by John Rae in 1895, the low-profile, comparatively uneventful life of Smith has been a prolific subject for modern biographers; however, this study is not a biography, but rather a history of specific economic ideas and their political uses.[23] For that matter, it is no coincidence that the first serious, full-length biography of Smith appeared with the culmination of the Victorian era—a period in which the United States was making its own initial foray into colonial empire-building (see Chapter 9)—since Smith's primary concern in *WN* was colonialism and its profuse socio-economic pitfalls. From the late 1800s moving forward, a steady stream of interpretative literature on Smith's legacy has made its way to the bookshelves, depending on the shifting winds of prevailing political opinion. During the early 1800s, even before contemporary studies had appeared, acute awareness of Smith or *WN* could pop up in some quite surprising (and prominent) places. Some of these include the contentious and drawn-out struggle over slavery abolition, the fierce political battles over the English Corn Laws (earlier criticized by Smith), and even the best-selling popular fiction of Herman Melville and Charles Dickens.

Smith's own books, letters, lectures, and anecdotes are naturally consulted as well. The main thrust of our analysis will be to underscore how Smith's literal texts are often directly at odds with the manner in which these have been presented by theorists, politicians, and media over the last three centuries. It will also be repeatedly emphasized (since it is so often forgotten), that Smith lived and worked within an 18th-century society completely different from ours, one yet to see the American War for Independence, by which time his two best known works had already been published. The mercantilist economy dissected and lambasted by Smith in large part transformed and disappeared during the Industrial Revolution of the late 1700s and early 1800s. Many specialists, with justification, would describe that vanished world as pre-capitalist. Nor should it ever be downplayed that Smith ended his life and career as a Scottish customs inspector (like his father before him), enforcing the restrictive international trade laws of which he had been so critical. Moreover, this final stage in his life's work occurred *after* 1776 (the year *WN* was published), thus Smith's customs house experience influenced the text only to the extent (if at all) that later editions of *WN* were slightly revised within his lifetime. Lastly, a recent trend towards examining the philosophical and ethical roots of modern economic study will be employed to bring Smith's sometimes paradoxical theories into a clearer focus.[24] To emphasize, however, this study is not intended as an academic exercise, but instead seeks to highlight the critically important and too often overlooked connection between classical economic thought and longstanding philosophic traditions which served as Smith's important starting point.

Study Objectives

Smith's intellectual legacy will be placed squarely within the framework of evolving Anglo-American political and economic history. In this respect, I believe this survey to be unique. Beginning with the American colonies' forceful breakaway from the British Empire, a chapter-by-chapter chronology of English-speaking capitalism will examine how each time period seemed to view Smith through its own unique bias. To give one example, Chapter 10 ("Trustbuster") will focus on a key turning point in American history when the U.S. first began to economically challenge Great Britain by expanding its global reach under the aggressive presidency of Theodore Roosevelt, even as Roosevelt himself, a wealthy pro-business Republican, began to realize that certain corporate special interests were becoming so powerful as to completely undermine state and federal authority. Simultaneously, the first body of serious scholarship on Adam Smith's life and work was by then proceeding apace, posing (among other difficult questions) how America might avoid the same mistakes as Great Britain in its new quest for economic and military global dominance.

Patient readers will hopefully have as much fun perusing this survey as I had assembling it. Since Smith is rarely read by anyone nowadays, and wrote during an epoch so completely different from our own, specific interpretations of his text and attempts at direct application of his ideas to contemporary problems often become a freewheeling, unaccountable business. "Smithian" references or quotations within the public sphere frequently seem as if these are being viewed through the looking glass, to borrow a catchy Victorian turn of phrase.[25] For that matter, almost any literary text can be turned on its head with selective quotation and lack of context. The same certainly holds true for the study of economics. By the time Smith's prestigious name and celebrated ideas articulated in *WN* had been over-simplified for decades by the exploitive special interests of Victorian England and Gilded Age America, Mark Twain could rightfully crack jokes in public about the "classics" (see header quote). Some of his fellow Americans were probably not amused. As for the Second British Empire, irreversible decline lay less than a generation into the future, even as it achieved the apex of its worldwide power and influence. A full century before these events, however, the moral philosopher Adam Smith was simply proposing a little more commercial freedom for a system that at the time allowed for little or none. Arguing for extremes was just not his stock in trade. Presently, as we all seem to be living during a time of extremes, moderating voices such as his need to be heard more clearly than in the past. In truth, Smith belongs to a longstanding tradition of western writers with markedly conservative temperaments, espousing liberal ideals.

1. Businessmen Become Revolutionaries (1764–1777)

"The wise and virtuous man is at all times willing that his own private interest should be sacrificed to the public interest of his own particular order or society. He is at all times willing, too, that the interest of this order or society should be sacrificed to the greater interest of the state or sovereignty, of which it is only a subordinate part."—Adam Smith[1]

Those inclined toward a politically liberal point of view often tend to forget that sharp tax increases were triggering events for the American Revolution; moreover, this deeply ingrained attitude against taxes in general remains part of the contemporary American DNA, for better and for worse. The unlikely coalition of Yankee traders and Southern planters—the latter unapologetically utilizing slave labor—who founded this country had one important thing in common: all deeply resented having their pockets picked by a distant central government giving them no representative say in the budget decision-making process. By the second half of the 18th century, the original 13 North American colonies were also beginning, after nearly two centuries of hard and dangerous work, to form their own cultural identity quite separate and apart from that of the mother country. To colonists it no longer seemed right or fair that they should be arbitrarily taxed or regulated by an overseas power merely in return honorary membership to the British Empire and the uncertain military protection which it afforded. Therefore they rebelled. To this day, almost all Americans, especially those of us tracing our colonial ancestors to pre–Revolutionary times, do not react well to the phrase "tax increase"—even when we are possibly receiving something of high value in return. While all developed societies have properly adopted some form of centralized taxing system, it may be fairly asserted that no nation on earth instinctively views such systems, no matter how equitable or justified, with more suspicion and mistrust than the United States of America.

Given the increasing failure of our educational systems to effectively teach history, combined with a growing, widespread ignorance of our republic's origins, it seems appropriate within these pages to give a very brief recap as to the agreed-upon facts regarding this signal event transpiring less than two and a half centuries ago. The French and Indian War (1756–1763) had been a lengthy and complex military struggle, setting the stage for the American Revolution much the same manner in which the Mexican War later set the stage for the American Civil War in the following century. In terms of huge financial expense combined with dubious results, the French and Indian conflict was also not unlike the U.S. wars in Iraq and Afghanistan during the early 21st century.[2] The Battle of Quebec in 1759, the same year that Adam Smith's *The Theory of Moral Sentiments* (*TMS*) was published, proved to be a decisive turning point, followed by the fall of Montreal in 1760, and belatedly, the Peace Treaty of Paris in 1763. Some historians plausibly argue that the concurrent (and impossibly tangled) Seven Years' War in continental Europe was in reality an outgrowth of the Anglo-French fight for supremacy in the New World, rather than vice-versa.[3] In either event, England emerged victorious from these high-stakes struggles—and deeply in debt. As for English and French-speaking Canada, later repeated American attempts to conquer the northern provinces for itself failed miserably; Canadian Quebec remains predominantly and proudly French-speaking to this day.

Someone of course had to pay for all of this. Most rational beings on both sides of the Atlantic agreed that the colonists should bear a significant portion of the expense, as the war had been fought primarily to protect their interests and liberties; however, the colonists themselves had little or no say in the matter, being unrepresented in the British Parliament. Beginning in 1764, that same distant Parliament attempted to impose its will on the colonists with a barrage of controversial legislation, culminating in 1767 with a heavy tax on American tea consumption. This in turn prompted a half-decade of civil unrest and disturbances only made worse by a new Tea Act of 1773, sponsored by Prime Minister Lord Frederick North (1732–1792) with the intent of moderating the burden of established duties, but instead provoking greater colonial outrage by their ongoing retention. The problem was exacerbated by the tea taxes also benefiting special interests represented by the British East India Company. The symbolic climax to these political and economic tensions occurred on December 16, 1773, when a rambunctious gang calling themselves the Sons of Liberty, nominally disguised as Mohawk Native Americans, forcibly boarded the British freighter *Dartmouth* parked in Boston Harbor and threw its imported tea cargo overboard in protest. In 1774, Parliament responded to the outrage by passing even more oppressive legislation (the "Intolerable Acts"), and by 1775, skirmishes between occupying British regular troops and newly-organized American militia had been fought at Lexington, Concord, and Bunker Hill, Massachusetts. This was the volatile political environment in which Adam Smith finalized and published *The Wealth of Nations* (*WN*). Four months later in July 1776, American independence was formally declared and colonial statues of King George III were hurled to the ground.

During the decade leading up to the American breakaway from the British Empire, Smith had been undergoing his own major re-education of sorts. In 1764—the same year that Parliament began taxing the colonies—he left his professorship at the University of Glasgow to accept a lifetime annuity from M.P. Charles Townshend (1725–1767) in return for providing services as a private travelling tutor and chaperon for his stepson, Henry Scott, 3rd Duke of Buccleuch (1746–1812), during the latter's projected grand tour of recently-vanquished France. Ironically, this was the same Charles Townshend who three years later, in 1767, would conclude a distinguished Parliamentary career by sponsoring (as namesake) the first unpopular tea importation tax on the American colonies. For two years prior to that, however, Smith enjoyed intellectual celebrity in France as the respected author of *TMS*, being entertained by leading French writers and freethinkers of the day, the most exotic of whom was probably Dr. François Quesnay (1694–1774), royal physician, leading Physiocratic philosopher, orientalist enthusiast, and acclaimed author of *Tableau Économique* (1758), considered by many to be the first serious treatise on western economic theory. In contrast to the British colonial system, which heavily regulated and taxed international commerce, Quesnay argued in favor of near total freedom, or *laissez-faire* (roughly translated, "leave it alone") as the best method for governments to promote private enterprise and international trade. Quesnay obviously made a big impression on Smith and it is said that Smith would have dedicated *WN* to Quesnay had it not been for the latter's death two years before publication.

Smith returned to Great Britain in 1766, settled at his mother's house in their home town of Kirkcaldy, Scotland, and began writing about international commerce as British hostilities with the American colonies continued to escalate. Upon his return from France, the former professor of moral philosophy had apparently decided that it was time to step down from his ivory tower, and by writing *WN*, he did so with a vengeance. In 1772, Smith moved to London and spent most of the next six years completing his ambitious project, overseeing its publication, and enjoying a surprisingly favorable reception, including a second edition.[4] Then in late 1777, he permanently returned to Scotland, in anticipation of his pending appointment as Customs Commissioner of Edinburgh, the very same post held by his father in a previous generation.[5] That the most eloquent English-speaking voice of that era in favor of free trade (as well as a moderate, inclusive state policy towards the colonies) should be rewarded for his efforts with a government post that, for all intents and purposes, interfered with and restricted free trade, must be viewed in hindsight either as devious punishment of sorts or a kind of twisted poetic justice.[6] As things turned out, Smith still had to earn a steady living, over and above his annuity payment from the Townsend family, even after having produced a well-received landmark in world literature.[7]

Meanwhile in America, occupying British and mercenary Hessian military forces, after chasing the ragged remnants of George Washington's defeated Continental Army clear across New Jersey, failed to deliver a quick knock-out blow. Instead, much to their surprise and chagrin, they were handed resounding defeats by the Americans at the battles of Trenton and Princeton in late 1776 and early 1777, respectively. Later in 1777, the Americans under General Horatio Gates (with future traitor Benedict Arnold playing a key role) won a stunning and signal victory at Saratoga, New York, thereby leading to French intervention in favor of the colonists, an alliance personally promoted in Paris by Benjamin Franklin since the previous year. Thus American and French mercantile interests, the bitterest rivals less than two decades prior, now became formal revolutionary partners against the British Empire. The French intervention insured that the conflict would be protracted, thus giving Washington a chance to successfully implement the type of Fabian military tactics for which he was ideally suited by temperament, training, and limited conventional resources.[8] Notwithstanding the mythos of Valley Forge (1777–1778) representing a low point in morale for the Continental Army, the fact was that by then the Americans had achieved a daunting strategic upper hand over the British.[9] It was to Washington's eternal credit that he knew exactly how exploit this golden opportunity presented to him by fortune or circumstance. Back in England, voices which less than two years ago had unsuccessfully argued for more moderation (Smith among them) were now being seen more and more as prophetic. The latest unwelcome events seemed to vindicate their earlier predictions and fears that yet another American colonial war would prove too long, too costly, and ultimately futile.

The former Professor Smith, it is worth repeating, had received his real world education in France not long before this. In *WN* he had warned of the prolonged, relentless fight that was sure to ensue if the American colonies were treated too harshly. The resulting quagmire, he wrote, would be comparable to that of the French Protestant King Henry IV's attempted subjugation of Catholic France during the 16th century Wars of Religion, a fierce and endless partisan struggle only resolved by the king's calculated and timely conversion to Catholicism. Drawing a direct parallel with British-American relations, Smith asserted: "Our colonies, unless they can be induced to consent to a union, are very likely to defend themselves against the best of all mother countries, as obstinately as the city of Paris did against one of the best of kings."[10] Touring France in the aftermath of its defeat by Great Britain had prompted Smith to worry. The French had recently gambled heavily on maintaining mastery of North America and lost in spectacular fashion. Furthermore, during the height of the French and Indian War, the forceful *laissez-faire* doctrine of Quesnay had argued that such total hands-on control was unnecessary for sustained economic growth and prosperity. Like Smith's *WN*, however, Quesnay's ideas did not find widespread acceptance until after his country began to suffer serious reverses in the field. When disaster finally struck, more people began to listen. A visiting Smith found himself among Quesnay's new growing audience, though it would be going too far to call him a Quesnay disciple or that he was uncritical of the *laissez-faire* model.[11] On the other hand, Smith clearly connected the dots in terms of Great Britain now facing a challenge in the New World very similar to the one previously faced and lost by France only a few years before.

Around the same time that Quesnay wrote *Tableau Économique*, Smith had written in *TMS* that all good citizens, regardless of religious or political opinions, owed certain moral obligations and duties to king, country, and society at large, obligations which took precedence over all personal interests, including those of financial gain (see header quote). This aspect of Smith's core beliefs would never change. One might well describe such a philosophy as the direct opposite of "greed is good" or any notion that free markets and private philanthropy can solve all problems with minimal government involvement. Quesnay no doubt would have agreed to some extent, but one must remember that Quesnay lived in a bankrupt nation on the verge of suffering devastating military defeat which, within a few short years, would overthrow its monarchy (and nobility) in a violent, near anarchic revolution. It is a good surmise that Smith's notions of duty and sacrifice were considerably broader than those of his French counterpart, particularly as he was writing before the Declaration of Independence had been signed. In short, Smith's strong beliefs on personal duties to society trumped his beliefs on free markets. When Smith returned to Scotland in 1766 on the eve of the despised Townshend

Revenue Act becoming law, his mind began turning as to how Great Britain might strike a better balance between free trade and government regulation, thereby avoiding a similar colonial catastrophe recently enveloping France.

Without mincing too many words, Smith places direct blame for the huge expense of recent American colonial conflicts on a relatively small but powerful group of special interests exerting disproportionate influence over the decision-making process of the British government. Moreover, Smith asserts that "The late war was altogether a colony quarrel, and the whole expense of it ... ought justly to be stated to the account of the colonies."[12] After giving an impressively exhaustive history of colonial trade over the course of western civilization from ancient Greece to Latin America, Smith turns his attention to British colonialism, persuasively arguing that the Anglo version of this mercantile system was the most benign and successful in history. Then despite characterizing the recent war as "a colony quarrel" with France, Smith argues, rather surprisingly, that a voluntary separation between England and the colonies might be economically advantageous for all (especially the British) but that such an event was unlikely given lack of similar historical precedent.[13] Alternatively, he proposes (even more surprisingly) that the colonies should be allowed representation in Parliament.[14] Assuring that no one will miss these controversial points, he reiterates them during the final pages of his treatise, declaring the unsustainable status quo as "a golden dream" from which "they should awake" and concluding with an ominous prediction that "If the project [paying for the colonies] cannot be completed, it ought to be given up."[15] These same ideas form a part of Smith's larger backdrop for Book V, Chapter III, in which he delivers a practical discourse on the ever-relevant subject of public debt, presenting fundamental concepts ignored by the British establishment of his own day, but with continual relevance for the U.S. or any other modern nation seeking to achieve economic objectives through foreign trade (see Chapter 11).

Smith attributes the unprecedented prosperity of the Anglo-American colonies to several factors, not the least of which is a strongly implied cultural superiority of English-speaking peoples over European and Native American competitors. After favorably remarking upon the wide availability of land, an official use-it-or-lose it policy, and comparatively liberal inheritance laws, Smith then delves into the items that he believes are primarily driving a seemingly irresistible engine of progress. The first of these (famously) is moderate taxation.[16] The second (almost as famously) is relative freedom of trade.[17] Both of these crucial factors, he proceeds to exhaustively demonstrate, had been recently damaged by overly-assertive mercantile interests enriched by government-enforced monopolies, in tandem with incentive-killing surcharges and regulations on any potential or perceived trading competition, whether it be foreign or home-grown. With a perceptible sigh, Smith laments that "It is unnecessary, I imagine, to observe, how contrary such regulations are to the boasted liberty of the subject, of which we affect to be so very jealous; but which, in this case, is so plainly sacrificed to the futile interests of our merchants and manufacturers."[18] Generations of economists following in Smith's wake, particularly in more recent times, have used these passages from *WN* to argue in favor of minimal (or no) taxation and regulation, but in actuality Smith was pointing an accusatory finger at the merchants dictating or perverting government policies, rather than government itself. It was the mercantile interests who were responsible for inflicting higher taxes and less trade freedom on their would-be competitors through a corrupting influence on Crown and Parliament. It is indeed hard to miss this relentless, overriding message if one takes time to read the text of *WN*, particularly Books IV and V.

It was therefore natural that colonial traders and planters being financially harmed by these aligned mercantile interests took notice when a respected intellectual on the other side of the Atlantic publicly expressed sympathy (in print) with their grievances and advocated a different official government policy. To be clear, the American Founding Fathers did not go out and buy copies of *WN*, then decide to sign the Declaration of Independence. On the other hand, many of them certainly read it, as well as Smith's earlier famous work, *TMS* (such as John Adams). It is documented that George Washington, Thomas Jefferson, Alexander Hamilton, James Madison, and Samuel Adams, among many others, all either owned copies of *WN* or had studied Smith's writings.[19] In short, most of the Founding Fathers playing central or key roles in the American Revolution were highly aware of Smith's new ideas.[20] What we know of their reading and reaction to Smith will be examined more closely in Chapter 2 of this study, as they grappled with their own attempt at forming a lasting, stable, and just form of central government in the aftermath of the Revolution.

With respect to events leading up to the Revolution itself, however, the one Founding Father worth taking a close look at in relation to Adam Smith is none other than Benjamin Franklin, unofficial elder statesman of the group and the man most personally responsible for securing the French intervention which proved essential to the long-term achievement of American independence.[21] It was a sixty-something-year-old Franklin who, sometime between 1771 and 1775, during his final diplomatic years in Great Britain, got wind of Smith's great work in progress (through mutual friend David Hume), and reportedly met with and urged the former Glasgow professor to advocate more British leniency towards the colonies. Various conflicting accounts, derived mostly from 19th century anecdotal sources, have Franklin either simply lobbying in favor of the colonials or outright assisting Smith in redrafting his arguments. These traditions would have us believe that not only did *WN* influence the Americans, but that it had originally been influenced by them via Franklin—a not totally implausible scenario (see Chapter 16).[22] Even at this late hour in history, however, Franklin had not yet become an outright revolutionary, favoring more accommodation and closer union based on the British-Scottish model achieved earlier during the same century. In any event, by mid-1776, Franklin was signing the Declaration of Independence and Smith's *WN* had been published to wide notice.

For a superpower making preparations of war against the fledgling United States, Great Britain responded to Smith's severe criticisms with surprising tolerance, if not outright admiration, or simply turned a blind eye. As one might expect, Smith's close friend and fellow Scotsman David Hume (1711–1776)—widely considered to be the Empire's leading philosopher (however dubious in theological reputation)—showered *WN* with praise. At this point, Hume only had a few months left to live. Smith would be at Hume's bedside at the end. He then publicly eulogized the controversial philosopher after his death, with little apparent realization what the fallout would be. On the other extreme of the political spectrum, Irish-born M.P. Edmund Burke (1729–1797), the father of modern conservatism, wrote a glowing review of *WN* for the *Annual Register*, just as he had 17 years earlier when Smith's *TMS* was published. One of the few things that both Burke and Hume had in common was sympathy for America's plight, probably based on the oppression that their own native lands had suffered at the hands of the English. They were also both fans of Smith's work, and Smith in turn had high regard for each of them, especially Hume. With respect to Burke, a dissenting member of the same Parliament that oppressed the colonies, Smith later admitted that, despite all of their other differences, he and Burke tended to think exactly alike on economic issues.[23]

Another leader among Smith's intellectual circle in London was the eminent historian Edward Gibbon, writing that *WN* was "an excellent work" with "the most profound ideas expressed in the most perspicuous language."[24] As for criticism, in England or otherwise, it was scarcely to be found. Most likely, the entrenched mercantile interests and subservient Parliamentarians attacked in *WN* tended not be book readers or especially concerned with new ideas. *WN* was simply not on their radar until much later in time, by which time its admonitions were too late for the originally intended targets, probably saving Smith a lot of grief in the process. Smith himself expected to be pilloried and soon afterwards expressed surprise that he was not, instead being rewarded with a British government customs appointment, but not before he was publicly censured for his recent eulogy of David Hume (see Chapter 2). One is uncertain whether to conclude he had more powerful friends or extremely devious enemies.[25]

Any reader doubting the relevance to the world of modern international commerce of the highly-nuanced issues addressed in *WN* need only glance at the daily headlines. For example, as the year 2013 drew to a close, PBS reported on the ongoing dispute between the U.S. state of Maine and domestic prescription drug manufacturers regarding the rights of public and private entities to import similar generic but less expensive drugs from Canada and other parts of the British Commonwealth. Residents and workers of Maine, with strong local and bipartisan political support, insisted on their prerogative to bypass existing F.D.A. regulations by importing comparable health care products and thereby saving on cost.[26]

At a glance, it would appear to be the 1773 Tea Act dispute all over again. Among these supporters are vocal members of the modern-day Tea Party political faction, although the irony of American citizens fighting their own federal government for the right to import mail order products from the British Commonwealth is probably lost upon most of them.[27] Nevertheless, there remains a connection between these contemporary events with the grievances of 18th century American colonists; namely, are the existing restrictive controls really to protect consumers from bad quality or to protect a designated group of domestic manufacturers from foreign competition? Adam Smith's response, were he alive today, would be fairly predictable: let international traffic flow and let the consumer market decide on the best deal. As for consumer protection, he would probably say that restricting international trade is not the answer, and would in fact likely prove a futile long-term exercise. On the other hand, most modern Tea Party apologists would never acknowledge the final chapters of Smith's *WN*, in which taxation for purposes of public education, public works and public defense are given top-priority, but that topic is best addressed within other sections of this study.

As for the 1773 Tea Party of Boston, Massachusetts—today possibly the most politically liberal major city in the United States—it has over the last three centuries demonstrated itself to be one of the most popular, if not *the* most popular subject matter for artistic interpretation dating from the revolutionary era. Among countless intriguing depictions, one of the more fascinating also happens to be one of the earliest and possibly the very first. In 1774, only a few months after the event transpired, noted British cartoonist Philip Dawe (?-1832), a former apprentice to the famous English engraver William Hogarth, produced a series of mezzotints portraying rebellious American colonists in less than a favorable light. Without going into too much detail, Dawe presents all of the rebels, more or less, as a group of murderous hustlers and whores, which no doubt some of their ancestors had in fact been before departing from England for America. The centerpiece of this striking series is labeled "The Bostonians paying the excise-man, or tarring and feathering."[28] In the background of this depiction we see faceless colonial hooligans wastefully pouring cargo crates of expensive imported tea into Boston Harbor. There is no sign of the Mohawk disguises supplying the most creative touch adopted by the historical protestors. More of interest is the central image, another factual event, specifically, the literal tarring and feathering of Boston Customs Commissioner John Malcolm while being force-fed hot tea by a gang of sadistic American Sons of Liberty.[29] A symbolic Liberty Tree (with a lynching noose) seems to preside over the violence. It is unknown whether Adam Smith ever saw this cartoon, although he had indeed moved to the city of London by that time. It is also worth repeating that Smith's own father had previously been a customs inspector (not unlike Malcolm), and Smith would himself accept the same position only three years after this cartoon appeared. In short, he likely did not write *WN* for lack of any sympathy with these beleaguered government officials.

Men like Washington, Franklin, and Jefferson did not start out in life as revolutionaries (far from it, in fact), but rather more like Smith, completely loyal to king and mother country, despite outlier social status as colonials or provincials. They recognized that to be a revolutionary was, in general, bad business, and above all, most of the Founding Fathers were good businessmen, entrepreneurs, and innovators. Most would have agreed with Smith's views from *TMS* on private sacrifice for the public good. In spite of this conservative inclination, however, all eventually found themselves pushed into a corner (or at least perceived themselves pushed into a corner) by a distant, centralized power in which they had no voice or representation. Suddenly, for them, revolution became a good business gamble. As a great novelist from the next century would later write, in order for everything to stay the same, everything had to change.[30] Within two years (1776–1777), the United States had progressed from an abstract idea with political support from perhaps a third of its citizens, to a stubborn military force formally aligned with France, sending a clear message to the British Empire that any attempted subjugation would be neither quick nor inexpensive. It would take another five years for Great Britain to admit defeat, or as Smith had written by 1776, "to accommodate her future views and designs to the real mediocrity of her circumstances."[31] Now that a new dynamic nation had been formed, these same businessmen-turned-revolutionaries began to discover and appreciate, just as Smith had eloquently pointed out back in 1776, that there were certain advantages to being protected and nurtured by a strong central government. Meanwhile, as the British were busy losing the American war, an unlikely firestorm was brewing for the former Glasgow professor, even as he enjoyed increasing public accolades and financial reward.

2. A New Republic Grapples with Old Issues (1778–1790)

"Sugar, rum, and tobacco, are commodities which are no where necessaries of life, which are become objects of almost universal consumption, and which are therefore extremely proper subjects of taxation."—Adam Smith[1]

On May 11, 1778, William Pitt the Elder (1708–1778), Earl of Chatham and former Prime Minister of Great Britain, passed away in London, having consistently advocated the avoidance of an ongoing, rapidly escalating war with the American colonists. It was Pitt the Elder who during previous decades had successfully guided his country through the lengthy parallel struggles of the European Seven Years War and the American French and Indian War. Though victorious in both, hard experience had taught him to dread the expense and risk of geographically distant conflict; moreover, this time around England was making war on its own people, the American colonists. For him, the time had come to step back and reach a compromise; unfortunately the new powers in the British government, including the Anglo-American mercantile interests which supported them, would have none of it, even after defeat at Saratoga had brought the French back into the American contest like a bad recurring nightmare. Later, it was very fortunate for the young United States that Pitt's son, William the Younger (1759–1806)—who mostly shared his father accommodating views towards the Americans—later became British Prime Minister during the final decades of the 18th century, thus allowing the U.S. to pass more or less unmolested through the formative phases of its federal government. As for the Founding Fathers of this country, after having dramatically won the Revolution, they found themselves quickly confronted with many of the same thorny and multi-faceted economic issues on international trade so recently vexing and diminishing to the British Empire.

2. A New Republic Grapples with Old Issues (1778–1790)

The historical overview of this period and place can be summarized in a few sentences. After Great Britain failed to quickly suppress the Revolution, the years 1778–1781 saw sustained French intervention in favor of the colonists and George Washington do militarily what he did best—wait patiently for his opponents to make a big mistake. That big mistake occurred in late 1781 at Yorktown, Virginia, when Lord Lieutenant General Charles Cornwallis allowed his large British force to be surrounded and bottled up by combined revolutionary ground and naval forces under the respective commands of Washington and the Comte de Rochambeau. British surrender formally occurred on October 19; then, after two years of petulant negotiations, England finally agreed to the 1783 Treaty of Paris, bringing the American Revolution to a triumphant, historic conclusion for the former British colonists. Defeating the British Army, however, proved to be only phase one in the independence process, as the next seven years (1784–1790)—also the last seven years of Adam Smith's life—witnessed the United States fitfully becoming a new nation in the truest constitutional sense. To accomplish this not inconsiderable feat, many old unresolved issues had to be addressed in a mature adult fashion, not the least of which were numerous, longstanding bread-and-butter economic questions regarding the proper roles of federal, state and local governments in the promotion of national economic growth and prosperity. It also so happened that Adam Smith, by then Commissioner of Customs in Edinburgh, had addressed many of these same questions on the eve of the Revolution while writing *The Wealth of Nations* (*WN*).

In many respects, the early economic development of this country in wake of the Revolution is far more interesting than the military aspects of the Revolution itself. The early American republic, without a strong centralized federal government under the short-lived Articles of Confederation, had severe problems paying its bills, not to mention sustaining domestic growth or maximizing employment of its vast resources, both natural and human. After three shaky years following the Treaty of Paris, a failed armed rebellion led by disgruntled Massachusetts army veteran Daniel Shays in 1786—the first in a long line of American war veterans protesting mistreatment by their own government—sent a psychological shock wave through the young nation's leadership.

By 1787, a new constitutional convention had convened in Philadelphia, personally presided over by Washington himself. By 1788, after a few months of haggling (modest by today's standards), the new U.S. federal constitution had been ratified by a majority of states, and the American national Congress, both House and Senate, convened for the first time in the newly-designated

U.S. capital of New York City. One of their first major official acts was to pass the Tariff Act of 1789, designed to combat the growing inundation of the American market with imported goods, thus protecting domestic manufacturers from foreign competition. The law pretty much went against everything that Adam Smith had long preached, thus imposing the same kinds of artificial restrictions on international commerce that had prompted the colonists to rebel against Great Britain in the first place merely 13 years prior to that. Meanwhile, across the Atlantic, a terrified England and Europe watched as the French Revolution violently erupted on the continent, caused in no small part by the French government's inability to effectively address widespread economic grievances similar to those loudly voiced by Daniel Shays in America only three years earlier.

The influence of Smith's work on the Founding Fathers was subtle yet tangible; nevertheless, even during his lifetime there was apparent disagreement over what Smith really meant to say, and to what extent that message should be adopted in practice. As one might expect, the Virginians led by Thomas Jefferson and James Madison applauded Smith's express glorification of agriculture over manufacturing, as well as his advocacy of limited restrictions on foreign trade.[2] As Southern planters, Jefferson, Madison, and their fellow slave owners did not need to be reminded that the wealth of the Piedmont region had been built around agricultural exports, especially tobacco. Consequently, the South depended more upon free-flowing trade and foreign manufactured imports than the comparatively self-sufficient North. Jefferson personally owned two separate editions of Smith's *WN* (1784 & 1815), frequently quoted from it, and in 1790 called Smith's treatise "in political economy ... the best book extant."[3] Today, Jefferson's image can of course still be seen on the nickel coin and (somewhat fittingly) two-dollar bill of U.S. currency.

Another reader of *WN* among the Virginians was none other than George Washington himself, whose signed 1789 edition (the last published during Smith's lifetime) is today housed in the Firestone Rare Book Library at Princeton University, not far from where Washington won signal victories over the British in early 1777 (see Chapter 1).[4] Washington's image continues to grace the U.S. one dollar bill. Though not himself known as a great reader, intellect, or theorizer, Washington was often a great patron and supporter of others who were. Consciously setting examples by his own behavior, he had as his most prominent protégé a rather unlikely individual who, probably more than anyone among the Founding Fathers, became the primary architect of the fledgling American economy.[5]

Alexander Hamilton (1755?–1804) was the illegitimate son of a Scotsman and a French woman, born into underprivileged circumstances outside of the American colonies in the British West Indies. After Benjamin Franklin, no other American of that era had more versatile, wide-ranging talent, and certainly none had more raw ambition combined with creative genius, or, as some have characterized it, creative madness. Arriving stateside as a teenager in 1772, within the breathtaking time span of four years, Hamilton had made New York City his adopted home, was admitted to Columbia University, wrote articles in passionate support of revolution, joined the militia as a volunteer at the first sound of gunfire in 1775, and by 1776, at age 21, had become Washington's chief of staff, seeing prominent action in all early official engagements from American defeat at White Plains through American victory at Trenton. Crucially, during this early period the low-born Hamilton became a kind of surrogate son to the older, childless Washington, the latter frequently fawning over the younger man's incredible energies and abilities. This, however, represented only the beginning stage of Hamilton's explosive career trajectory. By the time that Hamilton was appointed first U.S. Treasury Secretary by Washington in 1789, he had become, among many other accomplishments, a keen student (and critic) of Adam's Smith's economic theories. Today, he tends more to be remembered as the face of the U.S. ten-dollar bill and the man whom a furiously-offended Vice President Aaron Burr killed in a duel on the heights of Weehawken, New Jersey, in July of 1804.

Fifteen years before this melancholy event, however, soon-to-be Secretary of Treasury Hamilton was a major player in the passage of the 1789 Tariff, a law working in pronounced economic favor of his home state New York at the general, indirect expense of Southern agricultural interests. This in turn caused a breach of trust between Hamilton and longtime working partner James Madison, thereby leading to Madison's permanent breakaway from the Federalist Party and tentative beginnings of the two-party political system in this country, continuing (with a few bumps along the way) more or less unabated ever since.

Hamilton then spent the next two years drafting his most famous document, the *Report on Manufactures*, as justification for his recent actions and a proposed blueprint for future American industry (see Chapter 3). At the core of the debate in 1789 was whether the U.S. should economically align itself with France or England, an issue which would dominate U.S. foreign and domestic policy over the next 16 years. The Virginians, led by Jefferson, predictably favored France, while Hamilton more clearly saw what was then happening with the French Revolution, feared its instability, and preferred to mend fences with Great Britain. Each side laid their respective cases before newly inaugurated President Washington, who stood aloof from the fray, which is to say that in the eyes of Southerners he favored Hamilton, a northern interloper. It is further testament to Washington's greatness that he almost always favored Hamilton—an illegitimate foreigner by birth, subsequently adopting New York as his home—over most of his fellow Virginians, of whom he was known to have been highly critical. In any event, the Tariff Act became law on the 13th anniversary of the Declaration of Independence, which must have galled Jefferson even more, having been primary author of the Declaration. New England Yankee manufacturing and trade interests with Great Britain were thereby enhanced.

Meanwhile, the same time period in Great Britain witnessed Adam Smith's reputation as an economic advisor continue to grow, even as his country's military fortunes in the New World suffered irreparable reversals. Soon after British defeat at Saratoga in 1777, Smith was appointed to his government post as Customs Inspector in Edinburgh, then in early 1778 he was invited by solicitor-general (and fellow Scotsman) Alexander Wedderburn (1733–1805) to contribute a memorandum as to how trade relations with the colonies might be salvaged. The surviving memo (in Wedderburn's handwriting) is dated February 1778 and titled "Smith's thoughts on the State of the Contest with America."[6] Smith had basically condensed and reiterated his beliefs from *WN* advocating more freedom and leniency of trade. Though always cordial with Smith, this was the very same Alexander Wedderburn who in 1774, perhaps overcompensating for own his Scottish birth, had humiliated Benjamin Franklin before the British Privy Council, thereby instantly transforming the previously loyalist Franklin into an enthusiastic revolutionary.[7] If theories about Franklin's early influence on Smith's ideas are correct (see Chapter 1), then Wedderburn may well have been unwittingly seeking counsel from a source (Smith) imbued with similar opinions so publicly chastised by Wedderburn himself only four years previous.

Around this same time, as first noted by Smith's biographer John Rae, British Prime Minister Lord Frederick North borrowed several taxation ideas from *WN* for his beleaguered budget of 1778 to raise money in support of the faltering war effort against the American colonies.[8] Copies of the second edition of *WN* (from 1778) had reportedly been given both to North and British Treasury Secretary Grey Cooper. While North did not share Smith's views of pragmatic accommodation towards the colonies, he was clearly intrigued with the latter's suggestions regarding potential untapped sources of tax revenue. After the futile, expensive war against the colonies had finally been lost in 1781, the 1783 Treaty of Paris was largely negotiated for the British by William Petty, Earl of Shelburne, an early supporter of Smith's free trade theories.[9] Shortly after the Treaty was signed, Whig Party and war opposition leader Charles James Fox openly praised Smith's *WN* in Parliament.[10] The reigns of the recovering British government were then assumed by Prime Minister William Pitt the Younger (1759–1806), who like his namesake father before him, believed that the English should use their superior navy to out-trade the Americans, rather than outfight them (see Chapter 3). Like his political opponents, Pitt the Younger had studied Smith's economic philosophy, but seems to have taken its core message more to heart. Accordingly, he immediately realized that England's top priorities should be maximizing trade profits from India and the New World while focusing on the rising military threat posed by revolutionary France in nearby continental Europe. Indeed, the subsequent inundation of the American domestic market with imported British goods during the late 1780s probably did more overall to undermine American political and economic stability than any foreign declaration of war against the United States ever accomplished.

Regarding Smith himself, trouble and controversy soon came from a completely different direction, one probably least expected.[11] As an innocent homage and tribute to his recently deceased friend, mentor, and fellow Scotsman David Hume, Smith had written a carefully edited letter to his publisher William Strahan, subsequently printed in 1777, in praise of Hume's memory, elevating him by allusion to the level of an English Socrates.[12] The main problem was that Hume was widely perceived to have been an atheist, as well as a persistent critic of the Church of England. Worse still (for Smith), Hume had long been at intellectual loggerheads with the influential circle of Dr. Samuel Johnson (1709–1784), famed author of the first English Dictionary, and a man not well disposed towards the Scottish people to begin with, although a notable exception was his devoted young biographer and sidekick, James Boswell (1740–1795). While Boswell had once been a student under Smith at Glasgow University, this memory was not able to rescue Smith from Boswell's criticisms; moreover, Smith and Johnson had a long uneasy relationship, beginning with Smith's highly qualified review of Johnson's *Dictionary of the English Language* upon its first publication in 1755.

Apart from a sharp Anglo-Scots divide, Johnson (unlike Smith) was politically a staunch defender of the British government's right to lord it over the American colonies, as well as firm defender of the traditional Anglican faith. Perhaps crucially, and far less remarked upon by commentators, is the sad fact that Johnson, despite all of his brilliance, was a man who had fought tremendously hard against many obstacles and disadvantages in life to achieve everything that he accomplished, whereas Smith was a former academic later generously patronized by the nobility, then seemingly segued effortlessly into the interconnected worlds of commerce and political influence.[13] When the imminently successful Smith went on visible public record to eulogize a freethinker (Hume) standing against everything that Johnson represented, it probably proved too much for Johnson and, for that matter, anyone wanting to remain Johnson's friend, including Boswell.

The backlash and firestorm began shortly after Smith's Hume eulogy appeared when an unsigned public response was published in late 1777, penned by the future Anglican Bishop of Norwich and then-president of Magdalen College at Oxford, George Horne. Horne, as another pillar of the British establishment, had double reason to be upset with Smith. On one hand, any lionization of Hume was considered a slap in the face to the Anglican clergy, of which Horne was a prominent member. Secondly, and perhaps more crucial, Smith within the pages of *WN* from the previous year, during his lengthy commentary and criticism on public education (see Chapter 15), had made a surprisingly hard jibe at Horne's employer, Oxford University. Here, according to Smith, "the greater part of the public professors have, for these many years, given up altogether even the pretence of teaching."[14] Never mind that Smith was imminently qualified to make such comments as a former student at Oxford and a former academic at the University of Glasgow, or perhaps that is exactly why his criticism drew such an angry response. In any event, Horne proceeded in endlessly tedious prose—the opposite of Smith's typically lucid expression—to portray Smith as the embodiment of everything morally and intellectually wanting in the British Empire. It is noteworthy that Horne's shrill response was written in the immediate aftermath of British military defeat at Saratoga and French entry into the American conflict. As for Smith, he wisely ignored this outburst, but the worst was unfortunately yet to come.

The real hurt and rejection surely came later in the form of ostracized relations from Johnson's prestigious London literary circle, of which Smith had previously been an uneasy though allowed member through association.[15] As early as 1773, when Smith was living in London while completing work on *WN*, Boswell had privately complained that "It was strange to find my old professor [Adam Smith] in London, a professed infidel with a bag wig."[16] Boswell's use of the word "infidel" automatically linked Smith with Hume, the latter nicknamed by Boswell with a similar descriptor ("The Great Infidel"). Later Boswell reported that his hero Johnson had unflatteringly described Smith "as dull a dog as he had ever met with." In short, all of the old prejudices between Johnson and Smith flared up into a permanent breach. Things seemed to have reached an unpleasant crescendo by September 1779, when Boswell recorded in his journal that "Since [Smith's] absurd eulogium on Hume, and his ignorant, ungrateful attack on the English University education, I have no desire to be much with him."[17] At this stage, Boswell may have clearly realized that his own future fame rested on a continuing association with his friend and confidant Johnson, as opposed to his former (and now rather controversial) Scottish professor, as well as the even more controversial, posthumous reputation of David Hume.

According to 19th century correspondence from the novelist Walter Scott and other semi-reliable sources, Johnson and Smith, two of the greatest English-speaking intellectuals of their time and place, in the end parted company hurling verbal abuse at one another. Reportedly, in the presence of Boswell and others, bringing up Smith's public eulogy of Hume as an exemplary human being, calm and fearless in the face of death, Johnson called Smith a liar. Smith quickly retorted that Johnson was "a son of a bitch."[18] The embarrassing exchange allegedly took place in Glasgow circa 1773, but that would be an impossibility, given Hume was still alive. It is also quite possible that Smith's insistent defense of his then-living friend Hume against Johnson's character aspersions did in fact date back to that earlier period; nor can it be ruled out that these specific parting shots occurred at a later date in London sometime after Hume's passing. It would seem more likely, however, that the final breach between the two came in wake of Smith's post–1776 literary celebrity. On the other hand, to label it purely as jealous backlash by Johnson would surely be going too far, since Johnson himself had little left to prove or apologize for at that point in his long career. More likely, he was sincerely outraged by Smith's and Hume's unorthodox personal and political beliefs, now gone so unapologetically public. Johnson himself would outlive the American Revolution and Treaty of Paris by only a year, dying in 1784.

Smith's last seven years can be briefly summarized, although his quiet personal lifestyle belied a lively intellectual interaction with many contemporaries, all the while remaining actively engaged in his day-to-day duties with the affairs of international commerce. Perhaps the most exciting event of his later life came earlier in 1778–1779, when the successful naval raids of Scottish-born American privateer John Paul Jones (1747–1792) occasionally fell within his customs jurisdiction.[19] Soon after American revolutionary victory, Smith helped to found the prestigious Royal Society of Edinburgh in 1783.[20] Then in 1784, he added 24,000 words to a brand new edition of *WN* (one of the same editions owned by Thomas Jefferson). That same year his distinguished admiring visitors included British P.C. and Tory conservative leader Edmund Burke, whom his writings had greatly influenced (see Chapter 1).[21] Two years later, in 1787, came the death of his elderly mother, with whom he lived and was probably closer to than any other person.[22] Smith would not long outlive this blow, although during this last period engraver James Tassie and caricaturist John Kay were able to memorably record Smith's likeness for posterity before his passing.[23]

After the loss of his mother, Smith turned his attention to making final revisions for his *Theory of Moral Sentiments* (*TMS*), originally written during his days as a Glasgow professor of moral philosophy, and published in its final form in 1790.[24] To the very end Smith surprisingly maintained that his obscure tenure at Glasgow had been "by far the most useful, and, therefore, as by far the happiest and most honorable period of my life."[25] It had also been in Glasgow where Smith personally witnessed the tremendous personal fortunes being made from the American colonial trade, especially from tobacco. In the revised edition of *TMS*, Smith dwelled upon widespread admiration for the rich and powerful while virtue and wisdom were generally held in contempt.[26] By 1790, frequent, complicating illnesses made him realize that the end was near. He ordered many of his unpublished papers to be burned, bequeathed his extensive library to the son of a cousin who lived with and helped to take care of him, then finally lamented that "he had done so little" and "meant to have done more."[27] Before passing away in Edinburgh on July 17, 1790, according to witnesses, Smith's final parting words to friends present at his house for philosophical discussion were "I believe we must adjourn this meeting to some other place."[28]

Smith ideas on taxation represent some of the most highly debated (and frequently misinterpreted) writings in the economics canon, but there can be no doubt as to where he stood on certain luxuries or, as some might refer to them, vice items. In short, he believed that such commodities, especially if imported, should be regulated and taxed without hesitation. The top of this luxury list included sugar, alcohol, and tobacco. Making implied reference to the cherished American notion of equality, Smith declares that all citizens owe financial contribution to their government in proportion to their respective abilities (see Chapter 9).[29] Later Smith takes more direct aim at the colonies by writing to the effect that they should be granted parliamentary representation, but then promptly taxed and regulated for their most profitable exports.[30] While he believed that these kinds of import duties should be moderate, reasonable, and not protectionist in scope, he insisted that many mercantilists, Americans included, were simply not paying their fair share of taxes, at least according to their substantial and rapidly burgeoning means. One cannot help but wonder if the Americans would have foregone their rebellion if the British government had followed Smith's advice, and given the colonies parliamentary representation while taxing them according to their considerable wealth. On the other hand, it seems apparent that many of the key American revolutionaries—Washington, Franklin, Hamilton, Jefferson—were driven to rebellion in no small part by various personal slights suffered previously at the hands of British arrogance, rather than any pressing desire for maximizing financial gain.[31]

If the British Empire earlier tried unsuccessfully to force-feed American colonists with over-expensive imported tea from the East Indies, then the colonists retaliated (in a very real sense) by successfully exporting home-grown premium tobacco to the English until they were hopelessly addicted. No other commodity better illustrates the international economic power of 18th century America. In *WN*, Smith almost broodingly reflects on the spectacular success of Virginia and Maryland as tobacco exporters. This was an age in which the health risks of tobacco were merely being hypothesized, but any close read of *WN* leaves one with the definite feeling that Smith sensed something was wrong, in terms of commercial trade balance if nothing else. At both the beginning and end of the work he remarks upon the high market value of tobacco, which was used extensively as barter both in America and abroad.[32] Despite a conspicuous shortage of hard currency, Smith observes that "They [Virginia planters] are reckoned, however, as thriving, and consequently as rich, as any of their neighbors."[33] It goes almost without saying that many of the most important American Founding Fathers were Virginians and, to varying degrees, tobacco growers, including Washington, Jefferson, and Madison. The controversy has continued seemingly unabated over nearly the last two and half centuries. Recently in 2013, the Adam Smith Institute (ASI), a respected but libertarian-leaning British think tank bearing the name of the founding father of modern economics, fell afoul of public opinion when it was revealed that a large portion of its funding came from big tobacco interests. Not too surprisingly, its public stances of late on various tobacco restrictions had been allegedly somewhat less than enthusiastic.[34]

Some of the most dramatic artifacts of the robust 18th century Anglo-American tobacco industry can be today found in the British Museum, where advertisements proclaim with pride the manner in which these products were produced. One such ad (readily available on the Internet) is a woodcut entitled "Martin's Best Virginia at the Tobacco Role in Bloomsbury Market," presumably in reference to a vendor at the eponymous farmer's market in London. The illustration depicts African-American slave children happily harvesting tobacco leaves from a Virginia plantation, a smiling-faced sun shining overhead.

In fairness to the multitudes that once earned their livelihoods, and in some cases, amassed great fortunes, from this overseas trade, it should be added many things have not changed between the 18th and 21st centuries. Despite the abolition of slavery, and despite proven health risks, tobacco now dominates world markets far more than it did during Adam Smith's time. One can only come back to his stated belief in *WN* that such unnecessary industries should be carefully controlled and profits channeled into proper directions, a pragmatic view that even the entrepreneurial and less-than-virtuous Alexander Hamilton would likely have agreed with.

Exactly two months before Adam Smith's death in Edinburgh, Benjamin Franklin passed away in Philadelphia on April 17, 1790. Franklin and Smith came into contact before the American Revolution, and most scholars agree that there was some exchange of economic ideas between them (see Chapter 1). Franklin lived to see not only the victory of the Revolution, but the firm establishment of a strong and centralized U.S. federal government as well, both of which he vigorously supported. The result would be an American economy able to grow by participating in international trade without being crushed by foreign competition. With Franklin's passing began the gradual disappearance of the nation's founding generation, and the rise of a new one that would build upon their successes in spectacular fashion. For the next two and half decades, however, the pressing economic issue would be which European country was America's greater rival, England or France? The answer, as time would prove, depended on the particular moment and whomever happened to be in charge.

3. The British Empire Makes War Against Its Offspring (1791–1815)

"The great change introduced into the art of war by the invention of fire-arms, has enhanced still further both the expense of exercising and disciplining any particular number of soldiers in time of peace, and that of employing them in time of war."—Adam Smith[1]

By the early 1790s, the French *Ancien Régime* was in the midst of its final death throes thanks to a cataclysmic revolution inspired in no small part by the American example set less than two decades before. An unfortunate byproduct of this event in France was widespread violence both at home and abroad. While *Le Marseillaise* was becoming the new French national anthem, the rest of Old World Europe, along with their diminishing numbers of French allies, reacted with fear and loathing. Before the end of 1793, both King Louis XVI and Queen Marie Antionette had been guillotined while all-out war, for the third time in less than 40 years, commenced yet again between neighboring France and England. With a few pauses, this struggle would continue on several continents until Bonaparte's ultimate defeat at Waterloo in 1815 finally brought some lasting closure to Anglo-French hostilities.

Meanwhile, in America, the upstart United States of America was mostly allowed to grow and prosper, thanks in part to Europe's distractions with itself, and in no small part due to the wisdom and perseverance of the U.S. Founding Fathers. As the 18th century drew to a close and the 19th century began, it may well be said that the very same international trade issues addressed by Adam Smith during the 1760s and 1770s continued to play out on an even wider global scale. By the end of 1790, however, Smith was dead and his philosophical legacy was only for the first time being seriously pondered on both the American and European continents. Strangely, even in revolutionary France, the Anglo-American ex-patriot Thomas Paine (1737–1809) saw fit to favorably drop Adam Smith's name in his *Rights of Man* treatise from 1791, while attacking the anti-revolutionary sentiments of Smith's younger economic disciple, the Irish-British Parliamentarian Edmund Burke (see Chapter 1).[2]

In America the economic debate commenced, as it usually did in those days, with the unquenchable political rivalry between Alexander Hamilton (as Secretary of Treasury) and Thomas Jefferson (as Secretary of State). After the Tariff of 1789 gave a round one victory to Hamilton, he spent much of the next two years drafting an elaborate economic blueprint, published in 1791 as the *Report on Manufactures*, considered a classic in terms of its long range influence on public policy, although this influence was not immediate, nor even within Hamilton's lifetime. In the *Report*, Hamilton did not quote Smith by name (probably for political convenience), but did borrow extensively Smith's terminology, language and ideas from *WN*.[3] Conversely, Hamilton took express issue with Smith's belief in the supremacy of agriculture over manufacturing, as well as Smith's perceived advocacy of total free trade with no restrictions. Hamilton's compelling justification for this argument was that other foreign countries used tariffs against the U.S., and if the U.S. did not do the same it would be placed at a competitive disadvantage. In short, Hamilton proposed more (and generally higher) tariffs on designated imports—to be used, however, in a specific and moderate fashion—plus direct government subsidies for certain private industries. Most of the highest tariffs related to military spending—firearms, gunpowder, steel, iron—which President Washington supported.[4] Congress ignored the controversial suggestion for government subsidies, at least for the time being, but otherwise adopted wholesale Hamilton's recommendations for tariffs, as well as his proposed consolidation of the national debt. Both of these proved to be successful endeavors and both were made over the strenuous objections of Jefferson, Madison, and other Southerners.[5]

In 1795, as Washington's second term began to wind down—and after implementation of Hamilton's pet project, a National Bank—the combative Secretary of Treasury stepped down from the cabinet, probably knowing that he would not be reappointed by a new President. By then, it may have also dawned on Hamilton that he had no future in elected politics, and possibly had reached the pinnacle of his life's achievements, considerable as those were. Apart from having personally antagonized most of his peers (except for Washington), Hamilton's biggest problem was a messy, sordid personal life that made the later violent excesses of Andrew Jackson look like high-spirited fun. According to the letters of Abagail Adams—considered a highly reliable source by this author—Hamilton imagined himself an American Bonaparte, and dreamed of leading a great army against the French and Spanish as far west and south as the imagination could carry.[6] When this ambition was thwarted by President John Adam's secret peace negotiations with France in early 1799, a frustrated Hamilton found himself with a Major General's commission, but no great army to lead or war to conduct. Then he worked tirelessly behind the scenes to defeat the re-election of Adams—a co–Federalist Party member—in the presidential election of 1800. After Washington, his great protector, died in late 1799, the much younger Hamilton outlived him by less than five years before being killed in a duel by Vice President Aaron Burr.[7] After half a lifetime of offending powerful people everywhere, Hamilton had at last offended the wrong person, a co–Federalist and fellow New Yorker. Viewed in political and economic hindsight, he was the wrong messenger, but with perhaps the right message at the right time.[8]

America's delicate balancing of maintaining neutrality in escalating European conflicts continued into the early 19th century with the two-term presidency of Thomas Jefferson between 1801 and 1809. Both England and France were major U.S. trading partners, even as the two fought each other near continuously over economic turf and political ideals. It was the same kind of expensive, debilitating struggle that had so horrified Adam Smith during his Glasgow academic days during the late 1750s. Then in 1803, Jefferson accomplished through diplomacy and negotiations with France what Hamilton had only dreamed of doing through military conquest, namely, acquired for the U.S. over 800,000 square miles of land stretching from New Orleans north to the Canadian border.[9] The Louisiana Purchase nearly doubled the size of the country overnight, and helped to finance Bonaparte's war against England for years to come. Simultaneously, between 1801 and 1805, Jefferson authorized U.S. naval force to be effectively used against North African Barbary pirates in the Mediterranean ("the shores of Tripoli"), thereby asserting American trading rights in international waters. The net effect of these bold moves was to further antagonize Great Britain, both by giving money to France and having the presumption to insist that American shipping be allowed to navigate in the European sphere alongside the all-powerful British fleet. Although the Americans had not formally sided with the French—the natural thing to expect after French support of the American Revolution—they had not fought against them either; moreover, the U.S. had now become a forceful player on the international stage (much to British resentment) thanks to a domestic prosperity wisely promoted during the 1790s.[10] After the retirement and death of the comparatively pro–British

Alexander Hamilton, however, it rightfully seemed by the time of Jefferson's re-election as President that Anglo-American relations were in a state of serious, irreversible decline.

In a misguided effort to repair this damage in neutrality, Jefferson sponsored the unpopular Embargo Act of 1807–1809, aimed against both France and Great Britain simultaneously. The measure succeeded only in severely hurting the American economy, straining relations with France, and doing nothing to mollify the British, who retaliated with their own, long-term trade restrictions. The only people profiting were smugglers, who were earning unprecedented fortunes. Afterwards, it was one of the few documented instances in which Jefferson ever admitted to making a mistake. Although he was an enthusiastic student of Adam Smith's free trade theories, and Smith would have surely advised against making such a move during time of peace, Jefferson became temporarily carried away with his old conviction that the United States was a uniquely self-sufficient nation of gentlemen farmers like himself.[11] To his credit, once visible damage from the Embargo appeared on the home front, it did not take Jefferson long to recognize his error. Another incentive for repeal of the Act came when the presumed-dead Federalist Party made a surprising show of strength against the incumbent Democratic-Republican Party of Jefferson and newly-elected President James Madison in the 1808 election. Repeal of the Embargo, however, did not remove the growing popular outrage over brazen and widespread British naval impressment of American merchant marines. By 1812, the United States was effectively back to one-party governance, and one completely hostile to England. The American Congress, like a long-abused child, declared war, partly out of exasperation and partly out of hubris. England, preoccupied with Bonaparte at the height of his power, prestige, and arrogance, at first ignored the declaration. This prompted the Americans, as if in a plea for attention, to inaugurate hostilities by invading Canada with a rag-tag force that was quickly repulsed.[12] Great Britain at last responded by vigorously attacking American targets on land and sea, and the War of 1812 began in earnest.

It is a safe bet that Adam Smith would have taken a dim view of this unnecessary conflict, just as he had on previous British military excursions into North America. It is also hard to imagine Smith, as a Scotsman, sympathizing with the impressment of naturalized American citizens (many of them Irish-born) by the British Navy, even as part of the war effort against Bonaparte. On the other hand, he would have likely censored Americans for jumping into a fight for which they lacked both a standing professional army and adequate financial resources. In any event, after roughly two years of stalemate, both sides sued for peace. In between, having forever disabused the Americans of their Canadian territorial ambitions, the British enjoyed payback of a sorts by wreaking havoc against U.S. commercial shipping and burning the government buildings of Washington, D.C., to the ground in 1814, forcing President Madison and his government—the same which had declared war two years previous—to flee for their lives.[13] On the positive side of the ledger, the war led to the defeat and mass expulsion of Native Americans east of the Mississippi River, and concluded with General Andrew Jackson's spectacular victory over British regulars at the Battle of New Orleans on January 8, 1815, fought 15 days after the Peace Treaty of Ghent had been signed, but during an era in which trans–Atlantic communications took several weeks.[14] Interestingly, at New Orleans, Jackson had received significant help from an unlikely source whose fate and calling in life had been largely shaped by the unwise official trading policies of those times.

Captain Jean Lafitte has proven over time to be one of the more controversial, mysterious and interesting figures in American history. Born sometime during the American Revolution either in France, Hispaniola, or perhaps Louisiana—where his Jewish forebears may have been part of the great Acadian diaspora following the French and Indian War—Lafitte seems to have made a study of defying all easy stereotypes during his turbulent life. His romanticized legend has been largely shaped by the Hollywood screen biographies (*The Buccaneer*) of 1938 and 1958 by Cecil B. DeMille.[15] Although hard evidence is scanty at best, it appears that in wake of the Louisiana Purchase, Lafitte had been a respectable entrepreneur—at least in the New Orleans sense of the phrase—until Jefferson's Embargo Act of 1807 threatened to extinguish his livelihood as an importer. Rather than succumb to poverty, Lafitte did what many others did: turned to smuggling and piracy. He found himself quite adept at these activities, earning more money than he ever did as a legitimate businessman. Although quickly declared an American outlaw, his habit and reputation for square dealing, as well as for harassing the British and Spanish, earned him a substantial amount of local popular sympathy and cooperation. When the Embargo was lifted, Lafitte saw no particular reason to earn less money or throw himself at the mercy of American legal authorities. In his case the lines between commerce and piracy became clearly blurred. Some viewed him almost as a Robin Hood–like figure.

Lafitte's moment of glory came at the Battle of New Orleans, in which Andrew Jackson found himself badly outnumbered by an invading British expeditionary force. Jackson's main asset was heavy artillery, but the backwoods militiamen constituting the bulk of his army lacked the expertise to use it. Lafitte's sailors, on the other hand, knew exactly how to use these field pieces, and had no great love for the British besides. Accounts vary, but many agree that Jackson—famous for cozying up to marginal types when necessary—requested a sit-down with Lafitte in which it was agreed that his pirates would fight with the Americans in return for amnesty. During the battle, Lafitte's artillerymen wreaked havoc on British Highlander regiments assaulting the American-defended line. After victory and peace, Lafitte received his official pardon, but his previous lifestyle and enmity for petty government officials had accustomed him to living above the law. He moved his operations west, first to Galveston, Texas, and then later to Mexico, where most accounts have him perishing in naval combat while privateering for the Mexican independence movement away from Spanish rule. Today, a Louisiana National Park bears his name, as well as numerous other tourist attractions in the region.

It has been noted by a number of commentators that Smith, both in his writings and as an appointed customs commissioner holding free trade beliefs, displayed a certain sympathy with smugglers, and the same attitude would have likely applied towards Lafitte and his merry band of Franco-American outlaws. With respect to economic theory, however, the Battle of New Orleans in which Lafitte participated would have underscored one of Smith's core assertions regarding the art and science of modern warfare, namely, that skilled firepower nearly always trumped heroic manpower.

An infrequently remarked upon historical event (at least among economic historians) from Smith's younger days would have been crucial in the formation of his opinions on military spending. During the spring of 1746, as a 22-year-old and probably dispirited Smith made his way back home to Kirkcaldy, Scotland, from an unsatisfactory stint at Oxford University, the fabled Battle of Culloden was fought in the northern Highlands between combined British-Scot royalist forces under the Duke of Cumberland and Jacobite rebels led by Charles Edward Stuart, better known as Bonnie Prince Charlie or the Young Pretender (to partisans and critics, respectively). This engagement would prove to be the last in long series of organized clan uprisings crushed by the English, and they did so heavily aided by updated weapons technology.[16] Although the Jacobites had won several previous engagements with determined hand-to-hand fighting, and were engaging the British on familiar native soil with roughly comparable numbers, at Culloden they found themselves charging defensive lines composed of concentrated, disciplined musketry and heavy modern artillery. The shocking result for the rebels was a slaughter, and it may well be said that the disastrous, bloody rout left a permanent psychological impression on the Scots national sensibility. This same impression was perhaps even stronger for Scotsmen living further to the south and more traditionally loyal to the English crown, including Adam Smith and his immediate relatives.[17] In terms of military and economic strategy, Culloden also shared this commonality with the Battle of New Orleans fought some seven decades later on the North American continent, namely, the side possessing the bigger guns (and knowing precisely how to use these) won the contest notwithstanding other factors.

Smith's writings are unequivocal in this regard. In Book V, Chapter I, Part I of *WN*, he lays out, in uncharacteristic, succinct form, national defense as the number one, nonnegotiable justification for public taxation. After giving one of his typically thorough and far-reaching historical overviews, Smith concludes that, not only is a standing professional army a necessary thing, but usually a desirable thing as well, so long as its commanders have a vested interest in preserving the government under which they serve. Smith declares that a standing professional army even "may in some cases be favorable to liberty."[18] Then he proceeds to his main point, that tax dollars for military spending are best spent on the latest technology and skillful human use thereof. We would wager heavily that Smith had Culloden in the back of his mind when writing these words.

This dynamic of course makes military spending much more expensive than it used to be, or as Smith explained: "The military force of the society, which originally cost the sovereign no expense either in time of peace or in time of war, must, in the progress of improvement, first be maintained by him in time of war, and afterwards even in time of peace."[19] With bittersweet insight, he concludes this rarely-quoted section of *WN* by noting that, in stark contrast to the ancient world, "In modern times the poor and barbarous find it difficult to defend themselves against the opulent and civilized."[20] He may as well have been writing about Manifest Destiny in the American West, which began to noticeably accelerate from the moment war was declared between the U.S. and Great Britain in 1812.

Historians have disagreed on the underlying causes of the War of 1812, although most agree the British naval impressment of American citizens was a triggering factor. One might well argue that the underlying causes were very similar to the ones causing the American Revolution itself, namely, the 300-year struggle for economic supremacy in the New World between Americans, Great Britain, and France. In a very real sense, the 1812 conflict was a direct outgrowth of revolution in America (more so than in France), though coming 29 years after the fact. The years 1812–1815 arguably represented the climax of this struggle and, in hindsight, the United States was the clear victor, although this was certainly not obvious at the time. The new world order that Adam Smith had suggested in the final passages of *WN*—Great Britain trading with America as an independent state—had come to pass. At first this proved to be very advantageous to British in terms of international trading prowess, but by the early 19th century the Americans had learned to push back with no small help from a strong, newly-formed central government. In pure economic terms, this new dynamic of a U.S. federal government, one hardly imagined by the Founding Fathers (with a few exceptions), had been the brainchild of Alexander Hamilton. He must also receive major credit for politically ramming it into existence. In order to examine how this altered balance of international power might have been viewed by Smith, one could do no better than summarize the opinions of Hamilton himself, even though he had been dead eight years before overconfident and poorly-organized U.S. forces marched north over the Canadian border, the very opposite geographical direction in which Hamilton would have had them marching were he still alive.

While adopting wholesale language and analysis from Smith's *WN*, Hamilton in his *Report* then did what no American before him had: dared to reinterpret, refine, and mildly criticize Smith's famous propositions.[21] With the appalling example of the French Revolution in recent memory, Hamilton argued that too much freedom could be a bad thing. Given the never-ending mess of Hamilton's personal life, the argument carried particular force coming from him. For one, Hamilton clearly foresaw that agriculture would play an equal if not supporting role to manufacturing during the unfolding industrial revolution. Secondly, Hamilton was one of the few contemporaries of Smith recognizing that the Scots philosopher was not an uncritical *laissez-faire* advocate, but rather a selective borrower of *laissez-faire* ideas. Accordingly, Hamilton stressed that the U.S. should only go so far in implementing free trade policies and that a strong federal government was essential to the well-being of national prosperity.

All this being said, Hamilton far more agreed with Smith than disagreed with him on general principles. In addition to being critical (like Smith) of the French *laissez-faire* doctrine in its pure form, Hamilton praised the ever-sharpening division of labor in the American economy and, above all, stressed the need for more public infrastructure as the key to national wealth. For this last item, Hamilton quotes from *WN* verbatim (without crediting the source): "They [Good roads, canals, navigable rivers] are upon that account the greatest of all improvements."[22] Perhaps the most tangible result of this precursor for public-private partnership in the United States was that, thanks to Hamilton's policies, foreign holdings of U.S. debt increased eightfold between 1788 and

1795, even as national economic growth and prosperity skyrocketed.[23] It was this same early prosperity which enabled the country to emerge during the early 19th century from the great Anglo-French conflicts of the past into a position of worldwide competitive strength.

Around the same time that Hamilton was writing his *Report*, another U.S. Founding Father was quoting Adam Smith in print, but in a considerably different context. Future President John Adams (1735–1826), apparently bored with his job as Vice President and left out of the loop while Washington, Hamilton and Jefferson were busy running the new government, took to writing anonymous installments in 1790–1791 for the *Gazette of the United States*, a periodical which President Washington subscribed to. In 1805 these essays were published as a collected volume, with handwritten annotations by Adams as late as 1812. Obliquely titled "Discourses on Davila," the series began as a new English translation of Enrico Caterino Davila's history on the 16th century French Wars of Religion—a topic today forgotten but one near and dear to the Founding Fathers—then eventually transformed into opinion pieces.[24] Therein Vice President Adams quoted Adam Smith at length verbatim (like Hamilton, without mentioning him by name), alongside the likes of Shakespeare, Voltaire, Pope, and Smith's old nemesis, Samuel Johnson. Interestingly, however, Adams did not quote from *WN*, but rather from Smith's earlier, well-received philosophical treatise of 1759, *Theory of Moral Sentiments* (*TMS*).

The passages of *TMS* that caught Adam's attention were Smith's gripping mediations on why mankind pursues wealth, fame, power so ferociously. In Book VIII of his *Discourses*, Adams quotes these at length, beginning with Smith's withering observation that "To those who have been accustomed to the possession, or even to the hope of public admiration, all other pleasures sicken and decay." Then he gets to the heart of the matter:

> Of all the discarded statesmen who for their own ease have studied to get the better of ambition, and to despise those honours which they could no longer arrive at, how few have been able to succeed? The greater part have spent their time in the most listless and insipid indolence, chagrined at the thoughts of their own insignificancy, incapable of being interested in the occupations of private life, without enjoyment, except when they talked of their former greatness, and without satisfaction, except when they were employed in some vain project to recover it.[25]

These words may well have been aimed by Adams at the likes of Alexander Hamilton, even though Smith originally wrote them around the same time that Hamilton was born. This was also the same year (1759) that Charles Stuart, a (by then) not-so-young pretender, vainly plotted yet another Scottish rebellion (from his French exile), news of which had surely reached a disapproving Smith in Glasgow.[26]

Smith's stature and reputation after his death in 1790 continued to grow in Great Britain, as well as America. William Pitt the Younger, British Prime Minister from the end of the American Revolution to the beginning of the 19th century (see Chapter 2), was well versed in Smith's philosophy, and put these beliefs into visible political practice during his long and influential administration. Paradoxically, in spite of Pitt's peaceful disposition towards the U.S., his liberal trade policies quickly allowed British imports to flood American markets, hence pushing the latter's economy to the brink of chaos. When Americans rose to the challenge by creating a new federal government and semblance of coordinated policy decisions (thanks mainly to Hamilton), Pitt continued to apply export pressure against the U.S. even while England waged all-out war against France. The net effect was to repair England's damaged finances after the costly North American conflicts of the previous century, as well as to goad the Americans into taking their first tentative steps towards protecting their economy while encouraging military spending and buildup. Perhaps the most famous anecdote regarding Pitt's veneration for Smith dates from the previous decade, which gives an account of Pitt, along with his political protégés, paying an honorary visit to Smith in Edinburgh late during the latter's life. Upon entering the room, Smith found his distinguished guests standing and refusing to sit down first because, as Pitt declared, "we are all your scholars."[27]

Another one of Smith's famous "scholars" was fellow countryman and Scotland's national poet Robert Burns (1759–1796), also destined to become one of the most popular modern English-language poets. Like the American statesman John Adams, Burns had been first influenced by Smith's *TMS*, and in the case of Burns, during his impressionable teenage student years. Some scholars have argued this influence carried over into his poetry. By the time that Burns began to make a name for himself as a poet during the late 1780s, Smith reciprocated the admiration by purchasing Burns' works. A prearranged meeting between the two great writers in 1787 turned into an unfortunate near-miss when sudden illness forced Smith to seek medical treatment away from his Edinburgh home.[28] Rarely remarked upon, but most fascinating, is Burns' subsequent appointment in 1789 as a customs inspector in Dumfries, a position that he held (like Smith before him) until his untimely death seven years later. Having failed at farming—an activity glorified by Smith in *WN*—Burns, like Smith and many a noteworthy writer before and after him, supported his family and his art with a steady paycheck from the civil service.

Within three short years of Smith's death appeared his first published biography by fellow Scotsman Dugald Stewart in 1793, *Account of the Life and Writings of Adam Smith L.L.D.*[29] Stewart, as a professor of philosophy at the University of Edinburgh (and fellow member of the Royal Society), had known Smith personally and was in a good position for the task of memorializing his friend.[30] Stewart is also said to have delivered the first university lectures on political economy, a newfangled subject matter more or less introduced to the English-speaking world by Smith. Stewart's biographical sketch on Smith, though abbreviated and incomplete, has formed the basis for longer biographical studies coming in its wake. Around this same period, big-name British economists of the next generation, such as Jeremy Bentham (1748–1832) and David Ricardo (1772–1823), began to study Smith's legacy in earnest, adding their own refinements and corrections, not unlike Alexander Hamilton had done. Our continuing focus will be on the political influence that economists like Bentham and Riccardo had on future Anglo-American policy-making, rather than the complex and unique theories of these writers. It is noteworthy, however, that as the pervasive influence of the Pitt administration in Great Britain receded during the early 1800s, along with the death of Hamilton and decline of the pro–British Federalist Party in the U.S., military tensions with the U.S. correspondingly increased.

Political cartoons leading up to the War of 1812 on both sides of the Atlantic are a trove of wit and irreverence, and a surprising number deal with bread-and-butter economic issues rather than British naval impressment of American citizens. This held particularly true with respect to the highly unpopular Embargo Act of 1807–1809. A notable example is the notorious "Ograbme" ("embargo" spelled backwards) cartoon from 1807, in which American public opinion humorously sways against the very same legal protectionism supposedly designed to protect its domestic economy from foreign goods, particularly British imports. An Anglo merchant on American soil, holding a barrel labeled "superfine," is bitten in the posterior by a huge American snapping turtle treading a trading license underfoot.[31] The turtle's American wrangler (presumably a customs official) gleefully exclaims "D—m it, how he nicks 'em," while the aggrieved merchant laments "Oh, this cursed Ograbme." The reverse spelling makes no attempt to disguise the object of its satire, but is intended as a bawdy pun. President Jefferson, the prime mover and shaker behind the embargo, but also a consummate politician, probably took one look at cartoons like this one and quickly realized that immediate back-peddling would be necessary. It was such misguided legislation that drove people like Jean Lafitte and thousands of other enterprising individuals into lucrative lives of crime, much the same manner in which naïve American Prohibition laws would do the same a little over a century later.

On June 18, 1815, less than five months after the Treaty of Ghent put an end to the senseless War of 1812, the Battle of Waterloo was fought and won by the British, forever ending the Napoleonic threat against Europe, and inaugurating the *Pax Britannica* of the 19th century. Never again would Great Britain and France make war on each other; never again would the U.S. and Great Britain fight each other, at least in the conventional sense. France and U.S. never had fought each other to begin with, and that still remains happily true to this day. By the summer of 1815, a new dynamic was emerging under the great competing world powers. Although the American and French Revolutions had ended, the Industrial Revolution was still ongoing. In short, there was money to be made, oftentimes great fortunes that would make or break nation states in the process. The number one line expense in all business endeavors, however, is usually the cost of labor. Unfortunately for the rapidly developing United States, much of this cost had thus far been perceivedly defrayed through the extension of an ancient social institution that was coming into increasing public disfavor worldwide.

4. Almost Free Labor (1816–1837)

"The experience of all ages and nations, I believe, demonstrates that the work done by slaves, though it appears to cost only their maintenance, is in the end the dearest of any. A person who can acquire no property, can have no other interest but to eat as much, and to labour as little as possible."—Adam Smith[1]

With the conclusion of the Napoleonic Wars in Europe, Great Britain and the United States went back to doing what they did best together: international trade and commerce. France did the same but, as a recently defeated country, had to settle for secondary status. For the United States, however, this meant sustained explosive growth, both in terms of territorial expansion and economic productivity, fueled primarily by Northern manufacturing in tandem with Southern agriculture. The Industrial Revolution, beginning in the late 18th century, now hit England and New England simultaneously with its irresistible combination of technological progress and higher profit margins, jumpstarted by the completion of the Erie Canal in 1820, linking the upper Atlantic seaboard with the Great Lakes region. Curiously, though, the new invention proving to most shape and provoke American political events over the next half century occurred, not in New England, but in the slave state of Georgia, where Yankee-born inventor Eli Whitney (1765–1825) patented his first cotton gin prototype circa 1794.[2] One unintentional consequence of this breakthrough was a powerful resurgence of slave labor below Mason-Dixon, even as legalized slavery had been abolished by all states north of the line as early as 1804.[3] By the 1830s, this trend unfortunately coincided with a widespread change in public attitudes towards slavery throughout the industrial world; in fact, the writings of Adam Smith during the previous century are among the earliest and most eloquent to be cited as an example of this notable shift in opinion.

The defining political symbol of this era in American history may well be summed up by the combative presidency of the Carolina-born, adoptive Tennessean, and Scots-Irish descended Andrew Jackson (1767–1845), hero of the Battle of New Orleans, whose lionized image today graces the American twenty-dollar bill. Jackson's two White House terms from 1829 to 1837 were marked by a raucous public and congressional debate over sweeping economic issues facing the rapidly expanding republic. By late 1836, the last surviving Revolutionary-turned-elected-official, Aaron Burr, was dead, and Jackson perfectly represented an entire new generation of American leaders drawn from the growing ranks of self-made frontiersmen.[4] Jackson may also be characterized as the feisty re-inventor of the modern Democratic Party, as well as the personal embodiment of all its virtues and shortcomings.[5] His natural and deeply-engrained prejudice against big business led him in 1833 to forcefully dismantle the Second Bank of the United States (BUSII), an institution endorsed, with qualification, by Adam Smith during the previous century and which many of the Founding Fathers, beginning with Alexander Hamilton, had worked hard to establish.

Jackson's successful but rash crusades against BUSII and the U.S. national debt in turn triggered dire economic consequences from which the country took seven long years to recover. Jackson's Democratic successors in office never made the same mistakes again; moreover, Jackson's anti-big-government feelings only went so far. Infrequently remarked upon was his unhesitant willingness to turn upon his own Southern constituents with the same ferocity he directed against British and Native American opponents. When Vice-President John C. Calhoun of South Carolina attempted to stir up a secessionist movement in 1828–1832 over imposed federal tariffs, Jackson not only ousted Calhoun as V.P., but publicly threatened to lead a federal army into South Carolina where, he said, all traitors would be made to hang. Everyone, especially Carolinians, took the threats of Old Hickory quite seriously, and were suddenly willing to compromise, thus averting a crisis. Later, an irritated Jackson wrote privately that the incident was a mere Southern pretext for asserting prerogatives over slavery—history would prove him correct.

In 1833, not long after President Jackson contemplated using U.S. troops against U.S. citizens, the British Empire abolished all human slavery within its jurisdiction. Twenty-five years earlier, in 1807, the British had abolished the trading of slaves as a prelude to outright abolition. A hundred years prior to that, in 1707, the official Union of Scotland with England (to form the United Kingdom) caused many Scots for the first time to be directly confronted with the evil practices of African-American human trafficking, although for decades there had been a bustling white slave trade from the Scottish Highlands to the New World. As fate would have it, around the year 1726, a three-year-old Adam Smith was temporarily abducted from his Kirkcaldy home, probably with intent to ultimately sell the boy into overseas slavery. Fortunately, Smith was rescued soon afterwards and brought safely back home to his frightened widowed mother. Also rescued in the process was the future of English letters and yet-to-be invented academic field of political economy. How much of this disturbing incident Smith personally remembered is not recorded, but there can be little doubt that as an adult he later must have often reflected upon it. More importantly, as a native Scotsman, no matter how otherwise loyal to the British Crown or sympathetic to the American colonists, Smith would have certainly taken a dim view towards any kind of perceived human oppression, with or without trauma personally experienced.[6] In his case, however, there was personal experience, progressive education, and a longstanding cultural tradition all combining to bolster his uniquely negative attitude towards any form of human bondage.

Smith was among the first writers, if not *the* first, to forcefully argue against slavery on the grounds that it was a counterproductive business practice. In *Wealth of Nations* (*WN*), Book III, Chapter II, he famously lays down his cornerstone principle that forced labor lacking profit incentive for the worker is the most inefficient and least desirable of its kind. In terms of pure dollars and cents, Smith emphasized that the maintenance and replacement costs of slaves were in fact much higher than generally acknowledged; moreover, that "wear and tear of a slave" was in reality a much greater expense to the master than that of a free servant or salaried employee.[7] In other words, there were hidden costs associated with slavery in addition to the moral arguments against it.[8] "It appears," wrote Smith, "from experience of all ages and nations, I believe, that the work done by freemen comes cheaper in the end than that performed by slaves."[9] Accordingly, he argues, "great improvements are seldom to be expected from great proprietors" and "least of all to be expected when they employ slaves for their workmen."[10] Despite these strong pronouncements, in recent years some commentators have tried to postulate that Smith was not an abolitionist in the traditional sense, based on preserved academic lectures he delivered from the early 1760s. Here, long before the American Revolution or *WN*, Smith reminded students that slavery had been a constant in the world since the dawn of recorded time and unlikely to be abolished anytime in the foreseeable future.[11] Nevertheless, some 43 years after his death, the British Empire did precisely that.

Anyone doubting Smith's absolute hostility towards slavery may refer not only to extensive passages from *WN*, but to earlier ones in 1759 from his *TMS*. Here, while exploring the pervasive influence of habit and custom on mutable human beliefs, Smith favorably contrasts the noble savagery of African slaves and Native Americans with the typically less-than-noble behavior of their European masters in the New World.[12] In reaction to Smith's writings—keep in mind this was over a decade before *WN* would appear—the London-based American diplomat and spy, Arthur Lee (1740–1792), published in 1764 his ponderously titled *Essay in the Vindication of the Continental Colonies of America from a Censure of Mr. Adam Smith, in His Theory of Moral Sentiments*. Lee, that rarest of breeds, a Virginian abolitionist, nevertheless took umbrage at Smith's egalitarian views on race and felt a need to refute them. Instead, however, he comes off as a prime example of what Smith was writing about in the first place, that is, a privileged and highly-educated person whose opinions nevertheless seem to drastically shift depending on whatever surrounding circumstances happen to be. Twelve years later, at the dawn of the American Revolution, Smith's anti-slavery remarks in *WN* appear to naturally tie into one of his great secondary themes, namely, that free enterprise left unguided by rules of law or morality tends to be, in the long-run, short-sighted and self-defeating. That is to say, pro-slavery or pro-race theory apologists, despite their loud and often violent advocacy, were in fact defending a counterproductive and inefficient approach to economic development.

Smith's view of slavery was consistent with his theories on labor and human history in general. Early in the pages of *WN*, he unequivocally pronounces (somewhat controversially in the eyes of later economists) that "Labour is the real measure of exchangeable value."[13] In keeping with Smith's generally low opinion of overrated precious metals (see Chapter 10), he emphasizes that the value of gold and silver pales in comparison to the value of labor, and that "It [labor] is their [commodities'] real price; money is their nominal price only."[14] Within the context of medieval feudalism, with serfdom as its near equivalent to slavery, control of labor was the true key and lynchpin to the political power of kings and nobility. Once that specific control was gradually ceded to the rising merchant class, the days of absolute monarchy were numbered. In reference to this tectonic shift in history Smith wrote his famous remarks on "the vile maxim of the masters of mankind" ("All for ourselves, and nothing for other people"), in which medieval kings and barons began to swap total control of the workforce in return for shiny trinkets, and in the process accelerated their own downfall in terms of true clout and influence.[15] This bad choice once again ties into Smith's overarching theme in *WN* that unchecked economic prerogative, whether be in European royalty or Anglo-American merchants, tends to promote a kind of self-destructive implosion, however unintentional it may be. Thus in pure economic terms, Smith would have probably viewed slavery in the American South during the antebellum era as the last ditch hold-out of medieval feudalism in the modern western world, and consequently would have applauded its final overthrow as well.

Since the explosive economic growth of the American antebellum South was primarily founded upon cotton, tobacco, and other cash crops, Smith's negative view towards slavery also tied into his extensive writings on the closely intertwined relationships between agriculture and industry. Prominently (and somewhat notoriously), in Chapter I of Book III in *WN*, Smith proclaims the supremacy of agriculture over industry throughout the course of human history. Some commentators have argued that Smith thus failed to predict the consequences of the Industrial Revolution, but it would be more accurate to say that he foresaw these consequences and disapproved of them. During the Scottish Enlightenment of his own day, Smith personally knew men like James Watt, inventor of the steam engine, and Joseph Black, discoverer of carbon dioxide, and was well aware of what was beginning to happen all around him. As early as the 1770s, Smith in *WN* had complained that the "natural order"—that is, the traditional supremacy of agriculture over industry—had been "entirely inverted" and that the new "unnatural and retrograde order" had disrupted "the Natural Progress of Opulence," the direct result of governments and laws not keeping pace with technological advances.[16] Based as it was on slave labor, Smith would have characterized the Southern economy, despite its dazzling ascent during the 1820s and 1830s, as retrograde, inefficient, unsustainable, and essentially (in more contemporary jargon), a flash in the pan, in addition to being morally reprehensible. As for the northern (and British) industrial economies, these in turn became corrupted to whatever extent they relied on food, material, and luxury goods supplied by the agrarian antebellum South. One could say that in the long-run they were overpaying for imports that in fact could be produced more cheaply with comparable quality and without slave labor.

Anglo-American views on Smith's theories from the Jacksonian era are curiously in sync, yet deeply divided, over how exactly these theories should be interpreted and implemented in the real world. Smith, while criticizing the recurring abuses and failings of modern banking in *WN*, also acknowledged its necessity in all advanced societies, even referring at one point to the Bank of England as "a great engine of state."[17] In American politics of the early 19th century, no better example of this dichotomy in attitude can be found than in the Second Bank of the United States (BUSII), chartered by President James Madison in 1816 and then cantankerously dismantled 20 years later in 1836 by President Andrew Jackson. A detailed analysis of BUSII is well beyond the scope of this study; however, a few general points of observation suffice to underscore its controversial reputation, even to this very day. The shifting attitudes of Madison himself are another good example. Originally dead opposed to Alexander Hamilton's grand vision of state-sponsored central banking, Madison altered his views significantly—possibly to the astonishment of political ally and fellow Virginian Thomas Jefferson—after congressional failure to reauthorize the original BUSI in 1811 precipitated major cash flow problems for the U.S. military during the War of 1812.[18] After peace was made, one of the first orders of business for Madison was to support the re-chartering of BUSII. The subsequent presidencies of James Monroe and John Quincy Adams (son of Founding Father John Adams) in many respects represented the passing of the old guard in American politics. By the election of 1828, a new breed of leaders had ascended to prominence, and no one embodied this new American spirit better than Andrew Jackson.

Jackson did not see modern banking, either state or privately sponsored, as an engine of progress; he saw it as a scam by the rich aimed against everyone else. Nor did the average American frontiersman of that era read Adam Smith.[19] As a western land speculator, Jackson had been financially damaged by pro-creditor bank foreclosure policies during the 1790s; moreover, he was cognizant of how many others had been hurt in a similar manner by similar policies of BUSII during the otherwise relatively mild Panic of 1819. As the international market temporarily adjusted to shifts in supply and demand, BUSII in effect took sides with big moneyed interests, particularly Southern cotton, at the expense of small farmers, businessmen, and investors. Soon after this, lightning rod BUSII President Nicholas Biddle (1786–1844), appointed by President James Monroe in 1822, during his 14-year tenure did little to controvert Jackson's hostile views—quite the opposite in fact. Elitist in manner, privileged in background, and not particularly concerned with the lower classes, Biddle in many ways symbolized a throwback to the less attractive aspects of the original republic, as well as everything that Jackson personally despised and wanted to do away with.

One of Jackson's first initiatives as new President following his historic popular election of 1828 was to inaugurate the "Bank War" of 1829–1837 by announcing that any renewal of the government charter for BUSII should be seriously questioned. By 1832, Jackson had vetoed congressional efforts to re-charter the bank, and by 1836 he had "killed" it, to use his own turn of phrase.

By 1835, Jackson had also proudly succeeded in paying off the U.S. national debt for the first and only time in history. The reward and end result of these perceived achievements was the Panic of 1837–1844, the first sustained economic depression endured by the young nation, one to be inherited as an albatross by Jackson's unfortunate, hand-picked successor in the oval office, Martin Van Buren (1782–1862), as well as his Whig Party opponents William Henry Harrison (1773–1841) and John Tyler (1790–1862).[20] Then again, widespread insolvency and economic hardship marked by a balanced national budget and a Fed-less banking system would have come as no surprise to Adam Smith.

Probably the most famous American Whig politician of them all, however, was Henry "I would rather be right, than be President" Clay (1777–1752) of Kentucky, whose defection to the previously marginal Whig Party in 1833 as a reaction against Jacksonian policies helped to lay the groundwork for the modern Republican Party of the next generation.[21] Clay's cobbled together economic philosophy, which he dubbed the "American System," was a curious blend of backwoods, pro-slavery agrarianism combined with disciplined federal intervention to promote growth. The three primary components of Clay's "system" were subsidized infrastructure, centralized banking, and protectionist tariffs—the first two of which Adam Smith would have surely supported, and the last from which he would have likely recoiled. Some insight into Clay's decidedly non-academic approach to economics—one that he shared with his great opponent Andrew Jackson, for that matter—can be gleaned from a eulogy delivered to his memory many years later by one Colonel Alexander K. M'Clung, in a speech delivered to the Mississippi State House of Representatives after Clay's death in 1852. Using a comparison that seemed to come out of the blue, the Scots-descended M'Clung declared that "Mr. Clay was undoubtedly a far greater man than the Scotch economist, Adam Smith; yet it is not probable that any extent of education, or any amount of labor, or any length of study, would have enabled him to write Adam Smith's book."[22] The obvious reference was to Clay's limited formal education, a quality that would mark many a prominent U.S. statesman and President from Andrew Jackson to William McKinley. In short, Henry Clay and his kind did not write books, they decided the fate of nations. The corollary to this statement was that even some 19th century backwoodsmen knew that Adam Smith had prodigious amounts of education.

In contrast to Clay, his great Senatorial adversary, Presidential rival, and occasional political ally, Daniel Webster (1782–1852) of Massachusetts, was highly educated (Exeter, Dartmouth) and had nothing in his resume to feel insecure about, except perhaps a noted willingness to compromise whenever he believed that a greater good could be achieved. It was mainly through the skillful legislative efforts of Webster and Clay that fighting the American Civil War over slavery was delayed for over 40 years. Regarding foreign trade issues, Webster repeatedly bucked Clay's vaunted American System by his opposition to the escalating tariff restrictions of 1816, 1824, and 1828, the last of which helped propel Andrew Jackson into the White House that same year with its widespread unpopularity. Unlike Clay, who probably found no time to read Adam Smith, Webster found the time but concluded that the dismal science itself had little place in real world American politics. Writing privately, Webster admitted, "I believe I have recently run over twenty volumes, from Adam Smith to Professor Dew of Virginia, and from the whole, if I were to pick out with one hand all the mere truisms, and with the other all the doubtful propositions, little would be left."[23] Nevertheless, Webster generally opposed stricter tariffs (as well as the spread of slavery), just as Smith would have likely advised. Excepting Woodrow Wilson (see Chapter 11), Webster still stands as one of the highest ranking elected American officials ever claiming to have read Smith's *WN*. We see no reason here to doubt his word on the matter.

Meanwhile, the art and science of political economy continued to develop in Great Britain with the likes of Thomas Robert Malthus (1766–1834) and John Stuart Mill (1806–1873), both of whom studied Smith as a starting point for their own elaborate, original theories. More of interest in Great Britain, however, were those who read Smith or personally knew Smith in their youth and later held the reigns of political power. The dramatic abolition of slavery throughout the Empire in 1833 was led by a broad and diverse coalition of pragmatic insider-reformers, but none more influential than Yorkshirian M.P. William Wilberforce (1759–1833) and Lord Chancellor Henry Peter Brougham (1778–1868).[24] Wilberforce had actually met and known Smith, and was a political protégé of former Prime Minister William Pitt the Younger, himself a Smith disciple or "scholar," as he once put it. Brougham's adherence to Smith's unusual proposition that slavery was bad for business should come as no surprise given that he was born, reared, and educated in the same Edinburgh in which Adam Smith had spent the last 12 years of his life. Elected as a Fellow at age 25 to the same Royal Society of Edinburgh which Smith had helped to establish during the 1780s, Brougham went on to a long and highly distinguished career, first in law and politics, then in law and letters. In 1855 his *Lives of Philosophers of the Time of George III* was published in Glasgow, featuring the first extended biographical account of Smith's life since that of Dugald Stewart from the 1790s, followed in the same work by an extensive commentary by Brougham on Smith's work, "Analytical View of the Wealth of Nations."[25] History will best remember Brougham, however, as the headstrong leader helping to ensure Parliamentarian passage for the Slavery Abolition Act of 1833, a full 29 years before Lincoln's Emancipation Proclamation, and with little bloodshed in the process.[26]

Around the same time the British Empire was in the process of abolishing slavery, a young Frenchman by the name of Alexis de Tocqueville (1805–1859) was touring the United States of America at the contentious height of the Jacksonian era. A few years later Tocqueville's *De la démocratie en Amérique* ("Democracy in America") was published in two volumes (1835–1840), and literate Americans have been forced to take an unpleasant look at themselves through the lens of foreign viewpoint ever since. In his cool analysis of the Industrial Revolution in the U.S., Tocqueville does not mention Adam Smith by name but it is nevertheless hard to miss that he had read him. Directly alluding to Smith's intentionally mundane example of a pin-maker (from the opening chapter of *WN*), Tocqueville rhetorically asks "What should we expect of a man who has spent twenty years of his life making pinheads?"[27] Smith later in *WN* answers this question pretty much the same way that Tocqueville later did: that is, division of labor, taken to its extreme without the tempering counterbalance of education, would make citizens "as stupid and ignorant as it is possible" for them to become (see Chapter 15).[28] For Tocqueville, this unattractive prospect also provides the obvious answer to his applicable chapter heading "How Industry Could Give Rise to an Aristocracy."

Tocqueville, however, saved his most biting commentary for American slave owners, as well as his most Smithian of economic observations. In his provocatively titled "Some Considerations Concerning the Present State and Probable Future of the Three Races That Inhabit the Territory of the United States" Tocqueville at length for several pages emphasizes the same points about the myriad economic inefficiencies and hidden financial costs of slavery made by Smith in *WN* during the previous century. "In reality," Tocqueville writes, "the slave costs more than a free man, and his labor is less productive."[29] This was not to say that the slaves were not working hard, but rather that they were working under duress with no incentive or motivation except to avoid the lash or worse. And they had to be kept alive, which meant food, clothing, and housing, at minimum, for their entire productive lives. Free labor required none of these things, only wages at the discretion of the employer. The biggest hidden cost of slavery in the view of Tocqueville, though, was its debilitating effect on whites: too often it was beneath the personal dignity of whites to labor at much of anything themselves, except perhaps shooting and hunting.

Thus, he concludes, "...servitude, so cruel to the slave, was also fatal to the master."[30]

In one of the most celebrated passages from *Democracy in America*, Tocqueville sails westward along the Ohio River Valley, marveling at stark differences between the north bank of free state Ohio and the south bank of slave state Kentucky, also home state to the then illustrious Senator Henry Clay. Repeatedly on the north bank of the river could be observed prosperous modern capitalism at its best, on the south bank of the same river, regressive, backward feudalism. Tocqueville described the startling dichotomy as "the ultimate demonstration of this truth"—namely, that free labor—as opposed to slavery or serfdom—was a vastly more profitable and dynamic economic system.[31] Consequently, "To the south [labor] is degraded, to the north honored" while "Today only the North has ships, factories, railroads, and canals."[32] Mainly because of this superiority, Tocqueville predicted, slavery in America would eventually be abolished "not in the interest of the Negro but in that of the white man."[33] Lending poignance to his comments, as Tocqueville was travelling down the Ohio River, some of the greatest personalities of the still-to-be-fought American Civil War—Lincoln, Grant, Sherman, and others—were coming of age in that very same region of the country.[34]

This is not to say that the early 1830s was not an era of extreme political rancor in America. Political cartoons during the Jacksonian Age reached unprecedented levels of scathing ruthlessness, and their wide range of topicality suggests another book waiting to be written. A surprising number of these biting cartoons relate to controversial economic debates of the day. For example, following President Jackson's veto of congressional legislation to renew the charter for BUSII in 1832, a depiction appeared of "King Andrew the First" decked out in full royal regalia, subtitled "Born to Command"— almost in mockery of Jackson's signal victory over the British at New Orleans 17 years earlier. Another lampoon from *Harper's Weekly* in 1834 shows "Old Hickory" and BUSII President Nicholas Biddle squaring off bare-fisted in the boxing ring, frontier style, with Henry Clay and Daniel Webster on the sidelines both cheering against Jackson. A sly, elaborate 1836 cartoon depicts a frantic Jackson and associates in the act of killing BUSII, shown as the mythical hydra, with each state representing a hydra head and Biddle as the biggest head of all. The not-too-subtle point of "General Jackson Slaying the Many Headed Monster" was that federal banking was in fact impossible to actually "kill" by that point in American history, as subsequent events over the next century would conclusively demonstrate.

As startling as these images now seem, arguably the biggest cartoon legacy of Jackson's Bank War was the birth of the very political symbol for the Democratic Party. Contrary to widespread opinion, the Democratic donkey did not begin, strictly speaking, with the cartoons of Thomas Nast during the late 19th century. While Nast was the first artist to depict Democrats and Republicans as donkeys and elephants, respectively, he was in fact drawing upon an older tradition in the case of the former. Some point to the infamous 1837 lithograph by H.R. Robinson, "The Modern Balaam and His Ass," portraying Jackson as a biblical false prophet and robber of sorts, spurring and beating a donkey with a stick while trying to make a quick getaway from failing banks and the brewing Panic of 1837. The true origin of the donkey moniker in association with Jackson, however, appeared as early as 1833 in the brutal barnyard parable "Let Every One Take Care of Himself (as the Jack ass said when he was dancing among the chickens)." Here, Jackson is the donkey, gleefully stomping chicks to death as the mother hen (BUSII) cackles in futility, apparently unaware that it is being closely stalked by Jackson's anointed Presidential successor, Martin Van Buren, portrayed as a fox. Jackson himself, from all accounts, took personal pride in his reputation for mulishness, and adopted the donkey as a personal badge of honor. It has stuck ever since, and Thomas Nast would much later only amplify that which had already been firmly established within the public imagination.

As the memorable presidency of Andrew Jackson came to a close in early 1837, so began the British reign of Queen Victoria (1809–1901). With the blanket, landmark abolition of slavery throughout the British Empire in 1833, and other European countries soon to follow its example, the eyes of the world began turning towards the United States. There, cotton finally surged past tobacco and sugar to become the number one American export, and by the 1830s the United States, according to almost all estimates, had become the world's leading supplier of cotton, and certainly the leading supplier for the British Empire. The issue of slavery had therefore become clearly defined as a case of moral principle versus short-term profit or, as many leading thinkers coming in the wake of Adam Smith now postulated, inefficient short-term profit versus efficient long-term profit. Horrified and panicky American apologists for slavery reacted with every argument or distraction that could be mustered against abolition. Whereas the American importation of tea had helped spark the American Revolution, U.S. exportation of cotton, tobacco, and sugar now threatened to tear the country apart less than a century after its foundation. Meanwhile, the newly established Republic of Texas had achieved independence from Mexico in 1836 under the inspired leadership of Jackson protégé and Scots-Irish descended Sam Houston (1793–1863).

Overseas, in the United Kingdom of Great Britain and Ireland, there was a growing sense of impending Irish catastrophe. The international scene was now poised for multiple tragedies to unfold on both sides of the Atlantic. If some defined "free labor" as wage-earners, others defined it as slavery, or somewhere between the two extremes. True to the American character, the ongoing debate would soon be decided by military force, first abroad, and then, as if by retribution, at home.

5. Might Makes Right (1838–1850)

> *"Whoever examines, with attention, the history of the dearths and famines which have afflicted any part of Europe, during either the course of the present or that of the two preceding centuries, of several of which we have pretty exact accounts, will find ... that a famine has never arisen from any other cause but the violence of government attempting, by improper means, to remedy the inconveniences of a dearth."*—Adam Smith[1]

In 1843 the British Empire abolished the last vestiges of human chattel within its domains through passage of the Indian Slavery Act, aimed specifically at the very same East India Company that had played such a central role in provoking the American Revolution during the previous century. Thus within the space of 40 years, with minimal bloodshed and financial expense, the English set a great precedent for the rest of the civilized world to follow—or not to follow. France, a constant U.S. ally ever since American independence, had been experimenting in abolition ever since its own Revolution during the 1790s, and made the final leap in 1848, when all French dominions at home and abroad officially became slavery-free zones.

In former colonial North America, however, the political debate, as well as internal tensions, only escalated. Unlike European powers, the United States appeared to be making a lot of easy money from an economy half-geared towards seemingly inexpensive slave workers. More importantly perhaps, and again unlike the Europeans, Americans found themselves mid-century staring into vast expanses of contiguous, wide open territories. All of these expanses were nominally controlled by comparatively primitive and inter-warring Native American tribes, weak and corrupt Mexican officials whose authority extended little beyond their seats of residence, or still-loyal British colonialists having no real interest (unlike Americans) in spilling more blood over territorial conquest. In short, half a continent was there for the taking, and, in the end, the restless populace of the United States could not resist the temptation.

During the first half of 1842, on the eve of the greatest American territorial expansion in its history, English novelist Charles Dickens (1812–1870), like the Frenchman Alexis de Tocqueville a few years earlier, toured a good part of the United States east of the Mississippi River. Soon afterwards, the 30-year-old Dickens reported his findings in *American Notes for General Circulation*, the basis for the 2005 television documentary *Dickens in America*, hosted by Miriam Margolyes. Dickens, despite a professed affection for the American people, found much to criticize in the United States, making a subtle case that rapid economic growth had outpaced the nation's ability to wisely manage its people and resources. Pejoratively labeling Americans as a "trading people," Dickens disapprovingly noted that American literature and the arts must forever "fade to the stern utilitarian joys of trade."[2] He saved his most scathing criticism, however, for the final chapters, in which the entrenched institution of human slavery was roundly condemned. Like Tocqueville and Adam Smith before him, Dickens concluded that legalized bondage was inflicting psychological damage on complicit whites as well as on blacks, even suggesting a direct connection with what appeared to be a uniquely American propensity for violent behavior.[3] During his tour through Washington, D.C., Dickens was granted a brief interview by the 10th U.S. President, John Tyler (1790–1862), who as Vice President had succeeded to the White House upon the premature death of William Henry Harrison in 1841—the first American V.P. to do so.[4] Tyler made a favorable impression on Dickens as being a principled, dignified man, but one also completely overmatched by the cascading crises of his day. He represented yet another in a continuing line of early U.S. Presidents with a professed admiration for Adam Smith's *The Wealth of Nations* (*WN*), particularly with respect to Smith's advocacy of free trade and low tariffs. Tyler had probably first encountered Smith's work during his university days at the College of William and Mary in Virginia, home state to many of the original American Founding Fathers, as well as home state to his deceased predecessor and recent Presidential running mate Harrison.

The largely forgotten Tyler presidency is interesting in hindsight. Though not a compelling personality himself, Tyler's administration and policies perfectly encapsulated the common prejudices and occasional virtues typical of his time and place. Tyler was as a product of the old Virginian aristocracy and hereditary member of the Democratic-Republican political party founded by the likes of Jefferson and Madison. Later, as it suited him, he became a Jacksonian Democrat, then switched to the Whig Party of Henry

Clay when he realized that Jackson would without hesitation use military force to crush any attempts at Southern secession. Tyler's brief association with the Whigs landed him on same winning Presidential ticket as the victor of Tippecanoe (Indiana), William Henry Harrison in 1841. Expelled from the White House after less than one term by the same party that had brought him there, Tyler ended his long, controversial career as a slave-owning Confederate apologist, the only then-living ex–President to do so. Little known today, however, is the undisputed fact that Tyler first opened up U.S. diplomatic trade relations with China in 1845, reverberations of which are still being felt after two centuries.[5] Like Jackson before him, he staunchly opposed all federal banking, and like most Southerners, consistently favored low tariffs with unrestricted trade, the latter being the most tangible legacy of Smith on Tyler's political and economic philosophy, notwithstanding their differences on so many other issues, not the least of which was the legitimacy of slavery itself.

Although Dickens and Tyler did not discuss Smith when they met, there was nonetheless a Dickensian connection with Smith. In 1841, the year before he toured America, Dickens was in Edinburgh for a public reading. Killing time before the event around twilight, Dickens strolled through the Canongate Churchyard where Smith is buried, and stumbled into the headstone of Smith's grandnephew and former British government contractor, Ebenezer Scroggie (1792–1836).[6] Beneath Scroggie's name the young celebrity novelist saw an inscription appearing to read "Mean Man" and stopped in his tracks. Thunderstruck, Dickens later recorded the experience in his journal. What a horrible thing to have on one's tombstone, and in Scotland of all places, a country synonymous with parsimony! Two years later in 1843, after returning from America, Dickens completed *A Christmas Carol* and the rest is history, with the pre-reformed Ebenezer Scrooge becoming perhaps the world's most familiar personification of heartless greed. During the 21st century, conservative defenders of Smith have come to Scroggie's defense, however, arguing first that Dickens misread the tombstone, which supposedly read "Meal Man," as in corn merchant, the profession that Smith justified in *WN* but noted also tended to attract an "inferior set of dealers."[7] Unfortunately, Scroggie's headstone disappeared sometime during the early 1930s. Conservative apologists now like to emphasize that the historical Scroggie appears to have been more of a dissolute party boy than a Scrooge-like miser. In any event, that the modern debate over the personal character of Adam Smith's grandnephew continues even today only serves to heighten the comedy and durability of Dickens' brilliantly imaginative invention.[8] The subsequent bulk of his mature work as a storyteller and novelist, one so focused on the socio-economic concerns of his times, was further clearly reinforced by his Scottish and American touring years of the early 1840s.

Smith's frequently glossed-over chapter in *WN* critiquing the 18th-century Corn Laws of England also deserves brief examination, if for no other reason than to provide insight into his views regarding world hunger in relation to market-driven forces of supply and demand. To oversimplify somewhat, the Corn Laws subsidized British food exports, consisting of bounties generally opposed by Smith, while later during the 19th century also actively restricted foreign imports. Beginning in 1846, not long after the British Empire abolished slavery, it gradually repealed its Corn Laws, totally effective by 1849. Thus came to pass another one of Smith's ideas originally proposed many decades before. Serious political opposition to these laws in Great Britain had appeared as early as 1843 with the formation of the Anti-Corn Law League, which in turn sparked the founding of *The Economist* magazine that same year.[9] Back in the 1770s, however, in reaction to political praise of Corn Law policies, Smith had attacked the legislation as being illogical and counterproductive, even going so far as to declare that government ineptitude was the most frequent cause of large-scale famines, rather than bad harvests (see header quote).[10] Distinguishing between scarcities or "dearths" caused by "unfavorable seasons" with famines (or, as the Irish would say, "starvings"), Smith asserted that most government intervention tends to interfere with the naturally efficient division of labor, hence causing more problems than it solves.[11] As for populist support of legislation intentionally diverting resources during periods of scarcity, Smith labels these emotional convictions akin to beliefs in "witchcraft" and compares the Corn Laws to other misguided statutes, such as those interfering with freedom of religion.[12] The tone of Smith's commentary in these passages is unusually strident, given his typically dispassionate and restrained standards. Ending on a slightly more conciliatory note, Smith concludes the chapter by conceding that all legislation tends to be like the ancient Greek laws of Solon (as recounted by Plutarch), in which popular superstitions must always be partially catered to despite their falsity or barbarity.[13]

The stark foil to Smith's stern convictions is that only 79 years after *WN* was published, the Irish Great Famine of 1845–1852 struck the island with such devastating force that, in retrospect, the event is widely considered to mark one of the major turning points in Anglo-American history. Although Ireland had previously experienced periodic, severe famines, including during Smith's own lifetime (1740–1741), the great "starving" of the mid–19th century is rightfully viewed as being in a class by itself.[14] Some estimates, with little or no refutation, hold that over one-third of the Irish population died of hunger and disease or were forced to immigrate. Oddly, the specific potato blight in question is now thought to have been unintentionally imported to Europe from America, wreaking especial havoc in Ireland where potatoes comprised an unusually large portion of the local diet. Perversely, as the Irish potato crop was being wiped out for some five consecutive years, Ireland continued to export other foodstuffs throughout the famine, sometimes with Corn Law subsidies attached. Official British government responses to the escalating crisis began with indifferent denial and ended with incompetent half-heartedness, although it is a safe bet that many informed Anglo leaders wanted the island to depopulate, preferably through covertly forced immigration. Smith, had he lived to witness the event, would have been appalled. In *WN* he had advocated Irish Union with the British Empire, incorrectly believing that Union would benefit Ireland the same way it had previously for Scotland. In 1800–1801, this political Union had become a reality, but Ireland, an island nation with its own language and customs, proved not be Scotland. In retrospect, Smith's professed views on famines (notwithstanding his opposition to the Corn Laws), come across as one of his few philosophical blind spots, not accounting for ecological catastrophes, underestimating the power of strong central government to assert itself, and to some degree, even blaming the victims for their own misfortunes.

Meanwhile in America, other evils were transpiring. During the years 1846–1848, while Ireland was depopulating, the United States fought an aggressive, victorious war of conquest against Mexico, in the process acquiring California and the American southwest, vast expanses of land to this day referred to by some as "occupied territory."[15] Mexico itself had recently achieved recognition from Spain as an independent country in 1836, the same year that Texas declared and won its independence as a republic.[16] This set off a decade of foreign policy maneuvering, during which Irish-American journalist John L. O'Sullivan wrote in 1845 that it was the "Manifest Destiny" of the United States to, first, grant statehood to Texas, and then ultimately, extend itself from one ocean to another. Newly elected U.S. President James K. Polk (1795–1849) of Tennessee, another Jacksonian protégé, was the right man for the job. His four years in the White House saw the geographic size of the country double—an unprecedented expansion—through unprovoked war with Mexico in the south and opportunistic diplomacy with the British in the northwest.[17] Polk survived his presidency by less than three months, dying prematurely after a brief illness, some would say in divine retribution for what the country did or did not do during his tenure in office. One searches the pages of *WN* in vain for any condemnation by Smith of territorial conquest for empire's sake. He seems to take it for granted as a given reality of life, from the times of the ancient Greeks to those of the colonial British. It is even possible that he may have agreed with Manifest Destiny at a time in which the world was far less populated with civilized peoples than it is today, although he would have surely added that with great power always comes great moral responsibility.

The Scottish famines of Smith's personal experience had mainly been the result, not of blights, but of rebellious political upheavals. For him, a bad harvest was little more than a mandate to consume less and save more. Moreover, though Smith was not a Christian Protestant in the conventional sense, he would have observed a cultural Scots-Protestant frugality from the environment in which he came of age. This attitude manifested itself in an almost comically modest lifestyle despite routine interaction with some of the most extravagant personages of his day. One of the most influential of these personages on Smith's thinking, if not the most influential, was his old professor and mentor at the University of Glasgow, the noted philosopher Francis Hutcheson (1694–1746), having Smith under his tutelage during the latter's formative years. Interestingly, Hutchinson was born and died in Ireland; however, he hailed from County Down in the north, was Presbyterian, educated in Scotland (Glasgow), and spent his professional life there as well. Hutcheson's writings were also influential on the American Founding Fathers independently from those of Smith, although to what precise extent is still debated. Another strong Irish-born, Anglicized influence on Smith was Jonathan Swift (1667–1745), whose popular satirical writings made an acknowledged, lasting impression on throughout Smith's lifetime. Swift's anonymous 1726 masterpiece, *Gulliver's Travels*, appropriately delved into timely themes of colonialism and power that would later so preoccupy the thoughts of Smith and later English-speaking generations to come. Both Swift and Hutcheson belonged to an earlier, pre–Great Famine era of Irish-born intellectuals tending to be pro–British Union and seeking to assimilate themselves with the British Empire, rather than distance themselves from it. These were the writers helping largely to shape Smith's beliefs. Though Smith would have certainly opposed the spread of American slavery as a regressive use of labor, he would not have necessarily opposed the American takeover of former Spanish colonies in the New World. Indeed, a quick perusal of the colonial history chapters from *WN* often reveals Smith's low regard for the Spanish-speaking system and economic methods used in the New World, as well as his repeatedly outspoken beliefs in the superiority of those used by the British and their colonial satellites.

5. Might Makes Right (1838–1850)

Smith in his writings seems to take for granted the expansionist policies and aggressive behavior of all powerful nation states. To what precise extent he approved or disapproved is hard to discern, although there are hints that, in some cases, he viewed it as a prerequisite for a country's rapid economic growth beyond its established borders. "Plenty of good land, and liberty to manage their own affairs their own way," observes Smith, "seem to be the two great causes of the prosperity of all new colonies."[18] Without naming the American colonies by name, Smith unequivocally notes that "The colony of a civilized nation which takes possession either of a waste country, or of one so thinly inhabited, that the natives easily give place to the new settlers, advances more rapidly to wealth and greatness than any other human society."[19] The assertion has hardly been challenged before or since, though rarely spoken aloud. Roughly a century after these words were written, and less than a century after its initial establishment, the United States would well serve as living proof of Smith's general maxim. The prelude, however, would be the explosive U.S. territorial expansion of the 1840s. After that, it would become a question as to how that "waste country ... thinly inhabited" should be properly developed. As Smith had also written, "To prohibit a great people, however, from making all that they can of every part of their own produce, or from employing their stock and industry in the way that they judge most advantageous to themselves, is a manifest violation of the most sacred rights of mankind."[20] Pro-slavery Southerners would unapologetically argue that such "stock" included human chattel.

Curiously, by this same time period in Great Britain, Smith's doctrine of free trade, or at least how the doctrine was perceived, had come into wide acceptance on both sides of the political aisle in British Parliament. Prime Minister Robert Peel (1788–1850), Tory-Conservative Party leader, presided over successful repeal of the Corn Laws in 1846, but at the cost of his own constituency and hold on office. In doing so, Peel went against the very same special interests bringing his party into power in the first place, monetary descendants of the same special interests of which Smith had been so critical prior to the American Revolution. Peel began openly opposing protectionist corn measures as early as 1842, quoting from Smith's *WN* while giving a speech to the House of Commons, and no doubt to the astonishment of many Conservative colleagues.[21] Crossing the political aisle to make common cause with Whigs and Radicals, Peel finally won his cause in Parliament in 1846, after which he stepped down as Prime Minister, his political career effectively over. Comparable in unlikelihood to Richard Nixon's fence mending with the People's Republic of China during the next century, Peel's fateful decision to break with official party line in matters of agricultural trade was probably the natural outgrowth of a superb and privileged education which combined (rather unusually) both classics and mathematics.

Peel's partner in this memorable enterprise was a man normally opposed to him on most other issues, the famous Radical-Liberal M.P. Richard Cobden (1804–1865), co-founder of the Anti-Corn Law League in 1838. Cobden's long and distinguished career produced a number of historical achievements, several of which reflected his consistent veneration for Adam Smith.[22] Like Peel, Cobden quoted Smith in Parliament (circa 1843) while supporting repeal of the Corn Laws, specifically, another one of the well-known passages from *WN* linking free trade with the fundamental rights of free men:

> The property which every free man has in his own labour, as it is the original foundation of all other property, so it is the most sacred and inviolable. The patrimony of a poor man lies in the strength and dexterity of his hands; and to hinder him from employing this strength and dexterity in what manner he thinks proper without injury to his neighbour, is a plain violation of this most sacred property. It is a manifest encroachment upon the just liberty both of the workman, and of those who might be disposed to employ him. As it hinders the one from working at what he thinks proper, so it hinders the others from employing whom they think proper.[23]

Descended from poor farmers and tradesmen, the mostly self-educated Cobden became a prominent self-made man in the printing industry but never forgot his origins. Nor did he lose a persistent fondness for quoting Smith as an authority on a variety of political issues. Cobden owned a personal annotated copy of *WN*, promoted its study to anyone who would listen, and actively fought against its misinterpretation as well. A staunch, lifelong abolitionist, Cobden died in early April, 1865, only a few days before Lee's surrender to Grant at Appomattox.

The same year that Great Britain began to open up its agricultural trade policies (1846), newly-elected U.S. President James K. Polk was sworn into office. Despite a good university education (Chapel Hill), Polk was not the type of politician known for quoting Adam Smith, or any other philosopher, for that matter, as he presided over, through simultaneous war and diplomacy, one of the largest territorial expansions by any country in history. Polk did see fit, however, to appoint as his influential Secretary of the Treasury, Robert J. Walker (1801–1869), a man quite familiar with Smith's *WN*, and in many ways, as much of a political contradiction as had been former President Tyler. Born, reared, and educated in Pennsylvania, Walker as a young man moved to Mississippi, where he became a wealthy pro-slavery, pro-expansionist U.S.

Senator, before being tapped by Polk for his considerable expertise in business law and creative finance. Later during the War Between the States, Walker's old Unionist sentiments got the better of him, though, and he remained surprisingly loyal to the federal government, raising money for the Lincoln administration, and ended his long career as a respected Beltway attorney. Under Polk, Walker, like most of his Southern colleagues, opposed any revival of a Hamiltonian U.S. Bank, but alternatively supported a euphemistically-labeled Independent Treasury System established in 1846. In effect, it allowed Walker to oversee funding of the Mexican War without being overseen himself.[24] More in the true spirit of Smith's free trade doctrine, the Walker Tariff of 1846 was promptly enacted as well, significantly lowering U.S. import duties as Great Britain simultaneously phased out its Corn Laws. After leaving public office in 1849, Walker was invited to England in 1851, where he praised Adam Smith, Robert Peel and Richard Cobden, all in the same breath while giving speeches there.[25]

By the 1840s in England, popular artwork had reflected recent changes in public attitudes towards widespread poverty and hunger, and politicians were therefore obliged to take notice. In 1843, Charles Dickens' *A Christmas Carol* began to take firm hold of the reading imagination. This was two years after Dickens had encountered the gravestone of Adam Smith's grandnephew Ebenezer Scroggie in Edinburgh, and one year after his grand tour of America, where he had seen both the high and the low. The first edition of *A Christmas Carol* featured five skillful engravings by John Leech (1817–1864), including "The Second of the Three Spirits," depicting an amazed Scrooge as he confronts the Ghost of Christmas Present accompanied by two starving children, symbolically named Ignorance and Want, needing protection from the likes of Scrooge himself. The ghost mockingly accuses Scrooge of consigning needy children to the prisons and workhouses of early Victorian England. Dickens in fact lived during an age in which there was plenty of material to choose from in terms of finding inspiration for Scrooge, including the oft-misinterpreted philosopher-economist Thomas Malthus (1766–1834), himself being influenced by Smith's earlier work, or the notorious, unreformed English miser and member of British Parliament during the American Revolution, John Elwes (1714–1789), a near exact contemporary with Smith.

Then a few years later, during the mid–1840s, the Great Irish Famine (*An Gorta Mór* or "The Great Hunger") hit with full force, initially met with feigned or real skepticism by much of respectable English society. That false perception, however, was quickly disabused when British journalists were dispatched to the island and reported back vividly in both words and pictures.

Arguably the culmination of this opinion shift came in late 1849 and early 1850 when the *Illustrated London Times* published a series of articles and images on the condition of Ireland. Perhaps the most famous of these pieces appeared on December 22, 1849—just in time for Christmas—showcasing a harrowing sketch (by an unknown artist) of Bridget O'Donnel, huddling together with her two terrified children in County Clare, recently evicted from their home, emaciated, and dressed in tattered rags. Of such scenes, "I do not go out of my way to find them" wrote the anonymous London correspondent.[26] The pathos of the tragedy had been largely captured in a single image, seemingly taken out of a Dickens novel, except this was reality. There was no Scrooge in the picture, only the victims themselves staring out at readers. Through sensational features such as these, all rumors of denial or exaggeration of the Irish catastrophe were effectively quashed.

While the Irish starved, Americans made war, and rather effectively at that. Indeed, things began to happen quickly. Even as U.S. military forces swept relentlessly through Mexico in 1846–1847, Mormon settlers led by Brigham Young began to take physical possession of a Utah Territory still formally owned by the Mexican government. Immediately after peace terms had been dictated to the defeated Mexicans by the victorious Americans in 1848, the newly acquired Bear Republic of California became the national focal point of frenzied gold rush in 1848–1849, culminating with a grant of statehood in 1850. That same year, the Compromise of 1850—the last of its kind—was forged by an aging Henry Clay, along with energetic help from up-and coming Illinois Democratic Senator Stephen Douglas (1813–1861).[27] In truth, U.S. pro- and anti-slavery interests had begun to fight each other over Mexican War spoils before the conflict itself had even concluded. Although the 1850 settlement would postpone civil war another decade, everyone still seemed to know it was coming.

All moral arguments to the side, it was a question as to which economic model would be adopted for the new territorial acquisitions: the northern, more modern and primarily industrial model supported by wage earners, or the southern, more traditional and mainly agricultural model propped up by slave labor. One would eventually have to take back seat to other, or so many captains of industry viewed it. Adam Smith would have instantly recognized the conflict of ideas. The vehemence and violence of the participants, on the other hand, might have surprised him. It is no coincidence that one of the first recorded modern usages of the English phrase "Might Makes Right" came in 1846, when Unitarian minister and abolitionist Adin Ballou (1803–1890) reacted in horror to the bald-faced military aggression of his own country.[28]

6. Northern Industry Tames Southern Agriculture (1851–1865)

"The most opulent nations, indeed, generally excel all their neighbors in agriculture as well as in manufactures; but they are commonly more distinguished by their superiority in the latter than in the former."
—Adam Smith[1]

With the sudden, unexpected death of Mexican War hero President-elect Zachary Taylor (1784–1850), colorless Vice President Millard Fillmore (1800–1874) was sworn into the oval office and would serve out the remainder of Taylor's term until 1853.[2] Taylor and Fillmore would prove to be the last American Whig Party members elected to the White House. The remainder of the 1850s would be filled out by the ineffectual presidencies of Democrats Franklin Pierce (1804–1869) and James Buchanan (1791–1868), the latter being the last American chief executive born during the 18th century. Economically, the country had changed beyond recognition since the time of Buchanan's birth, when Alexander Hamilton was busy forging maiden domestic and foreign policies for the startup nation, many of which were semi-protectionist in nature. By 1851, new waves of immigration, led by the Irish, were flooding into North America, even as the British Empire tightened its grip on global trade. Curiously, at this crucial juncture in Anglo-American history, there seemed to be widespread agreement among statesmen and politicians of all persuasions that the free trade advocacy of Adam Smith was a desirable thing, especially as there appeared huge profits and fortunes to be made if government barriers were lowered. More controversial was Smith's condemnation of slavery as an inefficient use of labor, at least in the United States, where Southern planters clung to the old business customs of their forefathers. In the U.S., it was becoming increasingly clear that the slavery question would be settled not through compromise (as it had in other developed countries), but rather by force of arms.

In March of 1861, a month before Confederate guns bombarded Fort Sumter, Czar Alexander II (1818–1881) freed the Russian serfs by royal decree.³ The Czar had decided that his country would not be torn apart, at least under his watch, by this particular issue and, using authoritarian prerogative, put a final end to it.⁴ Thus within the span of less than two decades, Great Britain, France, and Russia had all resolved the great pressing moral and economic question of the era with minimal bloodshed and maximum semblance of due legal process. Not the Americans, however. By the time the most bitter and destructive war in American history (by far) had been unleashed amongst its own people circa 1861, there were 34 states in the union, 15 of which had legalized slavery, with plenty of undecided western territories still hanging in the balance.⁵ The vast majority of this geographic expanse was agricultural or undeveloped; most of it would have still been recognizable to Adam Smith in terms of casually-glanced vistas and fledgling technologies. The Industrial Revolution of the early 19th century, however, had transformed northern urban centers into manufacturing powerhouses, the squalid social consequences of which had so horrified a touring Charles Dickens back in 1842 (see Chapter 5), though not so much as had the entrenched slavery institutions of the antebellum South. Wealthy American business interests now tended to fall into one of two broad categories: Northern industrialists exploiting progressive free labor (a growing majority), and Southern planters exploiting regressive coerced labor (a diminishing minority). The latter tried to reassure and justify themselves with the popular slogan "Cotton was King"—a tremendous economic fallacy about to be revealed on a worldwide scale as the national tragedy played itself out on countless American battlefields, mostly located south of Mason-Dixon.⁶

The prelude to these terrible events would begin on the printed page. In 1852, Connecticut abolitionist Harriet Beecher Stowe (1811–1896) released her blockbuster novel *Uncle Tom's Cabin, or Life Among the Lowly*, written as a scathing indictment of the Fugitive Slave Act of 1850. To this day, every time modern audiences witness a performance of the Rodgers & Hammerstein musical *The King and I*, they also behold *Uncle Tom's Cabin* ("Small House of Uncle Thomas") as a play-within-a-play. Northern public opinion on slavery, to whatever extent still undecided, was galvanized. Southerners reacted mostly with outrage, denial or defensive hysteria. The novel was also a big hit in Great Britain during the war years, according to American then-ambassador Charles Francis Adams (grandson of John Adams), where it proved a significant factor in swaying British public opinion in favor of the Union, at a time when "King Cotton" might have easily swayed it the other direction. Adam Smith, as both a government customs inspector and lover of Jonathan Swift-satire, would have well appreciated how both imported goods and imported literature were capable of influencing foreign policies. As for Stowe's *Uncle Tom*, critics have since noted the book's many offensive stereotypes, now making the title synonymous with political incorrectness as it applies to race relations.

Far more realistic, though much less noticed by comparison at the time, was the riveting 1853 memoir by Solomon Northup (1808?–1863?), *Twelve Years a Slave*, dedicated to Stowe and recounting (in surprisingly objective manner) the free-born, kidnapped Northrup's time in forced servitude (later made into an Academy Award–winning feature film by director Steve McQueen in 2013).[7] In the recently re-released Penguin edition of the book, a splendid introduction by Professor Ira Berlin highlights the many unexpected economic themes boldly delineated by Northrup: "True to the abolitionist indictment of slavery, he [Northrup] demonstrates how slavery subverted the work ethic and undermined the values of self-improvement that white Northerners believed central to the creation of the good society."[8] Northrup shows how slaves ridiculed their master's incompetence in both business matters and everyday chores, lack of work ethic, inability to multitask, and above all, the ignorance of whites, as "a model of inefficiency" in which "the plantation regime could never match the productivity and profitability of free labor."[9] All of this harks back to Smith's dispassionate critique of slave labor in *WN*, as well as those of subsequent foreign eye-witness observers such as Tocqueville and Dickens. As for Northrup himself, perhaps he said it best when writing that "I have no comments to make upon the subject of Slavery. Those who read this book may form their own opinions of the 'peculiar institution.'"[10]

The same year that Northrup's astonishing narrative appeared in print, hostilities broke out between Russia and a broad allied coalition consisting of Great Britain, France, and the Ottoman Empire. The fight was not about slavery; rather, the Crimean War of 1853–1856 began as a wide regional attempt by Russia and Czar Nicholas I to take land away from the Ottoman Empire, cynically using alleged lack of Turkish religious toleration as an excuse. It ended up, however, centering on a geographic area (the Crimean Peninsula) that had been conquered away from the Turks by the Russians only 70 years previous, and today (161 years later) remains a very real and symbolic flashpoint for Russian territorial expansionism. The conflict also became, in many respects, a harbinger of true modern warfare finding more full expression in the American Civil War not long afterwards. Tactically, Great Britain and France appeared to prevail in no small part because of industrial superiority. It was also the first time in memory that Great Britain and France had fought a war together on the same side, representing progress of a sorts that Adam Smith would have likely given approval to. After all sides were quickly exhausted with casualties and financial expense, peace was negotiated (in Paris), essentially maintaining the prewar status quo. The main tangible results of the Crimean War were found in two new world leaders brokering the peace, the more-enlightened Czar Alexander II, coming to power after the death of his father in 1855, while Great Britain saw the rise of its dynamic new Prime Minister, John Henry Temple, 3rd Viscount Palmerston (1784–1865). Great Britain, widely perceived as the world's greatest superpower at the time, had intervened primarily to block Russian regional ambitions, and had succeeded in doing so.

Meanwhile in America, the political situation was spinning out of control. In 1857, the U.S. Supreme Court issued what was surely one of its worst decisions ever in *Dred Scott v. Sandford*, upholding the legality of the Fugitive Slave Act under the most extreme of circumstances. In 1858, the election for U.S. Senate in Illinois saw former U.S. Congressman Abraham Lincoln (1809–1865) challenge incumbent Stephen Douglas, co-author of the 1850 Compromise (see Chapter 5), including a memorable series of public debates. Douglas won the election, but many felt the anti-slavery Lincoln had won the war of words. In 1859, John Brown (1800–1859) launched his failed raid against Harpers Ferry, Virginia, proving that abolitionists could be just as fanatical and murderous as their pro-slavery opponents. In the historic general election of 1860, the six-year-old Republican Party won a stunning (though not overwhelming) victory, mainly through a fatal North-South split in the Democratic Party, thus catapulting Lincoln into the White House. For the South, Lincoln's victory was the last straw, and within a few short months formed their own country. The resulting military conflict had some parallels with the Scottish Jacobite Rebellion of Adam Smith's younger days in that an older, more feudal order of society was trying to maintain its independence from a newer, more progressive one. The main difference, at least in military terms, was that the Confederate States of America had far greater support from its rank and file citizenry, as well as a far more formidable army than the 18th century Jacobites.

The self-educated and voracious reader Lincoln is not known to have ever read Adam Smith. Lincoln's anti-slavery views appeared to have been an outgrowth, not of reading, but rather his formative years in same Ohio River Valley that had unsettled foreign travelers such as Tocqueville and Dickens during the same time period. The same may be said for Grant, a man also possessing great literacy and eloquence. Most of his biographers, however, would agree that, at least in military matters, Grant perfectly fit Smith's characterization of the "prudent man" from *The Theory of Moral Sentiments*, who "When distinctly called upon, he will not decline the service of his country, but he will not cabal in order to force himself into it."[11] The armies that Grant commanded during the war represented good case studies in some of Smith's basic ideas on the subject. Grant's Virginia Overland campaign of 1864 was another classic example of industrial might prevailing in warfare (see chapter 3). On the other hand, it had been his earlier strategic breakthroughs in the West that made it all possible in the first place. There, from Mississippi to Georgia, western federal armies, with encouragement from their commanding officers, adopted a live-off-the-land strategy that more or less appropriated Southern agriculture for its own use, thus depriving the Confederates of their own resources in one stroke. Thus one could say that the North won both through industrial superiority and agricultural efficiency combined. It was in fact an important lesson that Grant had learned while serving in the Mexican War under General Winfield Scott, part of that time having quartermaster duties.[12] As for the Confederate rank-and-file, such as Tennessee Infantryman Sam Watkins, his self-descriptors as "an automaton" and "a machine" serves as reminders that participants fighting on the ground for both sides in the conflict personally felt like a minuscule parts of a much larger industrial complex (see Chapter 15).[13]

In terms of agriculture versus manufacturing, there can be little doubt as to where Smith's personal sympathies firmly laid. Scotland of the 18th century was a sparsely populated, mainly agrarian society. Glasgow, today's largest city in Scotland, was then significantly smaller than the capital Edinburgh, although the western port of entry was beginning to gain significant ground on its eastern rival, thanks mainly to burgeoning imports of tobacco, sugar, and cotton from America.[14] At that time there were no other urban areas of significance north of the English border, and Scotland itself paled in terms of both population and industry in relation to Great Britain as a whole. Yet it was this same undeveloped rural environment that produced the Scottish Enlightenment, including Smith. It should therefore come as no surprise that he viewed agriculture as the wellspring of all economic progress, both in terms of his contemporary society and classical history. Although he could clearly see the Industrial Revolution taking shape by the end of his lifetime, there would be no reason for him to believe that rural society would lose its primary place in the overall scheme of things. His argument still carries force some three centuries later, even as technology and industrialized urban society assumed a far more dominant role worldwide during the early 1800s, and agriculture, a certainly less dominant and perhaps more subservient one.

Book III, Chapter IV of Smith's *WN*, entitled "How the Commerce of the Towns contributed to the Improvement of the Country," dwells at length upon these intertwining economic relationships, without diminishing the primacy of rural agricultural. Smith gives, however, three concrete examples in which rural economies benefit from prosperous urban centers. These include having a market for their goods, spillover physical improvements from urban wealth and, last but not least, good government which tends to extend from cities outward, the latter, Smith takes trouble to note, having been previously written about by his revered older colleague of the Scottish Enlightenment, David Hume.[15] Then Smith rolls up his sleeves and delivers one of the most stinging passages of *WN*, though one since quoted hesitantly with a bit of embarrassment and apology by philosophic defenders of rich society:

> But what all of the violence of the feudal institutions could never have effected, the silent and insensible operation of foreign commerce and manufactures gradually brought about. These gradually furnished the great proprietors with something for which they could exchange the whole surplus produce of their lands, and which they could consume themselves without sharing it either with tenants or retainers. All for ourselves, and nothing for other people, seems, in every age of the world, to have been the vile maxim of the masters of mankind.[16]

In effect, wrote Smith, manufacturing undermined the power of feudal lords by tricking them into trading away their political power, which had been based solely on agricultural delivery systems. Thus he credits the origins of modern industry with bringing down feudalism, similar to the manner in which the feudal American South would later be brought to heel by the industrial American North. This passage in *WN* was a moral criticism of excessive greed, but also a shrewd commentary on its inherent self-defeating (or self-correcting) nature—an "invisible hand" working in natural opposition to the forces of excessive greed.

In Book IV of *WN*, Smith wrote prophetically of the manner in which the slavery issue would later become such a hot button for the young United States of America, perceptively pointing out that republican slavery is the worst of all, because slaves, as private property, will receive less protection from abusive masters than under an arbitrary dictatorship, where they are treated more as common state resources.[17] Then he ties it all together. A careful study of history, maintained Smith—and no one, to the best of our knowledge, has ever contradicted him—revealed that slave labor in the ancient world was a drag on manufacturing (which exclusively employed slave labor) because of its expense and inefficiency. This in turn held back ancient agriculture, because the three major aforementioned benefits derived from urban industry were considerably less or completely non-existent. Accordingly, concludes Smith, to maximize agriculture in the modern sense one also had to maximize industry, and that implied doing away with slavery.[18] He summarizes by reiterating the very first sentence of Book III, Chapter I: "The great commerce of every civilized society, is that carried on between the inhabitants of the town and those of the country."[19] Antebellum planters of the American South would have responded that northern industry could have its free labor, while southern agriculture retained its "peculiar institution," but this is obviously not what Smith had in mind. More importantly, American northern industry had clearly come to the reasonable conclusion that it was paying unnecessary social and financial expenses by tolerating slavery in southern agriculture. As political pressure mounted to do away with it, the South did the North two tremendous favors, first by seceding, and then by firing upon Fort Sumter, thus sparing them the trouble of legislating away the problem, as had been earlier done by their European rivals. Smith's "vile maxim of the masters" had manifested itself yet again in dramatic historical fashion.

In hindsight, it seems a minor miracle that Europe, and Great Britain in particular, did not intervene in the American conflict, given their dependence on American agricultural exports. Other than the obvious fact that Grant's intrepid western federal armies had penetrated Mississippi within a year of the war commencing, other behind-the-scenes factors appear to have been at work as well. This important topic is another study unto itself, but perhaps the most notable role played by Smith's teachings in this regard were implied rather than written or spoken out loud. No individual better represented this tendency than John Henry Temple, British Prime Minister under Queen Victoria both during the American Civil War and at the successful close of the earlier Crimean War. Embodying an unusual case of an English politician progressing from Tory to Liberal over the course of a long career, Temple was Irish-descended and Scots-educated, having attended the University of Edinburgh during his youth. It was there, in the town of Adam Smith's final years, that Temple was formally trained in political economy by none other than Dugald Stewart, younger friend of Smith and his first biographer. Having an instilled aversion to slavery, Temple had learned during the Crimean War, from which he had shepherded his country's honorable exit, that foreign military intervention was rarely predictable, often risky, and always expensive. With respect to economic matters, Temple did not like the idea of Great

Britain being dependent on anyone for anything, although many of his constituents profiting from the status quo felt quite differently on the matter. Given all of these factors, there can be little doubt that Temple's early indoctrination of Smith's economic theories via Stewart had made him adverse to becoming politically entwined with the American War Between the States, just as Smith had been highly adverse to England provoking the American colonies into revolution during the previous century.

Temple's American counterpart in London at the time had similar sympathies. After Lincoln's election, the U.S. Ambassador to Great Britain became Charles Francis Adams (1807–1886), son of former President John Quincy Adams and grandson of former President and Founding Father John Adams. Previously, the youngest Adams had been former President Martin Van Buren's V.P. running mate in their unsuccessful 1848 bid (against James K. Polk) as Free Soil candidates. Like his grandfather before him, Charles Francis Adams was an enthusiastic reader of Adam Smith. One example of this tendency can be found in the 28-year-old Adam's diary entry for November 2, 1835, at the height of the Jacksonian era, in which he characterized Smith as "a powerful thinker," adding "I know of few men of modern times who excel him."[20] By 1861, as the American Civil War erupted, Adams found himself face-to-face with Temple's British government in London, trying to persuade them not to intervene in favor of the Confederacy. It is unknown whether the subject of Adam Smith ever came up during these negotiations (probably not), but even so, it surely did not hurt that Ambassador Adams was dealing in part with men who had a similar education in the field of economics, especially with respect to the influential British Prime Minister himself. Ambassador Adams' success in this daunting endeavor may be comparable to, though not quite as great as, Ambassador Benjamin Franklin's earlier effective persuasion of France to intervene in favor of the colonies during the American Revolution.

Back on the American home front, Lincoln's appointee to oversee the initial financing of the federal war effort was political team rival Salmon P. Chase (1808–1873), Secretary of the Treasury, and later Chief Justice of the U.S. Supreme Court. The combative, creative, and occasionally treacherous Chase was also anti-slavery, a longtime student of Smith's writings, and a strong advocate of American free trade in the Smithian tradition. Like Ambassador Adams, Secretary Chase recorded studying Smith in his younger formative years during the Jacksonian era. For example, on March 2, 1831, Chase's journal notes that he read *WN* in preparation for a presentation he was giving in Cincinnati, Ohio.[21] Chase successfully raised money for the war, in the process reintroducing a federal banking system, creating paper money, and strengthening government bonds. Then Chase had yet another falling out with Lincoln, this time over his own frustrated presidential ambitions, but was pacified once again, this time with a lifetime appointment to the Supreme Court, replacing as Chief Justice the late Roger B. Taney, who had presided over the odious *Dred Scott* decision shortly before the war.

As for Lincoln himself, probably too much has been made of his political acquaintance with fellow Republican and pioneering American economist Henry Charles Carey (1793–1879), who wrote several preserved letters to the new President-elect in early 1861 before Fort Sumter was fired upon.[22] Less remarked upon has been Carey's likely impact on Reconstruction policies after the war. While there can be no question that Lincoln and Carey held many ideals in common, Lincoln had probably been far more influenced by the earlier work of Carey's more widely-read American contemporary, Francis Wayland (1796–1865), particularly his *Elements of Political Economy* (1837). For this information we have the usually reliable but often disconcerting testimony of Lincoln's former and slightly disreputable Illinois law partner, Billy Herndon.[23] Significantly, Wayland had favorably cited Adam Smith and *The Wealth of Nations* in his own much shorter book with respect to the proper usages and equitable implementation of public taxation. The connection is noteworthy given that Lincoln was the very first President in American history to implement, with assistance from Secretary Chase, federal income taxes to support the Union war effort, as well as the initial establishment of the Internal Revenue Service.[24] The War Between the States eventually went away but the income tax would return, and has since become one of the more controversial aspects of the modern domestic economy, at least among American voters.

In terms of persistent, grass-roots level agitation, however, no person better represents the American Civil War era than Frederick Douglass (1818–1895), an eloquent speaker and writer born into slavery but escaping into northern freedom and international celebrity by the time he reached young manhood. Upon achieving liberty, Douglass travelled widely, including to Great Britain and Ireland during the Great Famine. Having written the first of three autobiographical installments in 1845, Douglass followed with a second in 1855 (*My Bondage and My Freedom*), following the success of Stowe's *Uncle Tom's Cabin* and Northrup's *Twelve Years a Slave*. After Lincoln's Emancipation Proclamation of 1863, and after the North had finally begun to assert its military superiority in late 1864, Douglass, in a Maryland speech, made a surprising reference to Adam Smith. Bypassing the usual and obvious moral arguments against slavery, Douglass instead focused on Smith's view that forced labor was a wasteful misuse of resources. The timing made sense, since universal American wage labor was about to become a reality, and border states such as Maryland, not to mention the American South in general, needed some reassurance. Douglas also made a subtle allusion to Smith's "vile maxim of the masters," paraphrasing a similar idea with "the contemptible notion, that every crumb of bread that goes into another man's mouth, is just so much bread taken from mine."[25] Thus Douglass, a man with no formal education to speak of, had not only read Smith but recognized as well that defenders of slavery fell into the same category as Smith's feudal lords, effectively trading away their own power through excessive greed and mismanagement of rural fiefdoms.

Selecting representative artwork from this period (which includes modern photography in its infancy) as good exemplars of these particular themes is difficult. Nevertheless, in terms of pure widest public exposure, the illustrations from Stowe's *Uncle Tom's Cabin* are without competitors. The original 1852 publication featured engravings by the artist Hammatt Billings (1818–1871), arguably the most memorable of which was "The Auction Sale," portraying human trafficking on the antebellum auction block in all of its demeaning context and sordid pathos. It was probably the first time that many readers living above or below Mason-Dixon had ever seen such a thing represented on the printed page. Realizing that many purchasers of the book were looking at the pictures as much as (if not more than) the text, publisher John P. Jewett and Company released "The Illustrated Edition" of *Uncle Tom's Cabin* the following year in 1853, in which Billings increased the number of total engravings from seven to a staggering 124. Limited space prevents going into the richness of detail and variety presented by these images. Suffice it to say that many deal directly with the obvious conflict between profitable slave commerce and preservation of the slave family unit, one in which the latter almost always came out on the losing end. Whether in words or pictures, it made for very effective agitprop. In the long run, however, factual depiction would prove even more powerful than the fictionalized version.

For Solomon Northrup's *Twelve Years a Slave*, released the same year as the fully illustrated *Uncle Tom's Cabin*, publisher Derby and Miller retained sketch artist Frederick M. Coffin (1822–?) and wood engraver Nathaniel Orr (1822–1908) to produce several images no less striking than those appearing in its more well-known literary rival. These illustrations are interesting and sometimes surprising in their departure from stereotypes, but surely the most wrenching is "Separation of Eliza and Her Last Child," a scene also movingly portrayed in the 2013 film by Steve McQueen.[26] That Northrup's real-life Eliza shared the same name as Stowe's fictional heroine, but with a more unhappy fate, only served to underscore the depth of human tragedy that he unwillingly witnessed. The fact that Northrup had himself been forcibly separated from his own children surely struck a chord, creating a permanent memory that gave his own personal suffering a certain perspective. Adam Smith had written about this same phenomenon nearly a century before in his *Theory of Moral Sentiments*. To witness the suffering of another being akin to one's own was, in terms of natural reaction, to sympathize with that other being, hence the foundation of all great moral teachings and the proverbial Golden Rule itself. In terms of worldly commercial dealings, however, tangible self-interest tended to prevail, especially where moral foundations were lacking—or worse, specious—no matter what the extreme cost to others, and this indeed proved to be the case with the real-life Eliza and her child's purchaser in Northrup's gripping firsthand narrative.

When Frederick Douglass travelled to Ireland during the onslaught of the Great Famine, he witnessed that African-Americans were not the only ethnic minority in western civilization experiencing oppression and discrimination. It was this realization, in fact, that often gave Douglass' oratory much of its gravitas and persuasiveness. And it would not have escaped him that many of the Irish immigrants coming to the United States in wake of the famine would be conscripted into the same federal armies that forcibly brought American slavery to an end.[27] Just as many whites began to feel empathy for enslaved blacks, so too did many blacks (such as Douglass) begin to feel empathy—or, as Smith would have termed it, "sympathy" in the philosophical sense—for those who died fighting for the Unionist cause.

As for Southern planters, they had to be forcibly persuaded that their customary way of doing business constituted a regressive and counterproductive economic system. Consequently, the most destructive by far of all American wars was fought, with American cities put to the sack and American fields laid to waste. Ultimately, the South had only damaged itself. In the earlier view of Adam Smith, it was simply a mistake that could (and would) be repeated if history were ever forgotten, hence his lengthy background on ancient Greece and Rome in this particular context. In many respects, the United States is still coming to grips with the aftermath of this convulsion, over 150 years after the fact. By the mid–1860s, for the first time in U.S. history, the original vision of the Founding Fathers—life, liberty, and the pursuit of happiness—was being extended beyond a relatively small group of white property-owning males.

7. More Competition, More Oppression (1866–1877)

> *"They [the wealthy] are led by an invisible hand to make nearly the same distribution of the necessities of life, which would have been made, had the earth been divided into equal portions among all its inhabitants, and thus without intending it, without knowing it, advance the interest of the society..."*—Adam Smith[1]

Had Abraham Lincoln not been murdered in 1865, it is still nearly impossible to say with any certainty how Reconstruction would have played out. There is some evidence to suggest, however, that had Lincoln lived, he would have been a strong proponent of leniency and appeasement towards those very same individuals who instigated the rebellion, even at the expense of those former slaves whose recent freedom had been so dearly achieved. By this point in American history, swift economic recovery from the war took precedence over all other social concerns, and this was one of the few points that most politicians at the time could agree upon. Although northern industry and markets had been transformed by the conflict, manpower had been decimated by unforeseen casualty rates. Even those benefitting most from preservation of the Union were now, for the most part, desperate for a return to some kind of normalcy.

As for the South, its lagging infrastructure had been wrecked, international trade virtually eliminated, and an entire generation of white Southern workers—those lucky enough to survive—had been drastically reduced in numbers with many physically disabled, not to mention personally embittered. Most worrisome for the old guard, however, was that the Southern labor force had been simultaneously replenished thanks to emancipation. It was a great economic opportunity for freedmen, but not so much for poor whites unadjusted from the old paradigm. Given a level playing field without the old social constraints, Southern workers of all colors, for the first time ever, would be in direct competition with each other over limited resources and job opportunities.

The 1865 formation of the Ku Klux Klan in the aftermath of Appomattox represents one of the more disreputable chapters in American history; looking past the sheer ignominy, however, clear economic motivations can be seen behind the racism. Confederate army veterans needed immediate work and land in order to recover from deprivations of the war, as well as broad latitude in utilizing depleted resources, and newly enfranchised freedmen represented a serious complication in this regard. Viewed from the newly leveled playing field, the average, typical Confederate veteran was not a highly educated or skilled laborer; in fact, contrary to many of their perceived self-images, they often compared unfavorably to freedmen as potential workers. Moreover, the penalty for unemployment in the Reconstruction South was frequently starvation. With such high stakes, fear drove a de facto decision among most Southern whites that black labor would be restricted mainly to sharecropping and certain designated services provided to their own people. As an important corollary to this decision, African American voting rights would be forcibly curtailed.

Although greed frequently trumps racism over the course of human affairs, Reconstruction was a lamentable instance in which the two vices seemed to naturally go hand in hand. Adam Smith might have recognized certain cultural aspects of the Klan, given documented Scottish origins for many of its rites, terminology, and symbolism.[2] He also would have strongly disapproved of the secret association, just as he had disapproved of slavery and the Jacobite rebellion. Klan apologists, by contrast, have always maintained that its existence was necessary, or perhaps a necessary evil.[3] Unfortunately, what began as an alleged and possibly even legitimate civil defense league for whites quickly devolved into a highly decentralized and violent terrorist organization. By the early 1870s, public opinion, especially in the North, had firmly turned against the Klan, and federal legislation aimed against it began to appear, such as the Civil Rights Act of 1871. Many Southerners who initially approved of or helped to organize the Klan, such as former Confederate general Nathan Bedford Forrest, found themselves disgusted and repulsed by its crude words and deeds.

The tumultuous, chaotic era of Reconstruction can hardly be given any justice within such a short space as this, let alone the rapid expansion of British colonialism during the same time frame, but both represented good examples of larger-scaled economic issues directly addressed by Adam Smith during the previous century. In the United States, the incompetent postwar administration of President Andrew Johnson (1808–1875) found itself in a constant reactive mode against numerous, unforeseen negative developments between 1865 and 1868, not least of which was a (barely) unsuccessful attempt by Congress to impeach the President himself. In the South, emancipation had produced a host of unintended consequences, all dramatically at odds with the original abolitionist vision of a free and equal American society. Beginning with the formation of the Ku Klux Klan in 1865, Southern pushback against federal policies culminated in a successful public relations campaign aimed against invading northern "carpetbaggers" threatening to exploit Southern vulnerability and to upset its traditional social order. Instead of receiving "40 acres and a mule" as recompense, new freedmen were lucky to be allowed participation in an oppressive sharecropping system—as opposed to being terrorized during the night by former Confederate army veterans.[4] Meanwhile in the North, the embryonic beginnings of the modern labor movement were taking shape.[5] The presidency of Civil War hero Ulysses S. Grant (from 1869 to 1877) saw a stabilization of sorts, but also unprecedented political corruption further marred by the Panic of 1873, brought on in significant part by Grant's lifelong ineptitude concerning anything that involved money. The year 1876 marked the 100th anniversary of the American Republic, as well as a stunning defeat of General George Armstrong Custer (1839–1876) by a improvised coalition of Native American tribes at the Battle of the Little Big Horn in modern day eastern Montana. Adam Smith knew nothing of Indian warfare, but he wrote extensively about agriculture, labor, and rent—the driving factors behind many of these better known socioeconomic events.

In Europe, political developments were somewhat less dramatic but no less consequential, especially to future generations of laborers and tradesmen. As the Victorian era continued to roll along in Great Britain, British politics and economic policies came to be dominated by the great political rivalry between Conservative Party leader Benjamin Disraeli (1804–1881) and Liberal Party leader William Ewart Gladstone (1809–1898), with one or the other holding the office of Prime Minister for a good part of the remaining 19th century. During this same period, the Suez Canal of Egypt was completed in 1869, ultimately providing yet another boost for English naval dominance of the world, despite French initiatives in constructing it. More interesting, however, was the simultaneous rise of unified German nationalism under Chancellor Otto von Bismarck (1815–1898), culminating in Germany's crushing victory over France and Louis Napoleon in the Franco-Prussian War of 1870–1871. Germany has remained at the forefront of western capitalism ever since, while France has ever since been forced to settle for a secondary role. Less enamored of western capitalism was the German-Jewish intellectual, Karl Marx (1818–1881), whose massively influential and endlessly controversial treatise *Das Kapital* was first published in 1867. Marx's bitter critique of the post–Industrial Revolution western economy still resonates with open-minded readers; however, his proposed alternatives for the future have left far fewer impressed, yet enough to inspire several major revolutions across the globe. On the other hand, it may well be said that the socially-conscious and so-called fictional works of Charles Dickens (see Chapter 5) have done just as much over the ages (if not more) to temper the cruel excesses of unregulated commerce.

All of this may seem far removed from Smith's *The Wealth of Nations* (*WN*), published almost exactly 100 years before celebration of the U.S. centenary; nevertheless, many of the basic issues confronted by Smith during the 1770s continued to be relevant through the 1870s and beyond. For example, the enforced union of Northern and Southern American states under Reconstruction offered a number of interesting parallels with the (mostly) voluntary union of Smith's native Scotland with England in 1707. One of these was that absolute control by a former local ruling class had been considerably weakened to the benefit of their former servants, notwithstanding the best efforts of the Klan. As Smith memorably wrote, "By the union with England, the middling and inferior ranks of people in Scotland gained a complete deliverance from the power of an aristocracy which had always before oppressed them."[6] Similarly, in the American South, slaves had been emancipated and the old planter aristocracy taken down a big notch. In effect, feudalist institutions had been finally abolished in both places. But overall transformation continued to be gradual. In the South, landowners did not give away the farm (proverbially speaking), and were far from giving their own former slaves all rights due. Likewise, in Smith's 18th century Scotland, there was a severe counterrevolution by disgruntled elements the old aristocracy. The winter of Scottish discontent came in 1745 with the Jacobite uprising, a rebellion opposed by Smith and the entire Scots "middling" class which his own family represented. Smith attributed the uprising to the economic isolation of the Highlands. With more than a hint of exasperation, he describes one Jacobite rebel nobleman bringing no fewer than 800 retainers into the 1745 fight, merely because he held economic sway over them like a feudal lord. This power derived not from law or coercion but rather from an old, backward Scots tradition completely lacking in foreign commerce and rooted exclusively in local agriculture.[7] As things transpired, the Jacobites were decisively suppressed through military force, but their resentment continued to be felt by varying degrees amongst disgruntled elements of the Scottish population not benefitting (as had Smith and his own family) from the 1707 union with Great Britain.

Regarding the new dynamic forming between Reconstruction landowners and workers in the American South, i.e., sharecropping, this too had distant precedent in 18th century Scotland (and long before), although it would have likely been frowned upon by the father of modern economic thought. Smith had little to say about the yet-to-be articulated notion of collective bargaining, but plenty to say with respect to which side in these negotiations held the natural advantage. After stating a general principle that the natural wages of all labor are produce, he quickly adds that the very notion of large private land ownership ensures that any and all such produce will be divided to varying degrees between owners and workers of the land.[8] Then Smith, the presumed modern-day defender of all private enterprise, heavily criticizes "the masters" (as he prefers to characterize them), as well as the powerful advantage they enjoy over any labor employed by them: "The masters, being fewer in number, can combine much more easily; and the law, besides, authorizes, or at least does not prohibit their combinations, while it prohibits those of the workmen."[9] Recall Smith wrote during an age in which organized labor unions were unknown.[10] Nevertheless, he was highly critical of anyone denying the collusion of moneyed interests against labor: "But whoever imagines, upon this account, that masters rarely combine, is as ignorant of the world as of the subject. Masters are always and every where in a sort of tacit, but constant and uniform combination, not to raise the wages of labour above their actual rate."[11]

As for labor, he views them as pathetically inept at advocating their own interests: "...they [the workers] have always recourse to the loudest clamour, and sometimes to the most shocking violence and outrage."[12] In the American South, the Klan was formed in no small part to ensure such disturbances did not occur. Admitting that wage increases can in fact occur naturally during times of increasing labor demand combined with labor shortages, a few pages later Smith strikes a sobering cautionary note: "No society can surely be flourishing and happy, of which the far greater part of the members are poor and miserable."[13] Thus, in a nutshell, Smith effectively described the sharecropping system of Southern Reconstruction nearly a century before it was hastily implemented.

Smith's thoughts on fundamental labor-management relations take on a deeper resonance if one looks beyond *WN* to his earlier masterpiece, *The*

Theory of Moral Sentiments (*TMS*) from 1759. Here, within the space of a few extraordinary pages, Smith touched upon two simultaneous themes later receiving more famous expression in *WN* some 17 years later. First, without using the exact phrase, he describes the "vile maxim of the masters," detailing the manner in which insatiable greed, or even hoarding tendencies, can lead to unintended consequences in terms of a more even distribution of wealth throughout society:

> It is to no purpose, that the proud and unfeeling landlord views his extensive fields, and without a thought for the wants of his brethren, in imagination consumes himself the whole harvest that grows upon them. The homely and vulgar proverb, that the eye is larger than the belly, never was more fully verified than with regard to him. The capacity of his stomach bears no proportion to the immensity of his desires, and will receive no more than that of the meanest peasant. The rest he is obliged to distribute among those, who prepare, in the nicest manner, that little which he himself makes use of, among those who fit up the palace in which this little is to be consumed, among those who provide and keep in order all the different baubles and trinkets, which are employed in the oeconomy of greatness; all of whom thus derive from his luxury and caprice, that share of the necessaries of life, which they would in vain have expected from his humanity or his justice....[14]

Smith's quotation of the Elizabethan colloquialism "the eye is bigger than the belly" was appropriate, since it represented a popular and simplified paraphrase of his later, more judgmental "vile maxim" language, adopted for *WN*.[15] In effect, Smith argued, the unbridled avarice of property owners also necessitated their upkeep of tenants and all related support labor; moreover, taken to its illogical extreme, intemperate greed would eventually result in the dissipation of established wealth and its redistribution among the newly emerging middle classes. Whether applied to European feudal lords, the old Scottish aristocracy, or the Southern Reconstruction, the same idea applied. In the case of recently emancipated slaves, the process would be far more gradual, painful, and fanatically resisted by anyone else standing to lose from changes in the old status quo.

In the very same remarkable passage from *TMS*, Smith goes on to use, for the second time in his published works, the celebrated phrase, "invisible hand." The usage in *TMS* is especially noteworthy, since it comes much closer to the sense in which the phrase is nowadays typically quoted, as opposed to its precise context in *WN* (see Introduction). In 1759, Smith cited the Invisible Hand as a kind of divine guiding force, causing moneyed, property holding interests to redistribute wealth for the general good, not of its own accord, but as a result of its own shortsightedness and limited physical ability to consume everything themselves. One could say that Smith's "vile maxim of the masters" thus sets the "invisible hand" of wealth redistribution into motion. The final irony of this strange dynamic is that the impoverished, disenfranchised masses benefitting from the arrangement, in the final end, seem to achieve similar results but with far less exerted effort.[16] Smith marvels that:

> In what constitutes the real happiness of human life, they [beggars] are in no respect inferior to those who would seem so much above them. In ease of body and peace of mind, all the different ranks of life are nearly upon a level, and the beggar, who suns himself by the side of the highway, possesses that security which kings are fighting for.[17]

Smith's observation may well be described as cynical in the classic philosophic sense. The text makes close allusion to the chance encounter between the Greek Cynic Diogenes of Sinope and Alexander the Great, recounted by Plutarch (an author well known to Smith) and other ancient sources. Alexander, an admirer of the indigent Diogenes, asked the sunbathing philosopher if a favor could be granted, and the reply was a request that the conqueror of the western world move out of his sunlight. With respect to Southern Reconstruction, it must be added that many of the previously hard-laboring freedman and not-so-hard-laboring whites had no particular interest in sunning themselves like Diogenes. Many wanted to work and earn money; many wanted to get rich and become (or remain) "masters" themselves. Unfortunately, Southern economic opportunities were now becoming severely rationed through political oppression.

Evolving views of Smith's theories in Great Britain around this same time began (interestingly enough) to perceptibly shift in emphasis from content to style. Almost every literate person in the English speaking world now openly admired *WN*, possibly in no small part because one could now easily interpret Smith's ideas so many different ways, especially since the western economy had changed so much one century after *WN*'s publication. The perfect case point in this regard was the 35-year British political rivalry between Benjamin Disraeli and William Gladstone. Disraeli, the quintessential Conservative Tory of the Victorian era, was himself a living example of self-reinvention and political evolution, beginning with his outlier social status as an Anglicized Jew. Embodying a rare combination of successful English politician and successful English novelist, excellent clues to Disraeli's complex worldview can often be found within the pages of his published fiction, beginning with *Vivian Grey* (1826), and extending to socioeconomic issues in *Coningsby, or the New Generation* (1844), and *Sybil, or Two Nations* (1845). The latter work, written about the same time as Charles Dickens' first socially-conscious works (as well as early Marxist literature), portrayed the same widening wealth gap in English society that was coming under increasing criticism from multiple directions.[18] For his last completed novel *Endymion* (1880), Disraeli nostalgically returned to the early days of his political career and the fight over the British Corn Laws, in which he stood as a protectionist. Within that context, in the story, the young Endymion is instructed by his political mentor Sidney Wilton: "I know you have read Adam Smith, and not lightly. Well, he is the best guide, though of course we must adapt his principles to the circumstances with which we have to deal."[19] By departing from free-trade principles in his support of the soon-to-be-repealed Corn Laws, the elderly Disraeli felt a need to offer explanations of sorts (at least in the form of novelistic fiction) for his youthful opposition to ideas later perceived as progressive, especially those ideas usually credited to an author with the acknowledged stature of Adam Smith.

Around the same time that then–Prime Minister Disraeli was being elevated to the House of Lords by Queen Victoria—and around the very same time the United States was celebrating its centenary in 1876—then-Liberal Party M.P. William Gladstone was invited to preside over the 100-year anniversary of Smith's *WN* by the Political Economy Club of London. Unlike Disraeli, Gladstone, as a minister under the Peel administration, had favored repeal of Corn Laws from the get-go. His lengthy praise of Smith and tribute to *WN* was preserved and published shortly after the event. Interestingly, Gladstone, a world class orator even according to his enemies, repeatedly dwelled on Smith's engaging style and eloquence, describing him as "...among other things, gifted with a most remarkable faculty of exposition."[20] Gladstone concludes, somewhat surprisingly and unnecessarily, that Smith was "...perhaps the very best, or almost the best, prose writer in the English language...."[21] Gladstone was not only impressed with Smith's ideas, but possibly more so with the persuasive manner in which these ideas were clearly expressed. Moreover, in examining the lengthy history of the Disraeli-Gladstone rivalry in detail, one is repeatedly forced to return to the Corn Law debates of the 1840s, and the thorny issue of when protectionism is justified and when it is not. In the book-chat rooms of English history it is often forgotten that Disraeli and Gladstone both began as members of the British Conservative Party before proposed repeal of the Corn Laws—a topic so central to Smith's analysis in *WN*—split them permanently apart.

Though German born, Karl Marx worked mainly out of London during his years of prime productivity after 1849. This exile had been prompted in part by the continental revolutions of 1848, as well as Marx's authorship that same year of the *Communist Manifesto*. As a Jew, suffice it to say, he could not have presented a more vivid cultural contrast with the likes of, say, Benjamin Disraeli. Marx was not a politician himself, but like Smith before him, a philosopher who influenced (or provoked) politicians. In a series of works between 1860 and 1880 (mostly published after his death), Marx took aim at the economic system praised even by liberals such as William Gladstone.[22]

At the risk of oversimplification, the Marxist critique of Smith in *Das Kapital* and other works can be summarized in a few sentences. Looking beyond a tedious prose style, which, even allowancing for the deficiencies of translation, cannot hold a candle to Smith's mastery of written expression, Marx's view of the post–Industrial Revolution economic model for western capitalism was relentlessly pessimistic. For him, the Industrial Revolution had been a destructive catastrophe for all of civilization, enriching the few and marginalizing everyone else. The specialized division of labor propelling it, one so highly praised by Smith in the opening pages of *WN*, had also, according to Marx, permanently stratified society, just as Smith had predicted it would unless tempered by taxpayer investment in public education (see Chapter 15). For Marx, there was no Invisible Hand, only the Vile Maxim of the Masters: the Rich got richer and the Poor poorer, or at best, stayed as they were.

In contrast to the scathing criticisms of Marx, American-born Henry Charles Carey (1793–1879) saw nothing but possibilities in capitalism, despite all of its shortcomings. Carey was a protectionist, pro-tariff, home-grown Hamiltonian of international renown, but with a typically Irish dislike for anything remotely British.[23] On the other hand, like Alexander Hamilton before him, Carey's reverence for Adam Smith has been generally underrated by economic historians. In a series of eight letters to the *London Times* in 1876, Carey praised Smith as the "greatest of economists" and "...a man who, in my belief, is entitled to stand side by side with Shakespeare as greatest of all the human productions of the British soil...."[24] Carey had also been impressed by the German nationalistic model (one so despised by Marx), a forerunner of the modern-day European Union, as espoused by economic visionary Friedrich List (1789–1846) and later successfully implemented by Chancellor Bismarck. Unfortunately, Carey, despite supposedly having the ears of presidents Lincoln and Grant, was also known to be bombastic, verbose, and overbearing, as well as brilliant. For example, in a long series of published open letters to President-elect Grant in 1868–1869, Carey urged upon him, among numerous other items, a flexible precious metals monetary policy that may well have avoided the Panic of 1873 had it been adopted, but to no avail.[25] Accordingly, it may well be said that Carey's influence on many issues was felt more after his death than during his lifetime.

Carey lived long enough, however, to see public opinion turn against the Ku Klux Klan. By the early 1870s, Klan outrages committed against innocent victims had caused even its early supporters to waver and question its legitimacy. Talented political cartoonists then joined the fray. Typical of this sudden reversal was "Visit of the Ku-Klux" by Frank Bellew, appearing in the February 2, 1872, issue of *Harper's Weekly*. Here, the Klan is most definitely not portrayed as protectors of the weak. Instead, a hooded rifleman steals into a humble freedman's cabin to take aim at unarmed women and children preparing dinner over a fire. Within two years, the Klan had become public enemy number one. On December 24, 1874, the famed Thomas Nast unveiled his not-so-allegorical "The Union as it was / The Lost Cause, worse than slavery," depicting Klansmen more or less as a motley collection of sore losers getting their thrills from vigilante lynching and torching schoolhouses. This latter item, one grounded in documented fact, would have particularly offended Adam Smith, who not only viewed slavery as an economically regressive institution, but also championed in *WN* taxpayer-supported public education as a necessary safeguard against the predictable excesses of specialized industrial labor.

In contrast to the extreme xenophobia of the Klan, its rumored original Grand Wizard, former Confederate hero, Lieutenant General Nathan Bedford Forrest, seems to have continued his own personal evolution on civil rights issues right up to his dying day. On July 5, 1875, the physically ailing but still imposing symbol of Southern resistance made his last public appearance near Memphis, Tennessee. Forrest had accepted a speaking engagement from, of all groups, the Independent Order of Pole Bearers Association, an African-American forerunner of the NAACP, to give some remarks on the current state of race relations in the South.[26] Having years before renounced and distanced himself from the Klan he had helped to organize, the former plantation owner, slave trader and man accused of war crimes against black federal soldiers, proceeded to deliver a short but hopeful message of conciliation, with emphasis on voting rights and equality in economic opportunity.[27] Then Forrest accepted a bouquet of flowers from the daughter of an Association officer, and reciprocated with a courtly kiss to the woman's cheek. Enthusiastic applause ensued. White supremacists have been trying to recover ever since.

Before his passing in October of 1877, Forrest lived to see the Great Railroad Strike of that same year, occurring between July and September. The burgeoning rail industry of the postwar era was a sector in which Forrest, a seasoned veteran of innumerable military campaigns, had tried his hand as an entrepreneur and utterly failed. Despite universally-acknowledged abilities as a leader of men, Forrest's best efforts had been overwhelmed by the economic upheavals of the 1870s, stemming from unseen market forces he could not have anticipated. By 1875, he was, in terms of mere dollars and cents net worth, little better off than the black freedmen inviting him to be their guest speaker. Now with the newly reunited country reeling from its first great labor disturbance, many a blameless victim east of the Mississippi probably decided that it was time to move wherever the grass appeared greener. The railroads would facilitate this. By 1869, the first Transcontinental rail line had been completed, and many more would follow despite temporary setbacks. Although Adam Smith had known steam-engine inventor James Watt in Edinburgh, Smith never lived to see the beginnings of modern transportation; nevertheless, in *WN* he had descanted at length on the virtues of taxpayer subsidies for transit infrastructure, as being a benefit and necessity for public prosperity. Few better examples of this idea can be found than in the United States during the late 1800s.

8. The Great American Relocation (1878–1890)

"How selfish soever man may be supposed, there are evidently some principles in his nature, which interest him in the fortune of others, and render their happiness necessary to him, though he derives nothing from it except the pleasure of seeing it. Of this kind is pity or compassion, the emotion which we feel for the misery of others, when we either see it, or are made to conceive it in a very lively manner. That we often derive sorrow from the sorrow of others, is a matter of fact too obvious to require any instances to prove it; for this sentiment, like all the other original passions of human nature, is by no means confined to the virtuous and humane, though they perhaps may feel it with the most exquisite sensibility. The greatest ruffian, the most hardened violator of the laws of society, is not altogether without it."—Adam Smith[1]

By the early 1880s, as the new Southern economic system of sharecropping calcified into the overt oppression of Jim Crow legislation, the American labor movement in the North began to simultaneously gain momentum as a direct consequence of new hardships caused by the Panic of 1873 and its aftermath. Everyday life east of the Mississippi River was becoming more challenging. As a result of these developments, ordinary Americans began to migrate or relocate west in greater numbers. While the myth of extensive wagon trains crossing the plains states are imbedded in the national consciousness—and indeed such dramatic movements did occasionally transpire—anyone who could afford to do so travelled west by railroad, or sometimes even by ship to the west coast. Railroad construction also meant steel production, as well as the vast apparatus of labor and capital that supported those industries. Although Adam Smith a century earlier could hardly have imagined infrastructure or transit on this scale, he was well acquainted with the forces that drove these, and wrote about it quite perceptively. He also seems to have sensed a tentative connection of sorts between western geo-economic expansion and the dramatic performing arts, to which we shall presently turn our attention. Like the ancient Greeks long before them, the former and present British colonials in all of their 19th-century manifestations, including Americans, felt a pressing need to see and hear their own true stories presented on the theater stage.

By the 1880s, the Second British Empire had reached the apex of its worldwide power and prestige, thanks in no small part to a modern navy that knew no rivals. Its considerable accomplishments during the century following the American Revolution were celebrated ostentatiously with a Golden Jubilee of Queen Victoria's reign in 1887, which condescendingly included an American Exhibition in London. This triumphal mood, however, had been marred by repeated colonial wars in Africa waged against both the indigenous population as well as other European settlers, most notably the Dutch Boers. Absolute British control of African resources appears to have justified any use of force, at least until it occurred to some British leaders that such use could be counterproductive and (in fact) more expensive than simply sharing the wealth to be had. While every literate British subject with half an education quickly acknowledged the supreme authority of Adam Smith's teachings in the realm of international trade, putting these same principles into practice appears to have been a mixed proposition, depending upon how much was to be gained by whom and how quickly. By the time the festivities of 1887 had subsided, the English had to step back and take stock of a world that was become increasingly volatile and strident in its demands for more equitable share of profits and resources. The British Navy, despite its legendary prowess, was finding that it could not fight everywhere at once. Within a decade, it would find itself challenged by an old competitor on the other side of the Atlantic.

Amid celebration of Anglo worldwide economic dominance, the influential Alfred Marshall (1842–1924) was appointed Professor of Political Economy at Cambridge University in 1885. Marshall was not a man given to self-congratulation. A unique blend of scientist and moralist, he is widely credited as the founder of modern economic thought in the strict academic sense. Though purely an academic himself, and despite suffering from bad health and bad nerves, Marshall's distinguished students would include John Maynard Keynes, later one of the most politically influential economists of the next century. Marshall's *Principles of Economics* (1890) would also become the standard textbook in its field for decades to come. His wife, Mary Paley Marshall (1850–1944), was one of the first notable female economists and likely an uncredited co-author of *Principles*.[2] Above all, Marshall explicitly held himself out as a direct intellectual descendant of Adam Smith, more or less subscribing wholesale to most of Smith's teachings, while refining them through utilization of Victorian advances in mathematics and data collection. His life's work was inspired by a negative reaction against the same extreme wealth inequality that had earlier shocked the likes of Charles Dickens and Karl Marx. Like Henry Charles Carey in the United States, Marshall had taken careful (though critical) note of the new school of economic thought coming out of Germany and orginally pioneered by Friedrich List, one that seemed particularly well adapted to practical use by the emerging European nation-states.

It was therefore fitting that Germany hosted the important Berlin Conference of 1884–1885, dealing with the growing importance of African colonial issues and presided over by Chancellor Bismarck. All the major European powers were present for roll call, with token participation from the United States and the Ottoman Empire.[3] Germany also broke new economic ground with the passage of its own Cooperative Law in 1889, offering an alternative, more egalitarian business model in contrast to the emphatically individualistic and strictly laissez-faire interpretation of capitalism then prevalent in other countries. Unfortunately for Germany, however, the new Kaiser Wilhelm II dismissed Bismarck in 1890 over disagreements on the expansion of German colonialism, which Bismarck believed should be undertaken very slowly, if at all. These were in fact the same issues that had faced Great Britain during the previous century, inspiring Smith to write *The Wealth of Nations* (*WN*) and, to a lesser extent, *The Theory of Moral Sentiments* (*TMS*). Meanwhile, neighboring France continued to excel in all of the arts and sciences while refusing to relinquish its own pretensions of colonial empire in Africa and elsewhere. The reality, however, was that recent unification of German-speaking peoples in northern Europe, combined with Prussian military superiority and continued British naval dominance, had effectively reduced France to second tier status in terms of political and economic influence. The full ramifications of this new power alignment in Europe would be fully felt worldwide in less than a quarter century, to the great distress of western civilization and far beyond.

Another major realignment taking place during this same time frame was the startling geographic expansion of the United States. Within the space of two years (1889–1890), six states were added to the Union—North Dakota, South Dakota, Montana, Wyoming, Idaho and Washington—contiguously linking the country from Iowa and the plains states to the Pacific coastline. Manifest Destiny was accordingly fulfilled.

Throngs rushed westward by any mode of transportation available, some more fit for survival than others. Among the less fit was future author of the beloved *Oz* books, Lyman Frank Baum (1856–1919), who led his beleaguered family into the wilds of the Dakota Territory in 1888, only to beat a quick retreat back to Chicago by 1891. Baum, like countless other Americans, had been a financial casualty of the Gilded Age in which economic upheavals caused the losers to far outnumber the winners. Perhaps the most prominent victim of this financial turbulence was former U.S. President and Civil War hero Ulysses S. Grant (1822–1885), whose considerable net worth had been extinguished almost overnight shortly before his death.[4] Westward migration, for those possessing the necessary resources and hardiness, was driven in no small part by this widespread misery.

Still another overt symptom of general misfortune, more so east of the Mississippi, was an uptick in violent labor upheavals. The definitive incident, in the minds of many at least, occurred May 4, 1886, at Haymarket Square on the Near West Side of Chicago, when a peaceful demonstration in favor of eight-hour workdays suddenly turned deadly for both police and protestors. Someone threw a bomb; no one knows who. After casualties and debris were cleared away, four organizers of the event were led to the gallows under pretense of law. Another committed suicide. Today in Chicago, 128 years later, discussion of the event can still cause heated partisan debate, beginning with semantics: was the Haymarket affair a "riot" or a "massacre"?

The American federal government of that era was simply not up to the challenge of containing these problems. Exacerbating systemic weakness in the Beltway were no fewer than five different White House occupants within the space of eight years from 1881 to 1889, the cumulative result of voter fickleness, electoral inefficiencies, or violent assassination.[5] This Presidential revolving door included Rutherford B. Hayes (1822–1893), James Garfield (1831–1881), Chester Arthur (1829–1886), Grover Cleveland (1837–1908), and Benjamin Harrison (1833–1901). As a result, consistent national policies, let alone forceful ones, were not to be found. In point of fact, big money was running the country, in nominal collusion with local government officials. Whereas Great Britain and Germany had no shortage of strong personalities in positions of national leadership during the 1880s, the United States seemed to be funneling its best talent outside the realm of government. What may have saved the country from itself was that the new class of proverbial robber barons rising to prominence, whatever their shortcomings may have been in terms of ruthlessness and greed, were certainly not lacking in common sense, energy, or creativity. All fully realized and appreciated that America had made them rich, and that American national government was something worth nurturing, if for no other reason than to help preserve their own unprecedented, accumulated fortunes.

Adam Smith was himself never a wealthy person, although he did respectably well for someone of his class and time in terms of earnings. Academia, writing, private tutoring, and government officiating, combined with a stereotypical Scots frugality and modest bachelor lifestyle, all enabled him to live a comparatively long life free of want. One aspect of Smith's relative security was an apparent lifelong ability and willingness to indulge his love of the performing arts, particularly theater. How and where exactly this began is open to speculation, but his first biographer, Dugald Stewart, suggested that the enthusiasm began during his unhappy student years as a young adult at Oxford University between 1740 and 1746, then reinforced during his French travels of the mid–1760s.[6] It might be added, that Smith's apparent fondness for the stage probably had earlier origins as well, particularly with former teachers Francis Hutcheson at the University of Glasgow or David Millar at the Kirkaldy Burgh School, not to mention his mother Margaret Douglas Smith, whom appears to have exerted more influence over him than anyone else from childhood onwards.[7] For example, it is known for certain that in 1734, when Smith was 11 years old, Kirkaldy schoolmaster Millar put on a play written by himself for the students, although it is unknown to what extent Smith actually took part.[8]

In this sense, Smith was entirely a man of his time and place. Indeed it is hard to imagine any gifted English-speaking schoolboy coming of age during the same era as British actor-impresario David Garrick (1717–1779) not to have taken a keen interest in the ongoing revival of English stagecraft.[9] In any event, by the time that Smith came of age himself, theater had become (and would remain) a favorite topic of his conversation, one that he intended later to write about extensively, but unfortunately never did. Stewart noted that for Smith, "The principles of dramatic composition had more particularly attracted his attention; and the history of the theatre, both in ancient and modern times, had furnished him with some of the most remarkable facts on which his theory of the imitative arts was founded."[10] Over a century after Smith's death, it therefore seemed entirely appropriate that the performing arts center in Kirkaldy, completed in 1899 and dedicated by none other than visiting Scots-American billionaire Andrew Carnegie, should be dubbed the Adam Smith Theatre. The facility continues to be an important community focal point into the present day.

Smith had a lot to say about wealthy people, both in *WN* and *TMS*. Regarding the sudden availability of wide open spaces (and in specific reference to the American colonies), he was quick to emphasize that there was no better way to fast-track economic development in tandem with job growth:

> Every colonist gets more land than he can possibly cultivate. He has no rent, and scarce any taxes to pay. No landlord shares with him in its produce ... which is thus to be almost entirely his own. But his land is commonly so extensive, that with all his own industry, and with all the industry of other people whom he can get to employ, he can seldom make it produce the tenth part of what is capable of producing. He is eager, therefore, to collect labourers from all quarters, and to reward them with the most liberal wages.[11]

The problem with this dynamic, Smith quickly added, if it could be considered a problem at all, was that labor in such situations tended to be a quick study of capital, and impatient of their own subservient status, as well as lost opportunities for their own rapid advancement. Thus, competition was quickly bred:

> But those liberal wages, joined to the plenty and cheapness of land, soon make those labourers leave him, in order to become landlords themselves, and to reward, with equal liberality, other labourers, who soon leave them for the same reason that they left their first master.[12]

In the case of the 18th century American colonies, this same principle ultimately led to their breakaway from the mother country. For the United States of the 19th century, however, this would not be an option. The Civil War had already been fought and decided. From then on, it would be merely an internal struggle between labor and capital or the "masters," as Smith preferred to term the latter. The issue, as it had always been and always will, would be equitable distribution of wealth and profits.

The spectacle of the North American continent being filled up by western civilization would also provide a new stage of sorts for theatrical drama. Although Smith never completed his grand projected work on the imitative arts, he managed to sneak in a fair amount of interesting observations in his surviving works, particularly with respect to the ancient Greek culture first spawning this distinctively western form of drama. The ancient Greeks were also similar to Anglo-American culture in that both were aggressively expansive colonizers who enjoyed burgeoning wealth and increasingly opulent standards of living. Smith was unhesitant in making selective comparisons between Hellenic and British economic models: "The progress of the ancient Greek colonies towards wealth and greatness, seems accordingly to have been very rapid. In the course of a century or two, several of them appear to have rivaled, and even to have surpassed their mother cities."[13] In *TMS*, Smith's fascination with ancient Greek culture is apparent throughout, beginning with theatrical allusions in the very first paragraph (see header quote), and then becoming more specific as the text progresses. In expounding his complex theory of the moral, sympathetic spectator in human affairs, Smith in *TMS* makes direct references to the dramatic works of Sophocles, Euripides, Shakespeare, Otway, Racine, and Voltaire. In reading these passages, one is tempted to conclude that his early interest in the stage later acted as a springboard for Smith's philosophic and economic thought. Although Smith never makes the assertion, one is also nearly inclined to draw a connection based on his comments between the progressive development of western stage drama and the explosive geographic spread of western colonial empire, whether it be Greek or British.[14]

Among the apologists for the second British Empire of the 19th century, perhaps none was more introspective or sage-like than John Edward Dahlberg-Acton, better known to history as Lord Acton (1834–1902), ending his long political career as a close advisor to Liberal Party Prime Minister Gladstone over the course of several decades. A regular correspondent with Gladstone's daughter, Mary Gladstone Drew, Acton's letters were later published after his death and have since become valuable windows into the mindset of late Victorian era liberal politics. Writing to Drew from Cannes in 1881, a full five years before the Haymarket debacle in Chicago, Acton warned of the dire consequences that could result from unequal bargaining power between labor and capital, citing Adam Smith as authority in the process: "Adam Smith set up two propositions—that contracts ought to be free between capital and labour, and that labor is the source, he sometimes says the only source, of wealth."[15] Taking Smith's assertion to its logical conclusion, Acton then offers simple justification for not allowing big money alone to run any government:

> If there is a free contract, in open market, between capital and labor, it cannot be right that one of the two contracting parties should have the making of the laws, the management of the conditions, the keeping of the peace, the administration of justice, and distribution of taxes, the control of expenditure, in its own hand exclusively. It is unjust that all the securities, all the advantages, should be on the same side. It is monstrous that they should be on the side that has the least urgent need of them, that has least to lose.[16]

With the advantage of hindsight, it is hard to argue either with Acton or with Smith on these notions; and yet, there were many at the time, perhaps even some today, asserting that labor was too ignorant, lazy, or violent to have any voice in government at all. Upon his passing in 1902, Acton's massive private library was purchased by none other than Andrew Carnegie (acting in a philanthropic capacity), who then immediately facilitated its donation to Cambridge University, which decades earlier had denied Acton academic admission because of his openly Roman Catholic religious beliefs.[17]

As hinted in the previous paragraphs, among the gaggle of American robber barons shaping world events during this period in history, Andrew Carnegie (1835–1919) in many respects stands apart. Though not the wealthiest, most paternalistic, or even the most ruthless of his breed, Carnegie was perhaps the most interesting, possessing all of the aforementioned harsh qualities combined with diverse philanthropic pursuits, mild philosophic tendencies, and close associations with distinguished literati of his day. It may be said that he popularized the notion that wealth should not be merely accumulated and reinvested, but selectively redistributed for the benefit of all society. This selective redistribution, of course, was dictated by the iron-fisted will and subjective judgment of the industrialist himself; but much of the wealth, in the final analysis, was in fact redistributed, not through any vaguely alleged trickle-down effect, but rather through direct and express charitable bequests. Over a century after his death, Carnegie's foundations still exist and continue to robustly promote his ideas and causes. His most famous legacy is the extensive chain of municipal public libraries built at his expense, most of which still exist and are used for their original purposes.[18] Carnegie was the robber barons' brazen response to the challenge of Karl Marx.

Born into abject poverty not far from Adam Smith's birthplace in southeastern Scotland the same year (1835) that Tocqueville's American impressions were being published, Carnegie is often cited as the ultimate rags-to-riches story. By late 1800s, he was the unquestioned American head of the largest steel empire the world had ever seen. His regular clientele included corporations, nation-states, and individuals both great and small. Though not a politician, he was among the elite group effectively running the country for a considerable length of time. After liberal donations of his vast wealth raised some eyebrows, Carnegie published a short essay in 1889, provocatively titled *The Gospel of Wealth*, melding semi-religious sentiments with faint echoes of Smith's *WN*, defending his philosophy against fellow capitalists who complained that his philanthropy was putting pressure on them to act in a similar manner. More significantly, in 1908 Carnegie's tightly reasoned and statistically supported "My Experiences with, and Views upon, the Tariff" was published in *Century Magazine*, in conjunction with his congressional testimony on the same topic.[19] Therein, Carnegie began by citing Adam Smith as "the greatest economic authority" in a predictably anti-tariff context. Carnegie took the trouble, however, to explore both sides of the issue, noting that Smith was not always "the bigoted 'free trader' he is generally supposed to be" and argued that Smith, were he still alive, would in fact support some protectionist legislation. In this respect, Carnegie's close reading of Smith, like Alexander Hamilton and Henry Charles Carey before him, was far more nuanced and complex than those given even by many of today's specialized academics.

As extraordinary as Carnegie's broad trajectory through life may appear, it pales in comparison to that of his younger, far less affluent contemporary, William Frederick "Buffalo Bill" Cody (1846–1917). Cody's career makes a better illustration of Smith's eccentric ideas, indirectly connecting epic-scaled economic growth with the pathos and tragedy of the public stage. He was at various times a Pony Express courier, abolitionist, Union Army teamster, U.S. Army scout, Indian fighter, bison bounty hunter, conservationist, Knight Templar, Scottish Rite Freemason, women's rights activist, author, promoter, family man, and entertainer—it is in fact difficult to comprehend how one human life could be more eventful or adventuresome than Cody's. Born in the Iowa Territory on what was then the American western frontier, Cody had all meaningful ties of kinship taken away from him by the time he was a teenager; nevertheless, his adult biography represents, in many respects, the last word in 19th century American success stories, though one impossible to pigeon-hole or precisely categorize. His enduring popularity is attested to by the ongoing stream of books, movies, plays, musicals, documentaries, etc., that continue to assess and reassess his cultural legacy. An unabashed, worldwide fan club included some otherwise highly acerbic and politically incorrect critics of Americana, such as Cody's fellow Midwesterner Mark Twain, aka Samuel Clemens. Finally, it should be observed that, among all of the people who subsequently made an excellent living by converting the saga of the American West into mass entertainment, Cody may well be described as the true pioneer and (by far) the most authentic of the entire lot. And all of this was accomplished in an age predating the motion picture industry.

After by some series of miracles surviving the first 30 years of his life, Cody turned full-time to playing a cowboy on stage, as opposed to being one in real life, the former proving to be a far more lucrative and secure occupation.[20] In 1883, he unveiled "Buffalo Bill's Wild West" as a barnstorming international road show, and never looked back. Cody was able to recognize and hire unlikely authentic talent—being one himself—that included stars such as sharpshooter Annie Oakley and Chief Sitting Bull. Like film director John Ford in the 20th century, Cody preferred to use real Native Americans in his performances.

The pinnacle of his success came in 1887, when Cody's Wild West became the featured act and indisputably the hot ticket at the American Exhibition of Queen's Victoria's Golden Jubilee celebration in London, one originally added almost as an afterthought by its organizers. In attendance at that command performance were present and future European royalty, including, rather ominously, Victoria's grandson Prince Wilhelm, to be crowned German Kaiser the following year and destined to lead his own powerfully growing country into a disastrous and prolonged world war roughly a quarter of a century later. It is tempting to postulate that Wilhelm, another young, excited member of Cody's fan base, saw his American first name counterpart in action that day to great applause and fantasized himself to be a future enforcer of European law and order, but we shall not go quite that far.[21]

Buffalo Bill Cody never read Smith, insofar as anyone knows, but his choreographed presentation of the American frontier at a moment when the "Wild West" was in fact being tamed and receding from history, contained forceful dramatic elements that Smith or any other connoisseur of the theater would have keenly appreciated. One of Cody's early centerpieces was his staged re-enactment of an 1876 skirmish at Warbonnet Creek, South Dakota, coming in the aftermath of Little Big Horn, in which he allegedly killed (and scalped) a Cheyenne warrior named Yellow Hair in single combat. This marked the end of Cody's career as an Indian fighter, and it appears he spent the rest of his life trying to rehabilitate the image of the Native American through entertainment and public relations.

Whether enacting this melancholy affair or Custer's Last Stand or any of the other countless, anonymous tragedies that played out in the westward expansion, Cody's performances, according to audiences, contained notable elements of pathos and sympathy for his countrymen, including mortal adversaries. For actors, audiences, and those whom they were memorializing, the experience had much in common with what Sophocles and Euripides were doing on Hellenic stages at the height of the Axial Age long before Europeans even knew that North America existed In essence, it represented the very same phenomena that Smith wrote about in *TMS* (the events beheld by the sympathetic spectator) and how subsequent feelings and behavior are shaped by them. In the unique case of Cody's Wild West, it eventually gave our culture the ubiquitous American Western, if nothing else, a continually viable economic engine in its own right.

The stage-worthy tragedies of the American West seemed to play out on a large scale for one final devastating day on December 29, 1890, near Wounded Knee Creek, South Dakota, where several hundred Lakota, including unarmed women and children, were senselessly massacred by heavily armed federal troops assigned to closely monitor their movements and whereabouts.[22] A few days earlier, Sitting Bull, personal friend of Buffalo Bill Cody and the man who had prophesized Custer's defeat, had been brutally murdered by law enforcement officials not far away in South Dakota on the Standing Rock Indian Reservation. After this orgy of violence, public opinion seemed to gradually sway, if not in favor of Native Americans, at least against their systematic extermination. Perhaps it slowly dawned on more Americans that the continent had finally filled up, and there was no place left in which to relocate, let alone re-relocate previous occupants. Accordingly, they began to look elsewhere for opportunities, plunder, and profits. The age of American colonialism was about to begin, and it was a subject on which Adam Smith had plenty to say.

9. A Clumsy Foray into Colonialism (1891–1901)

"Gold and silver, as they are naturally of the greatest value among the richest, so they are naturally of the least value among poorest nations. Among savages, the poorest of all nations, they are of scarce any value."—Adam Smith[1]

On September 28, 1891, a 72-year-old Herman Melville passed away quietly at his home in New York City. Considered one of the greatest American writers of the 19th century, Melville died in relative obscurity despite having published within his lifetime a voluminous and distinguished body of work. Forced to abandon writing as a livelihood by his late 40s, the author of *Moby-Dick* (1851) spent almost 20 subsequent years (1866–1886) earning a modest but stable living as a politically appointed port customs inspector, the same profession Adam Smith had turned to after publishing *The Wealth of Nations* (*WN*) to nearly universal accolades. Melville had not enjoyed a fraction of the acclaim that Smith had, but according to most accounts was an honest government official and, according to some, the only honest one working in the New York City harbor area. During his younger years, the mostly self-educated Melville had been a merchant sailor and had seen the world by the time he published his first novel (*Typee: A Peep at Polynesian Life*) in 1846.[2] Melville had not travelled west or longed to travel west like so many other Americans; his international vision was much broader than that, and it may have been a significant reason why so many ordinary readers still have trouble relating to him. Nevertheless, Melville had witnessed nearly everything during his long lifetime—slavery, the Industrial Revolution, the Mexican War, Emancipation, labor unrest, westward expansion, Native American persecutions—the works. What mattered most to him, however, at least as a writer, was the individual human being, and how individuals react to the moral challenges and choices presented to them during the course of everyday working life.

Many of these presented choices or dilemmas in Melville's best known prose stories have profound socioeconomic themes and overtones: *Bartleby, the Scrivener: A Tale of Wall Street* (1853); *Benito Cereno* (1855); *The Confidence-Man: His Masquerade* (1857); *Billy Budd, Sailor* (1891).[3] As early as 1849, however—the same year that the Great Irish Famine was reaching its terrible climax—Melville's fourth novel *Redburn: His First Voyage* was published to modest critical and financial success, despite the book having been sloppily written by its hard-pressed author strictly for (in his own words) tobacco money. *Redburn* also, rather surprisingly, has some passages devoted to lampooning Adam Smith's *WN*. Melville's heavily autobiographical main character, in an attempt to improve his mind while off-duty at sea, is given a musty old copy of Smith's famous work to peruse by a friend. Thinking the volume is a how to get rich quick manual, the disappointed Redburn concludes that Smith's "alleged wealth of nations" is "dry as crackers and cheese," becoming "dryer and dryer" the more he reads on. Then he reflects, "I wondered whether any body had ever read it, even the author himself...."[4] Redburn, however, judges *WN* to have some value as a sleeping aide, since he doses off every time that he attempts to trudge through it.

This Johnsonian reaction to one of the great masterpieces of western literature has in fact been leveled by some against Melville's own magnum opus *Moby-Dick*. Melville's publicly expressed opinion of *WN*, whether true or feigned (the former being more likely), is significant, if for no other reason, in that it reflects how Smith's lengthy secular sermon on the machinations of the international market place had little or no resonance for the average citizen of a growing, prospering 19th century nation such as the United States of America.

By the 1890s it was certainly true that the world economy had transformed itself into a technologically high-powered engine that Adam Smith, for all of his foresight, would have hardly recognized a hundred years after his death. The colonial mercantilism of which Smith was so critical in 1776 had gradually given way to a more impersonal, industrialized, and capitalist model producing a much higher volume of goods and services for far more people across the globe. In terms of pure global power, Great Britain and its state-of-the-art navy still dominated. Between 1896 and 1898, the venerable William Gladstone served out his final term as Prime Minister before death deprived Victorian England of its most able statesman. Gladstone's passing foreshadowed the end of that era in English history. The remainder of the 19th century for Great Britain would be marked by more colonial disturbances, particularly in Africa, where during the second Boer War a young

Winston Churchill found himself made into a POW by his Dutch Afrikaner captors.

More seriously from an international standpoint, the violent Chinese Boxer Rebellion of 1899–1901 required a military coalition consisting of Japan and seven major western powers to be forcibly suppressed. The United States contributed a numerically small but highly effective component to this intervention, causing many of its British allies to realize for the first time that the U.S. was not the same small upstart country it had fought eight decades earlier during the War of 1812. By 1900, Americans had in fact become quite adept at employing shock-and-awe tactics on foreign soil. As for the Chinese, they had realized too late (and to their sustained misfortune) that a new world order had arisen in which China and Asian markets were largely at the mercy of western industrialized powers. This position of weakness, however, would not last forever.

The great harbinger of American overseas might and prowess, however, had come in 1898, when a decaying and long-provoked Spanish Empire made the mistake of declaring war upon its persistent antagonist, the United States. Thus around the same time that journalist Winston Churchill was being detained in South Africa by Boer militia, the briefly but sharply fought Spanish American War was making a media hero out of the 40-year-old Theodore Roosevelt (1858–1919). The "splendid little war"—as Ambassador John Hay described it to Roosevelt—decisively won in less than three months by the recently modernized American Navy, overnight transformed the United States into an international power to be reckoned with. By the time the disintegrating Spanish Empire limped away from its theater of operations during the summer of 1898, the U.S. effectively controlled much of the Caribbean and a good part of the South Pacific, including the Philippine Islands.

U.S. motivation to intervene in Spanish colonial affairs was simple: it wanted to stabilize its own overseas commercial markets while establishing global military bases for its new showcase naval weaponry. In particular, a forceful demonstration by the Americans led by Commodore (and future Admiral) George Dewey at the Battle of Manila Bay had surprised and even dismayed European naval powers simultaneously converging in the South Pacific, particularly the Germans, who had reasonably expected to be the main beneficiaries of recent Spanish decline in that region.[5]

Although Adam Smith had always preached the superiority of technology over manpower in *WN*, it is doubtful if he ever imagined in his wildest speculations the speed, durability, and firepower brought to bear by predreadnought battleships of the late 19th century, including those of the U.S.

Navy. After a post–Civil War period of military dormancy, America in the 1880s joined a global arms race by fully modernizing its navy with steel provided by the sleepless production lines of Andrew Carnegie. No small part of Carnegie's vast fortune came from military contracts.

Other industrialized powers were unprepared for this sudden American ascendency, or simply were overmatched by its dizzying rapidity. When the American genie finally came out of the bottle during the Spanish and Chinese disturbances of 1898–1901, there was really little that these other aspiring superpowers could do except attempt to keep pace with their relentless New World rival. While ordinary American citizens debated whether gold or silver should form the basis of a uniform monetary standard, it was Carnegie's steel output that had placed the United States on the international economic map for keeps. This development would not have surprised Adam Smith, as he never had been much of an advocate for measuring wealth primarily (let alone strictly) in terms of precious metals or, for that matter, any other tangible, physical object or substance.

Predictably, America's spectacular achievement came with an unforeseen, heavy cost. The early 1890s were marred by a series of labor strikes unprecedented in their violence and their ruthless suppression. The first and arguably the worst of these occurred in 1892 at the Homestead Steel Works near Pittsburg, Pennsylvania, where organized labor learned to its dismay that any disruption of production affecting military contracts would not be tolerated by the federal government. At Homestead, the nation saw another side of Andrew Carnegie, one quite at odds with his philanthropic public image, in which the tycoon would unhesitatingly leave on-site management of operations to vicious henchmen if profit margins or national security were threatened to any significant degree. Not long after this dark chapter in American history receded, the utopian model company town of railroad baron George Pullman located near Chicago, Illinois, came to a depressing end when its workers learned similar, bitter lessons about disrupting national transportation infrastructure. Nor was the energy sector an exception to this harsh rule. That same year the United Mine Workers attempted to mount a nationwide coal strike in response to reduced wages but were crushed out of existence as a result. Although Adam Smith had been dead for over a century, none of these events would have surprised him, neither in terms of ownership's joint, grim resolve, nor the fledgling unions' inability to sustain peaceful, effective protests.

The devastating Panic of 1893 and subsequent social unrest had effectively wrecked the second-term presidency of Grover Cleveland (between

1893 and 1897), paving the way for a Republican Party political resurgence over the next decade. William McKinley (1843–1901), elected to the White House in 1896, represented the last in a long line of Civil War heroes hailing from the Ohio River Valley, then later achieving prominence in national politics. McKinley's opponent in 1896 had been William Jennings Bryan (1860–1925), who based most if not all of his campaign platform on the long-sighted proposition that American currency should not be based solely on a gold standard, thereby ensuring wider distribution of capital and credit among the less privileged.[6] Bryan's populist enthusiasm and single-mindedness won him large live audiences for his barnstorming speech rallies, but not enough votes to win the Electoral College. The debate over the gold standard had in fact been gradually building into a crescendo since the Civil War had ended, and the election of 1896 finally brought it to a head. Bryan was neither the first nor the last American political candidate attempting to sell bold economic theories sugarcoated with religious fervor or zealotry, but he was perhaps the most eloquent and certainly the most energetic. At the end of the day, however, more fiscally conservative voices in favor of a strict gold monetary standard and conventional protectionism won the day, setting the stage for sustained economic recovery under the victorious McKinley administration, along with major assists from the Spanish American War and subsequent hostilities abroad (especially in the Philippines), all of which suddenly seemed to have become serious concerns for American business interests.

Returning to the pressing question of a gold standard versus bimetallism (gold-silver) or other forms of government backed currency, Adam Smith had been surprisingly noncommittal in his views, though discussing in detail the historical origins, roles, and mechanisms of precious metals in *WN*. Smith merely made accurate observations as opposed to espousing doctrines. A good part of his detachment on subject matter known to send lesser mortals into Bryan-like reveries of passion—"You shall not crucify mankind on a cross of gold"—was traceable to his extensive philosophic training as a student which, until the 20th century, had been more or less a prerequisite to any kind of serious education in political economy.[7] Specifically, the three years (1737–1740) that the impressionable, teenaged Smith spent under the tutelage of famed lecturer Francis Hutcheson at the University of Glasgow had more than a little to do with Smith's consistent and rather unique ability to clearly distinguish between substance and symbolism. Close parallels between the teachings of Hutcheson and the later writings of Smith on money as a mere symbol of value, rather than having any intrinsic value in and of itself, have been noted by more than one commentator.[8] Also behind Hutcheson's overtly secular philosophy lay his own stern Presbyterianism, one with which he often imbued his students, treating any form of currency or trade—indeed all material things—as mutable, fleeting, and transitory. Much like Alfred Marshall would during the following century, Hutcheson was known to bring a religious intensity to the classroom, but for philosophical purposes, and his youthful scholars frequently took approving note. One of the many payoffs for Hutcheson's dedication was Smith later producing his own impressive written legacy.

Lengthy passages of *WN* are devoted to the mechanics of various hard and paper currencies, as well as how these currencies functioned within the mercantilist colonial system then known to Smith during the 18th century. Precious metals in and of themselves did not particularly impress Smith; instead, his continual focus was on investment, productivity, purchasing power, and standards of living.[9] His typical watchwords were "industry" and "opulence," not gold or silver.[10] Late 19th century American political debates over the gold standard or free silver would have interested him from an intellectual standpoint, but Andrew Carnegie's global steel empire would have interested him more. In one oft-quoted paragraph, Smith refers to gold and silver as "dead stock"—or "dead weight" in modern parlance—meaning that precious metals ("metal pieces") were expensive to produce and maintain while contributing nothing of real substance to true wealth.[11] Somewhat mischievously, Smith makes repeated reference to the use of iron and copper as hard currency by ancient societies, because these metals were once considered more valuable, primitive cultures being generally unimpressed by gold and silver (see header quote).[12] In fact, he begins his discussion on money by underscoring that precious metals eventually became money and replaced barter simply because of their unique combination of durability and divisibility.[13] In the same paragraph that Smith declares gold and silver to be "dead stock," he praises the judicious substitution of paper money (through banking apparatuses) as an efficient means to free commerce of the cumbersome burdens inherent to all hard currencies.[14] After several hundred pages of this discussion, it is tempting to conclude that Smith would have viewed any person possessing a bag of gold as being nonetheless poor, not to mention foolish, if that person were only willing to hoard the gold rather than to spend or invest it. It also calls to mind the Christian parable of the worthless servant who did not invest his master's money (Matthew 25:14–30), although Smith was never one to quote biblical scripture in favor of his arguments.

One distinguished British economist who did not shrink from employing biblical imagery in her expression was Martha Beatrice Potter Webb (1858–1943), usually credited with first coining the phrase "collective bargaining" in 1891, the year before the Homestead strike.[15] As early as 1886, however, writing privately not long after the Haymarket affair in Chicago, Webb marveled at the brazen manner in which Adam Smith had somehow, over the course of a century, been transformed into the new philosophical darling of the conservative business establishment:

> The Political Economy of Adam Smith was the scientific expression of the impassioned crusade of the 18th century against the class tyranny and the oppression of the Many by the Few. By what silent revolution of events, by what unconscious transformation of thought did it change itself into the "Employers' Gospel" of the 19th century?[16]

Webb's incredulous reaction at this stage in Anglo-American history is noteworthy. A cofounder of the London School of Economics, Webb, like her younger contemporary John Maynard Keynes, exerted a measurable degree of political influence over the course of her long career, at least within the United Kingdom.[17] Keynes, writing to George Bernard Shaw not long after Webb's passing in 1943 (and not long before his own), nor given to making easy compliments, called her "the greatest woman of the generation which is now passing."[18] It is significant that she, among many other experts of those times, believed that Smith's theories were being heavily misrepresented within the public sphere as early as the 1880s.

It is probably no coincidence that during this same late 19th century period of alleged widespread misrepresentation that the first seriously updated biography of Smith appeared, almost exactly 100 years after Smith's old colleague Dugald Stewart assayed the same elusive subject matter circa 1793. Thus in 1895 came *Life of Adam Smith*, published by MacMillan and written by the Scottish journalist John Rae (1845–1915), not to be confused with the earlier Scottish economist (1796–1872) or several other notable personages by the same name.[19] Rae was given access by institutions and individuals to many original materials for the first time, and incorporated data earlier uncovered by Henry Peter Brougham. Consequently, a far more complete, focused, and nuanced picture of Smith's life and work emerges. The accurate and presumed desired result of Rae's detailed portrait of Smith is a much more complicated personality than earlier suggested by Stewart, who had in fact gone to some length in emphasizing his friend's many-sided interests and diverse academic associations. Above all, Rae contextualizes, delineates, and frames Smith's philosophic theories within the late 18th century milieu in which the latter lived, a task for which Stewart, despite all of his ability and knowledge, lacked the historical distance to effectively accomplish, even had he wanted to. In short, anyone now wishing to pigeon-hole or oversimplify Smith for their own political purposes, publicly or privately, would be hard-pressed to find such ammunition with the pages of Rae's even-handed, dispassionate study. By 1895, Smithian biography had finally become serious business, and has remained so ever since.

This certainly did not prevent American or British politicians, however, from publicly dropping Smith's name on occasion in ways that were, to put it charitably, misleading or mystifying. An exception of sorts came on January 30, 1894, from, of all people, William Jennings Bryan, speaking before the House of Representatives as a Populist Democrat from Nebraska. As a proponent of what would have been the first peacetime, progressive income tax, Jennings took trouble to cite Smith and *WN* as a definitive authority to his no doubt stunned Congressional colleagues. In the midst of a debate which nowadays might be publicly broadcast on C-Span, Bryan pronounced:

> Adam Smith says: "The subjects of every state ought to contribute towards the support of the government, as nearly as possible, in proportion to their respective abilities; that is, in proportion to the revenue which they respectively enjoy under the protection of the state.... In the observation or neglect of this maxim consists, what is called the equality or inequality of taxation."[20]

Prefacing his remark with a reminder to less knowledgeable House members that Smith belonged to a very elite class of experts ("the most distinguished writers among political economy"), Bryan proceeded to bolster his energetic support of a progressive income tax bill with sober confirmation from *WN*.[21] Bryan neglected to mention that Smith wrote these words within the context of a pending 1776 revolution by American colonists against Great Britain over increased taxes; but no matter, the basic idea was still valid for the United States in 1894. Bryan's Democratic Party was attempting to reduce tariffs without creating a deficit by raising taxes on the rich. The measure passed Congress but was struck down by the Supreme Court, and a peacetime U.S. income tax would have to wait a few more years before becoming an unpopular but permanent reality.

The prelude to the income tax proposal had been the McKinley Tariff of 1890, effectively raising import duties in accordance with traditional Republican policy, and whose namesake sponsor was destined to become the 25th President of the United States in 1897. The tariff-income tax debate of the early 1890s foreshadowed the political showdown between McKinley and Jennings in 1896. Unfortunately for the Democrats, however, the administration of their sitting President (Grover Cleveland) had proven unequal to the task of preventing or stemming the debilitating Panic of 1893. The end result was a resounding return to national power for the GOP. As early as

1888, Ohio Congressman McKinley, leading his party in a two-year battle over tariffs, also dropped Adam Smith's name during a May 18th speech widely considered to be one of the greatest of his meteoric political career. Substituting visual aids—a suit of clothes with pricing unaffected by high tariffs—for academic authority, McKinley mocked the idea of free trade as an automatic price reducer: "It is the old story. It is found in the works of Adam Smith. [Laughter and applause on the Republican side.]"[22] "It" being code for free trade doctrine or lower tariffs, this moment may have marked the very first time in public discourse that Smith's name and *WN* were used for comic rather than serious effect. Appropriating the pro–American economic stance of Henry Charles Carey, McKinley did something that Carey would have never done, namely, treat lightly Smith's ideas, as opposed to merely complain of their widespread misrepresentation, as had Beatrice Webb only two years previous, and as had Carey even before that time. By the 1890s, the Democratic movement to lower tariffs had been successfully defeated by Republicans and replaced instead with legislation authorizing higher tariffs than ever.

Assuming the American mantle of economic expertise from Carey was Henry George (1839–1897), whose *Progress and Poverty* (1879) had been the first best-seller of its kind both in the U.S. and abroad. The mostly self-educated George was representative of a new breed of politically active economists, and is considered one of the intellectual fathers of what later became the Progressive Movement (see Chapter 10). By the early 1890s, he was hard at work on his ultimately unfinished tome, *The Science of Political Economy* (1898), containing in Book II, Chapter VI, a number of interesting passages devoted to the legacy of Adam Smith. Perhaps as a response to the question posed a few years earlier by Beatrice Webb, George offered a novel and not too implausible explanation as to how Smith had by then become, only a century after his death, the darling of big business and, for that matter, all opponents of government intervention into domestic everyday affairs of state. George was perhaps the first writer to emphasize that Smith wrote during a completely different era, one in which mercantile interests were separate from, and often perceived as a threat to, those of the English nobility. Consequently, Smith's *WN*, being aggressively critical of the mercantile interests (as well as of their provocation of the American Revolution), was well received, even embraced, by the nobility. By the late Victorian era, however, the two groups had become far more intertwined and interdependent. Therefore, according to George, it was much easier, and more convenient for that matter, to shift the emphasis on interpretation rather than condemn outright what had been long lauded as a masterpiece in Western literature and philosophic thought.

With respect to period news events, art never mirrored life better than in 1901, when the April 6 issue of *Puck* magazine featured a startling cover entitled "Columbia's Easter Bonnet," by S.D. Ehrhardt (1862?–1920), after an original sketch by Louis Dalrymple (1866–1905). Here, the formidable and disconcertingly attractive female counterpart to Uncle Sam sports one of Admiral Dewey's steel battleships as a headdress while admiring herself in a mirror. Emblazoned on her ship-hat are the twin mottos "World Power" and "Expansion." The effect is not unlike the Statue of Liberty, erected in New York City harbor only 15 years before, suddenly going mad with ambition and vainglory. *Puck*'s cheeky commentary came in the immediate wake of crushing American victories in the Caribbean, the Philippines, and China, the latter two being especially bloody and brutal.[23] To the eternal credit of the United States, not everyone stateside was cheering, applauding or boasting. Some clearly recognized a looming downside to these territorial gains. Just as the Mexican-American conquest of the 1840s had set the stage for the War Between the States, U.S. colonial expansionism of the late 19th century would presage American prominence in the highly destructive world wars of the early 20th century. *Puck* magazine itself was an appropriate venue for such double-edged commentary; named after Shakespeare's eponymous, supernatural troublemaker from *A Midsummer Night's Dream*, the popular publication's own motto, appearing directly above its provocative cover art, featured a direct quotation from the Bard, "what fools these mortals be" (III.II.115).

On January 22, 1901, three weeks into the 20th century, the 81-year-old Queen Victoria died, having reigned over the second British Empire at the height of its prosperity for more than six decades. She was succeeded by her son, King Edward VII. Most everyone at the time knew that Victoria's death marked the end of era, symbolically if nothing else. A few months later in the U.S., President McKinley was sworn in for his second term, having trounced William Jennings Bryan in the election of 1900 even more decisively than in 1896. Adding to the cache of McKinley's second term ticket was the addition of New York governor and Spanish American War hero Theodore Roosevelt, owing to the death of Vice President Garret Hobart in 1899. The Democrats never stood a chance. No sooner had Republicans celebrated their resounding triumph in 1900–1901, however, than McKinley was assassinated in September at a reception in Buffalo, New York, by a crazed anarchist.[24] Roosevelt was promptly sworn in and the new century was off and running. Though a pro-business Republican with a privileged upbringing, Roosevelt belonged to a much younger generation, and was cut from different cloth than his predecessors. Despite his family wealth, Roosevelt had been schooled in personal adversity and taught to empathize with those less fortunate than himself. As for big business and the robber barons, he knew their limitations and vices as well as anyone, as an insider, it might well be said.[25] While heartily approving of the great advances led by American and British capitalism over the last century, he was not blind to its extensive collateral damage. In many respects, there may have been no single person better suited to lead the young country in its newly-achieved status as a world power.

10. Trustbuster (1901–1913)

"It is thus that the single advantage which the monopoly procures to a single order of men, is in many different ways hurtful to the general interest of the country." —Adam Smith[1]

At the outset of the 20th century, the United States found itself with a new president, Theodore Roosevelt, and Great Britain found itself with a new monarch, King Edward VII. As the American Progressive and British Edwardian eras began to unfold, the English-speaking world asserted its will towards the rest of mankind on a previously unknown scale. Whereas Adam Smith had written during a time when the first British Empire, along with its restless American colonials, had fought long and hard to gain economic ascendency in the New World over its nearest —France and Spain— by 1901, the U.S. and the British Empire combined knew no real global competition, with the occasional exception of a recently-unified Germany. By the time Roosevelt, at age 42 the youngest president in U.S. history, had been swiftly sworn into office on September 14, 1901, he presided over a republic profoundly different from the one known by its Founding Fathers 125 years earlier.

While Smith, like many others, had envisioned the rapid geographic spread of English-speaking peoples over the North American continent, it is open to debate whether he could have foreseen their subsequent colonial ambitions realized on several other continents as well. Roosevelt, as former Assistant Secretary of the Navy and poster boy hero for the recently triumphant Spanish American War, perfectly embodied the ideals (as well as the pretensions) of the new national mentality. His family was also of Dutch ancestry, making his public image more marketable to a country largely comprised of newly arrived immigrants, even though the Roosevelts themselves had been in the New World since the 17th century. By contrast, the colorless King Edward VII of England (1841–1910) seemed to represent more of a throwback to the pre–Victorian age, one in which Edwardian England ruled its empire more by perceived right rather than true merit, even while its tenuous grasp on international power appeared to be loosening.

As if on cue, the geopolitical map of Europe began to shift drastically within the space of a few short years. Great Britain finally buried the hatchet with its old, weakened rival France and agreed to an alliance in 1904, followed in 1907 by a British treaty with Czarist Russia, coalescing into the so-called Triple Entente, a similar precondition to World War I. The old German-British solidarity, one so approvingly familiar to Adam Smith during his own time, had suddenly vanished within the space of three short years.[2] Whatever the true causes of the Great War (to this day still being debated among academics), there can be little doubt that European anxiety over the startling, meteoric rise of Germany as a world economic power fueled much questionable decision-making during the first 14 years of the new century. Germany's breathtaking ascendency on the world stage in less than half a century was simply too much too process for other European powers, particularly Great Britain, who stood the most to lose. The death of King Edward in 1910 was followed by the royal succession of his more competent and hard-working son, George V (1865–1936), the latter eventually taking trouble to rechristen his family the House of Windsor in order to distance itself from their German heritage. As for Germany, national success led first to hubris, then later, to military aggression, compounded by shortsighted leadership under Kaiser Wilhelm II that seemed to possess little understanding or appreciation for the volatile winds of socioeconomic change then swirling in every direction.

On the American side of the pond, a completely different kind of struggle was unfolding. Roosevelt, with single-minded energy, launched into a remarkable series of simultaneous reform crusades, usually successful and oftentimes against heavy political opposition, occasionally within his own Republican Party. Roosevelt's two-term (1901–1909) administration is rightfully remembered as the heyday of the Progressive Era or, as he himself dubbed it, a "Square Deal" for the American people. It also represents perhaps the ultimate casebook study of a perceived political conservative being able to achieve the most dramatic legislative results in terms of social domestic do-gooding. Most importantly, not since Lincoln had there been an American President who viewed the federal government as a primary implement of necessary change, and the executive branch in particular as a bully pulpit for swaying public opinion towards those ends.

In Roosevelt's case, however, this federal power was wielded during peacetime and frequently against the financial interests of the very same wealthy individuals supporting Roosevelt's candidacy in the first place. Contrary to Adam Smith's admittedly circumspect views on the proper designated roles of central government (defense, justice, education, infrastructure, etc.), Roosevelt saw federal intervention (or intrusion, some would say) as a necessary and desirable step offsetting the many evils brought about by modern industrial technologies and the economic changes attending these. The tangible results were enormous voter popularity for Roosevelt during his own time plus numerous useful institutions still with us today though now often taken for granted. More in line with Smith's express views in *WN* favoring government-sponsored infrastructure and transportation, Roosevelt initiated the American takeover of the ongoing Panama Canal project in 1904, an initiative that would a decade later reap huge economic rewards for both U.S. trading interests and the entire western hemisphere in general.

After declining a third term (a decision he would always later regret), Roosevelt was succeeded in the presidency by his protégé, William Howard Taft (1857–1930). Taft, despite possessing plenty of charm and amiability, lacked his sponsor's energy, brilliance, and idealism. The result was a considerable blunting of the Republican Progressive agenda. By 1912, Roosevelt had decided to reenter the fray of national politics. After being rejected for the presidential nomination by his own party—no doubt in part because of the special interests he had offended during his previous term in office—Roosevelt made the fateful decision to run as an independent under the Progressive or "Bull Moose" banner. The result was an acrimonious split in the electoral constituency which had—minus a few short intervals—run the country since the Civil War. This allowed the Democratic candidate, former Princeton University president Woodrow Wilson (1856–1924), a man of Southern birth and upbringing and Scots-Irish ancestry, to be elected 28th president of the United States in 1912. Perhaps the most important consequence of the 1912 election was that a career New York state politician on the make named Franklin Delano Roosevelt (1882–1945) openly broke with Democratic Party bosses to support Wilson's nomination. Teddy Roosevelt's fifth cousin, a member of the opposing political party and widely dismissed by his enemies as a foppish lightweight, had in 1905 married the president's favorite niece, Anna Eleanor Roosevelt (1884–1962), with his full approval. By 1912, FDR was himself poised to enter the stage of national politics, with significant economic reverberations to be felt for the remainder of the 20th century and well beyond, though these effects would not fully manifest until some two decades later.

The first year of the Wilson presidency in 1913 provides a good bookend to the Progressive Era in American politics. Though (for all practical purposes) a Southern Democrat, Wilson had taken careful note of the electoral support Roosevelt had enjoyed while in the White House, despite alienating some of his most financially powerful supporters. Borrowing a page from Roosevelt's political playbook, Wilson shrewdly appropriated any Progressive reforms that showed significant popular support among the voters. These first and foremost included lower tariffs on imports and then, to pay for the lost revenue, a peacetime U.S. income tax, enabled by passage of the 16th Amendment in early 1913. Later that same year came the Federal Reserve Act, and with it, the Federal Reserve Bank, a prominent staple in the American economy ever since. This was the first government-sponsored institution of its kind since 1836, when a totally different kind of Democratic President, Andrew Jackson, had so determinedly dismantled the Second Bank of the United States. Meanwhile, a defeated and disillusioned Theodore Roosevelt embarked for yet another adventure in the jungles of the Amazon, an excursion which eventually broke his health, nearly took his life, and probably shortened it as well. As for Roosevelt's young fifth cousin, Franklin, his early maverick support for Wilson landed him a prominent post in the new administration as Assistant Secretary of the Navy, the same stepping stone position previously held by Roosevelt.

Returning to Roosevelt in 1901, no sooner had he been sworn into office than he did what hardly anyone at the time could have expected, least of all those within his own party: he announced to a stunned Congress his intent to strictly enforce antitrust laws. Although the Sherman Anti-Trust Law had been on the books since 1890, it was widely viewed as symbolic rather than substantive.[3] Now, the public mood had changed and Roosevelt correctly gauged it. In many respects this shift represented a long overdue reaction against the previously tolerated excesses and injustices of the Gilded Age. Robber barons such as John D. Rockefeller and J.P. Morgan watched in astonishment as the man they had helped get elected proceeded to zealously break up their massive monopolies with sweepingly effective antitrust litigation.

In many other respects, through political necessity if nothing else, Roosevelt remained a strictly pro-business Republican, but his successful trust-busting crusade of the early 1900s was a notable exception. By leveling the competitive economic playing field—or at least reducing the extremity of its peaks and valleys—it allowed the pre–World War I U.S. economy to prosper more broadly than it otherwise would have. It also prevented the affected monopolies from having the same sort of destructive, ubiquitous political influence in Washington similar to, say, that of the East India Company in Great Britain during Adam Smith's day. It is unknown or unclear whether

Roosevelt ever read Smith's philosophical works; his literary tastes tended more towards military or historical subject matter. There can be little argument, however, that Roosevelt's trustbusting initiative would have met with full approval from the author who so publicly attacked the British trade monopolies of the 18th century.

No sooner had Roosevelt won this significant victory than he turned his attention to a host of other economic reforms. A national coal miner's strike that in the past would have resulted in widespread violence was peacefully mediated by the President in person, thus giving subtle, de facto recognition of organized labor's right to collectively bargain, much to the chagrin of mine owners more used to breaking such strikes with impunity and total disregard of worker grievances.[4] Numerous regulatory acts protecting consumers were implemented. Natural resource conservation and a National Park System were championed. In fact, no justice can be done in such a short space as this to Roosevelt's comprehensive legislative accomplishments. One of his few failed causes was a proposed inheritance or estate tax, an idea eloquently supported by Adam Smith in *The Wealth of Nations* back in 1776, but even this would later eventually become law under the Wilson administration in 1916.[5]

Significantly, the one area of economic reform that Roosevelt studiously avoided was tariff legislation, standing firm in the long Republican tradition of relatively high tariffs originally advocated by American economist Henry Charles Carey. Regardless of his evolving personal views on the tariffs, which always seem to have been sincere, Roosevelt the pragmatist recognized that the issue was politically divisive for the Republican Party in a way that few other issues were. It is a good surmise that he sincerely believed if business monopolies could be broken up or controlled on the home front, then foreign trade would take care of itself. As an original American expansionist, Roosevelt likely felt the best way to regulate international commerce was to regulate U.S. companies engaged in those activities. Unfortunately for the Republican Party, the debate heated up (rather than cooling down) after Roosevelt's premature exit from office, and would eventually contribute to decisive Democratic victory in 1912.

As for Adam Smith, the roots of his celebrated hostility toward monopolies of any kind are to be found in his unhappy days as a student at Baliol College, Oxford University, between 1740 and 1746. After a promising stint at the University of Glasgow, the 14-year-old Smith was awarded a scholarship to attend, as a visiting Scotsman, the bastion of English higher education, but ended up leaving Oxford after six years without taking a degree. Biographer Dugald Stewart glosses over this period in Smith's life, but significantly notes that he entered Oxford intending to become an Anglican clergymen, but instead found himself being punished for reading the controversial works of David Hume during his spare time.⁶ Both Stewart and Smith's later biographer John Rae agree that he managed to become proficient at languages while studying at Oxford, especially, Latin, Greek, and French. He enjoyed returning to the ancient classics for comfort and inspiration the rest of his life.⁷

Rae fills in more of the unpleasant details. Smith, as a young provincial, was continually away from home during those six years, lonely, impoverished and in poor health.⁸ As a Scotsmen during the Jacobite Rebellion, he was likely both looked down upon by the English for being Scottish and shunned by fellow Scotsmen sympathizing with the rebels.⁹ As a visiting undergraduate, he was not even permitted to use the Bodleian Library, but apparently made the most of the college library at Baliol.¹⁰ Rae usefully noted that Smith was not alone in his low opinion of the university, and that its critics included the likes of Edward Gibbon and Jeremy Bentham.¹¹ As a final critical touch, Rae adds that hardly anyone else of note attended Baliol at the time, and Smith was never granted an honorary degree after he became famous or even after his death.¹²

The most scathing criticism, however, comes from Smith himself, in the final sections in *Wealth of Nations* (*WN*) on public and private education. Smith essentially saw places like Oxford as educational monopolies in which there were no meaningful relationships between teacher pay and teacher performance. Teachers at Oxford were paid their fees regardless of results, usually to the impoverishment of their students; moreover, any private teachers attempting to offer meaningful competition to the establishment were marginalized. Smith later in *WN* compares the contemporary English system unfavorably with the ancient systems of Greece and Rome. Smith's last, memorable dig against his alma mater is that women, then totally excluded from the public educational system, often ended up receiving superior educations outside of the system because of their very exclusion.¹³ His Oxford sojourn must have been especially disappointing for Smith after being exposed to the Scottish Enlightenment firsthand via Francis Hutcheson. Indeed, Smith's torrent of harsh judgments against the monopolistic British public educational system of his day offers some of the most lively reading to be found within *WN*. For example, it was his acerbic dismissal of Oxford faculty to which contemporaries such as James Boswell took such strong exception. As astutely observed by Allan B. Krueger of Princeton University, "It may well be that Smith's Oxford experience ignited his belief in the virtues of competition."¹⁴

Smith's condemnation of monopolies is too extensive to catalogue here, but a few highlights are worth revisiting. In addition to being selfish at the expense of the greater good, monopolies were, in the long run, detrimental to the profits of their own shortsighted ownership, as the American Revolution would soon demonstrate to the special interests of mercantilist Great Britain. By the 20th century, this same idea might well be applied to labor, whose unnecessarily inflicted hardships were beginning to translate into production inefficiencies and disrupted assembly lines. The same could easily be said of consumers, often the same individuals clamoring for better wages and working conditions, and when these were not forthcoming, probably punished their employers most effectively with limited purchasing power and more reluctant, slacking demand for goods and services. In some respects, the situation was analogous to legalized slavery of the previous century, where increased, record production in fact concealed an outmoded and less profitable form of labor usage. Earlier than any of these developments, Smith had recognized that "Masters are always and every where in a sort of tacit, but constant and uniform combination, not to raise the wages of labour above their actual rate."[15] This held true both for slave masters of the 19th century, as well as for industrial robber barons and their serf-like workforce coming immediately afterwards. Smith was unequivocal in what needed to be done as a countermeasure: "...those exertions of the natural liberty of a few individuals, which might endanger the security of the whole society, are, and ought to be, restrained by the laws of all governments."[16] As a specific, primary example of these "exertions," Smith then cites "regulations of the banking trade."[17]

Anyone successfully running a business knows that labor is the most expensive line item and that efficient labor management (not marketing) is the most difficult, tedious task. In short, marketing or selling a product is one thing, but delivering that product to the satisfaction of consumers without competently managing a production line is hardly imaginable. Smith correctly acknowledged the centrality of labor in the profit equation by dividing all non-profit revenue into either labor (wages) or rent, in that order.[18] As for the rent component, he remarked upon its insidious nature in terms of frequent landlord tendencies to try and horn in on any successful tenant business enterprise: "As soon as the land of any country has all become private property, the landlords, like all other men, love to reap where they never sowed, and demand a rent even for its natural produce."[19] That is to say, landlords often covet a percentage rent over and above the base rent, a percentage rent typically calculated against tenant net profit or, worse for the tenant, gross production.

Without quoting Adam Smith—perhaps without even reading him—

Roosevelt recognized these tendencies in his wealthy constituents. For him, it posed a direct threat to the conservation or wise management of seemingly inexhaustible natural resources on the North American continent, resources which he so personally cherished. Accordingly, as president he moved to place defined boundaries on the powers of industry to acquire and utilize wide open spaces by converting some of these spaces into public lands. This action may have surprised and angered some of the more powerful sectors within the business community, but it also proved once again for Roosevelt to be a politically shrewd and effective move. The issue remains relevant. To this day, the acquisition by or leasing of public lands to private industry is a controversial topic; yet over a hundred years ago, to his credit, Roosevelt had the foresight to identify the problem and attempt to address it in a manner which still benefits the country as a whole.

In Edwardian England, the new century inaugurated itself with the first biography of Adam Smith written by an Englishman rather than a Scotsman. Journalist Francis Wrigley Hirst (1873–1953) was commissioned by Andrew Carnegie's old British political associate John Morley to produce a somewhat condensed overview of Smith's life and work, for Morley's *English Men of Letters* series in 1904, published by the originally Scottish Macmillan Company. Hirst drew upon material earlier presented in more longwinded fashion by Stewart, Brougham, and Rae to paint a concise literary portrait of Smith more appealing to the Liberal side of the aisle in Parliament. This had no doubt been partly motivated by Beatrice Webb's earlier complaint that Smith's philosophical legacy had been improperly co-opted by big business and those serving their special interests. Regardless of interpretations, the very fact that Smith's name was now being lumped together as a prominent literary figure with the likes of his old antagonist Samuel Johnson represented a shift of sorts in public perceptions. Now that the Second British Empire had reached its pinnacle of power and prestige, it was somehow more acceptable to acknowledge the greatness of English-language writers born and mostly living outside of England proper. In another very real sense, some one hundred years after the fact, the Scottish Enlightenment had finally gone mainstream.

American politicians during the Progressive Era tended to be far more blunt, and could afford to be so given that their constituents were often far more demanding and tolerant of change. No single individual better represented this tendency than Senator Robert Marion "Fighting Bob" La Follette, Sr. (1855–1925) of Wisconsin, a Republican progressive whose family's descendants are still prominent in local affairs.[20] Early in his national career, La Follette saw fit to drop Adam Smith's name in a speech to a no doubt startled

U.S. Senate on April 19, 1906. Making reference to the antagonized special interests then opposed to President Theodore Roosevelt's energetic reform agenda, La Follette observed: "...it is much easier to stand with these great interests than against them. This was true when Adam Smith wrote his Wealth of Nations, and it is true in 1906."[21] It is worth noting that by this point in time, Smith had been dead for 116 years and it had been some 130 years since the publication of *WN*; nevertheless, both were cited in a U.S. Senatorial debate over progressive reform legislation by a Midwestern politician.

La Follette's rhetorical ammunition in this instance is clearly traceable to his earlier education at the University of Wisconsin. There, he had been under the inspired tutelage of noted American educator John Bascom (1827–1911), president of the university between 1874 and 1887. Bascom, himself an economic thinker and writer of note, was steeped in the tradition of Adam Smith and the Scottish Enlightenment. His lengthy treatise, *Political Economy: Designed as a Text-Book for Colleges* (1874), names Smith as the true father of modern economic thought in its introductory pages. This was likely the same textbook used by La Follette as a student. It is interesting that in 1906, shortly after Hirst had written a short liberal-leaning biography of Smith in England, La Follette recognized as well that Smith had written *WN* in the face of disapproving opposition from powerful political forces, rather than out of any calculated flattery or perceived compliance with their narrow agendas.

The American Progressive Era left a treasure trove of socially or economically-themed political cartoons in its wake. Many are priceless in their biting satire, some worthy of Mark Twain, one of Roosevelt's many sharp critics up until the humorist's death in 1910. For example, there is the 1902 image depicting Roosevelt, as a big game hunter, turning his back contemptuously on a cutesy but restrained namesake teddy bear, or the 1906 caricature depicting Roosevelt, as self-appointed spelling reformer, physically booting an English dictionary out of the White House. More obscure, however, though far more prophetic, was a 1903 cartoon appearing in the *Brooklyn Daily Eagle*, subtly titled "Some Trouble with the Tariff Team."[22] Here, a very worried looking Roosevelt, in his incarnation as a cowboy rough rider, stands astride two mounts, each representing the conservative and progressive wings of his own Republican Party, and about to bolt into opposite directions. Dedicated reformer though he was, there was one reform he studiously avoided, namely, reducing tariffs since he accurately foresaw the destructive effect that it would have on party unity. During his re-election campaign of 1904, Roosevelt stayed with the old guard and higher tariffs, and later advised Taft to do the same after his election in 1908. Instead, Taft attempted to forge a grand compromise with Payne-Aldrich Tariff Act of 1909, but only succeeded in making all sides in the longstanding debate angry and dissatisfied. By 1912, a boisterous Roosevelt had re-entered the national political fray, and the Republican-Progressive coalition, always uneasy and one difficult to maintain, completely unraveled in the process. Thus the very same issues of free trade sparking the American Revolution during Adam Smith's day had by 1912 helped to also cause a crucial two-term (1913–1921) loss of political prerogative, both Presidential and beyond, for the U.S. Republican Party.

The world stage was now set for arguably the greatest shift in transcontinental economic power since the 1783 Treaty of Paris gave formal recognition to the newly independent United States of America. With the coming and passing of the Great War of 1914–1918, the Second British Empire would find itself being taken down a big notch in prestige, while Germany entered into one of the most traumatic phases in its long, extremely complex history. France would barely hold on to what little it had left. Simultaneous with these sudden and unexpected trends, the United States, somewhat against its own popular will, asserted itself to decisively influence international affairs in a manner that would have likely surprised (and appalled) many of the Founding Fathers, though not necessarily surprised Adam Smith had he still been alive. One of the great ironies of this transformation was that ailing former President Theodore Roosevelt, surely one of the most war-loving Americans to ever occupy the White House, was pretty much forced to watch the whole thing from the sidelines, even as his children were being killed and wounded in the catastrophic global conflict then unfolding.[23] Instead, Presidential oversight of American involvement in World War I was designated by fate to Woodrow Wilson, a former academic whose memories of Southern defeat during the Civil War less than half a century earlier were still fresh in his family's memory. Wilson would complete his task ably enough, but ultimately fail in a doomed quest to achieve lasting world peace, even as his own country quickly became the leading military and economic superpower within that world.

11. Anglo-American Power Shift (1914–1921)

"A country abounding with merchants and manufactures, therefore, necessarily abounds with a set of people who have it at all times in their power to advance, if they chuse to do so, a very large sum of money to the government. Hence the ability in the subjects of a commercial state to lend." —Adam Smith[1]

It was no doubt personally frustrating to Theodore Roosevelt, though certainly fortunate for the American nation, that he was never given an opportunity to lead during wartime. One might even argue that Roosevelt's "speak softly and carry a big stick" foreign policy helped to delay the European disaster which came to pass five years after he left office. Roosevelt the Trustbuster, a man who certainly loved war and spent most of his life overcompensating for self-perceived weaknesses, was instead forced to divert his irrepressible energies and boundless courage into the realm of domestic reforms, most of which we are all still benefitting from today. Nevertheless, after accomplishing that which he had been fated to do in life, former President Roosevelt was forced to sit back and watch while his country and family were engulfed in the Great War of 1914–1918.

It was probably just as well. World War I proved not be anything like charging up San Juan Hill during the Spanish-American conflict. By the time that the unprecedented destruction had subsided, his youngest son had been killed in aerial combat over Germany, two other sons wounded, and Roosevelt's health and spirits permanently broken, hastening his own death in 1919. As if all this were not enough tragedy for the Roosevelt family, a mere two years later, Roosevelt's fifth cousin FDR, at age 39, was permanently stricken with polio, not long after having put his celebrated marriage to Roosevelt's favorite niece Eleanor on the rocks through a combination of infidelity and neglect. By the end of 1921, conventional wisdom probably had it that the Roosevelt clan was finished as a force in American politics.

Nineteen nineteen was not a good year for the either the U.S. or the world. Although the war had ended in 1918 with defeat of the Axis Powers, the subsequent Peace Treaty of Versailles invited, with its harsh terms, a repeat of a similar but even wider conflict, which in fact came to pass a little over two decades later. Shortly after the Treaty was signed in 1919, a respected British official and former Cambridge pupil of Alfred Marshall resigned from the Treasury Department in protest, publishing an elegantly written book that more or less accurately predicted how the future would play out. *The Economic Consequences of Peace* by John Maynard Keynes (1883–1946) thus launched the international career of an economist who would remain at the forefront of world affairs over the next three decades, and one quite well versed in the theories of Adam Smith.

Meanwhile, President Woodrow Wilson's bid for U.S. entry into the newly formed League of Nations was met with hostile legislative defeat at home. By the end of his second term, like his former Assistant Secretary of the Navy FDR, Wilson had become a physical invalid, suffering a stroke while campaigning in favor of the League.

Also in 1919 came renewed labor and racial unrest on a scale unknown since the pre–Theodore Roosevelt era. The American national pastime suffered a blow in 1919 when the Black Sox Scandal rocked the professional sports world. The aftereffects of these cumulative misfortunes quickly led to the 1920 election of Republican Warren G. Harding, widely considered to be one of the most ineffective Presidents in U.S. history.

Overseas, Germany had within a few short years transformed from the most envied nation in Europe to the most abject, with crushing reparations imposed by its vengeful neighbors and over a million casualties suffered. Badly battered France survived only because the rest of the free world rallied to its defense. The Austro-Hungarian Empire, which had unwisely begun the conflict, vanished from the map.[2] In Russia, the Bolshevik Revolution destabilized the largest country in Europe and threw it into a chaotic and brutal civil war. The reverberations of this latter event in turn hit America, where the Red Scare of 1919–1921 caused still more unnecessary loss of life and property.[3] During the war, and going against its own strong isolationist traditions, the U.S. had been reluctantly drawn into taking sides with the European Allies, only to see one of those allies (Russia) turn Marxist. Although American manpower and industrial strength finally broke the stalemate on the Western Front in 1918, in doing so it earned the enmity of an entire German generation.

The biggest long-term loser in the Great War, however, was Great Britain, whose startling demotion in world status has never really since recovered. That demotion began with the English going into unsustainable financial debt to the United States. This process had been more efficiently facilitated thanks to the foresight of the Wilson administration by creating the Federal Reserve System back in 1913. The "great engine of state"—as Adam Smith had earlier characterized centralized national banking—was thus back in business for the U.S. and contributing heavily towards its world dominance.

Smith was no stranger to big geopolitical realignments, having lived through the American Revolution and Jacobite Rebellion, among other noteworthy armed struggles. In hindsight, however, perhaps the most sweeping and consequential during Smith's lifetime as a British citizen was the global Seven Years' War of 1756–1763, whose North American component included the French and Indian War, in which a young George Washington received his training as a military leader and strategist. Although Great Britain emerged victorious from this contest, both she and her vanquished longtime antagonist France amassed unprecedented levels of financial debt as a result of their colonial rivalry. Smith was never a soldier in this or any other war, having been appointed a professor of Moral Philosophy at the University of Glasgow in 1753. Later he described this period as "by far the most useful and therefore by far the happiest and most honorable period" in his career.[4] It was during the Glasgow years, and at the height of the French and Indian War, that Smith published his first masterpiece, *The Theory of Moral Sentiments* (*TMS*), in 1759.

Later in 1776, writing in *The Wealth of Nations* (*WN*), Smith commented at length upon the great public debts recently incurred both by Great Britain and France, with respect to the latter sternly noting that "notwithstanding all its natural resources, [France] languishes under an oppressive load [of debt]."[5] In the final chapters of *WN*, Smith hints that France in particular may be traveling down the same path of decline experienced by other previous world powers (such as Spain) making the same mistake, although Britain may be still be spared because of its robust economy and unique relationship between government and private enterprise. Subsequent history, however, confirmed Smith's worst fears. Within two decades of Britain's costly victory in North America, its colonies would be lost to revolution, while barely a quarter century after France's defeat, the Bastille would be stormed, inaugurating the overthrow of the French monarchy.

Smith dwelt at length in *WN* on the huge, constantly rising expense of modern industrialized warfare during the mid–18th century. In reality, he argued, normal government entities with normal systems of taxation are simply not up to the task of financing modern military technology: "The ordinary expence of the greater part of modern governments in time of peace being equal or nearly equal to their ordinary revenue, when war comes, they are both unwilling and unable to increase their revenue in proportion to the increase of their expence."[6] In other words, to raise such funding purely through increased taxation would be politically and economically unsustainable. Earlier in the same chapter, he calculates that

> When war comes, there is no money in the treasury but what is necessary for carrying on the ordinary expence of the peace establishment. In war an establishment of three or four times that expence becomes necessary for the defense of the state, and consequently a revenue three or four times greater than the peace revenue.[7]

Bear in mind that Smith wrote these words during the mid–18th century, not in 1914, let alone 2014. The expense multiple of three or four that he applies to wartime revenue has since increased to perhaps immeasurable amounts. Modern technological warfare waged on distant foreign soil knows no expense limits. Smith's general comments regarding national financial stability in the aftermath of war, however, remain as applicable today as ever.

Next follows a tough critique of human nature from *WN* in which Smith notes that citizens of "great empires" (including the British Empire) living in areas directly unaffected by war, far removed from the suffering, often do not mind paying some extra taxes in return for the entertainment and fantisizing provided to them by media during wartime. Scathingly, he observes:

> To them this amusement compensates the small difference between the taxes which they pay on account of the war, and those which they had been accustomed to pay during time of peace. They are commonly dissatisfied with the return of peace, which puts an end to their amusement, and to a thousand visionary hopes of conquest and national glory, from a longer continuance of the war.[8]

Smith never served in the military, but it is likely he witnessed this kind of behavior in provincial Glasgow during the course of the Anglo-French conflict. In short, he cared not for civilian arm-chair generals. By the 1750s, many of his Scottish countrymen were in fact serving in the British armed forces abroad, but whether he knew any personally is uncertain. More certain is that these very same issues (and embarrassments) continue to plague modern western societies into the 21st century.

Great Britain had significant foreign debt even during Smith's day. In *WN* he refers to the Dutch and other countries as holding "a considerable share in our public funds," adding that purely domestic public debt would not represent an improvement in the overall situation.[9] Either way, he considered excessive public debt to be an ominous sign of things to come:

> When national debts have once been accumulated to a certain degree, there is scarce, I believe, a single instance of their having been fairly and completely paid. The liberation of the public revenue, if it has ever been brought about at all, has always been brought about by a bankruptcy; sometimes by an avowed one, but always by a real one, though frequently by a pretended payment.[10]

For England and France—the respective "winner" and "loser" in the French and Indian War conflict, which quickly rang up debt for both—Smith's analysis proved prophetic during the late 18th century. Great Britain managed to rebound during the 19th century in the form of the Second British Empire, thanks to talented leadership able to learn from past mistakes, as well as vast international resources retained after a costly victory in the Seven Years' War. Fast forwarding to the Great War of 1914–1918, however, Smith's same dire warning applied both to England and Germany. Both emerged from the conflict deeply in debt, well beyond their means to pay, though one had "won" and the other had "lost" in the conventional sense. Curiously enough, it would be Germany, not Great Britain, eventually emerging as a global economic powerhouse some 70 years after the Treaty of Versailles.

Before leaving the topic of Smith's observations on the relation between wartime expenses and national debt, it would be remiss not to briefly address the threshold question as to why the U.S. fatefully decided in World War I to take sides with England rather than Germany. The question is not asked frequently enough, and these pages will comment upon the decision, in a rhetorical manner if nothing else. Although longstanding ties of blood, language and culture certainly bound together the U.S. and Great Britain, these factors alone were far from ensuring any military alliance between them. Not counting nominal cooperation during the Chinese Boxer Rebellion at the turn of the last century, the two nations had never seriously fought together before, and had in fact fought against each other on several past occasions. During the American Civil War the British had veered dangerously close to supporting the Confederacy, and were probably discouraged from doing so only by the unexpected victories of U.S. Grant's western federal armies in 1862.[11] By 1914, a huge segment of the American population was non–Anglo—indeed, many were German-American—and many of these were fiercely anti–Anglo, in addition to being staunchly isolationist or outright pro–German. In terms of international commerce and naval power, the U.S. and Great Britain by then were serious rivals, plain and simple. Despite a prosperous economy at home, Wilson had to fight for his reelection in 1916, merely because it had been suggested that the U.S. might take sides with the Allies in Europe.

The consequential American decision to side with the Allies was not an easy one, and perhaps Smith's views on what he termed "Moral Sentiments" can offer some insight. For Smith, human "sympathy" or lack thereof was a complex psychological process that often took time to resolve itself and oftentimes with surprisingly unconventional results. As American public opinion slowly shifted in favor of intervention against Germany, a number of complex factors came into play, and it was a full three years into the war before the decision was finally ratified. France and the Low Countries, both which the U.S. had close ties with, had been victims of German aggression from the moment that war was officially declared. For most Americans, they were easy to sympathize with, far more so than the British. Then unrestricted submarine warfare by the Germans began killing Americans directly either by accident or with intent. Finally, German diplomacy and public relations proved disastrous, culminating in the infamous Zimmermann Telegram of 1917, which promised Mexico restoration of territories lost in the Mexican War in return for Mexican support against the United States. By this time, the only Americans still opposed to Allied military support were isolationist ideologues, and Wilson seized the opportunity by having Congress declare war. Adam Smith would have probably seen it as a textbook case of the Allies winning American sympathy through a combination of German transgression and Anglo-French virtue under duress.

Woodrow Wilson, who presided over this crucial and prosperous period, was a former academic, the only president to have held a doctorate degree, and in all likelihood the one best versed in the writings of Adam Smith.[12] It was his administration that created the Federal Reserve Bank, granted women the right to vote, introduced the peacetime income tax, and kept a tight regulatory reign on private enterprise both in preparation for, and during wartime.[13] It was also his administration that first elevated a young FDR to high responsibilities in government. While earning his Ph.D. at Johns Hopkins University, Wilson wrote a paper on Adam Smith and later developed it into an article for teaching purposes at Bryn Mawr College, titled "An Old Master."[14] In this essay, interesting enough, Wilson the aspiring academic focuses mainly on Smith's eloquence, as had British Prime Minister Gladstone before him. Wilson saw Smith as a great teacher, and a great generalist: "It is this power of teaching other men how to think that has given the works of Adam Smith an immortality of influence."[15] He continues: "In this day of narrow specialities, our thinking needs such men to fuse its parts, correlate its forces, and centre its results...."[16] Ultimately, for Wilson, Smith was compelling because his written communication skills: "In a word, such men must write *literature*, or nothing."[17] Given that Wilson the academic would embark on a successful political career some 25 years later, his particular admiration for

Smith's majesty style and broad sweep appear to foreshadow Wilson's own ambitions.

Wilson's teacher (and rough contemporary) at Johns Hopkins University was the distinguished American educator and economist, Richard T. Ely (1854–1943), for whom Wilson seems to have held a lukewarm regard at best.[18] Nevertheless, it was for Ely's class that Wilson originally wrote "An Old Master" and it was Ely who would continue to be a prominent, respected voice in favor of Progressive and New Deal policies during the first half of the 20th century.[19] Not long after Wilson had established his own academic career, Ely was invited by Charles Dudley Warner in 1896 to write his own introduction to the works of Adam Smith, as part of the hyperbolically titled *Library of the World's Best Literature*.[20] After Ely's introduction to Smith, large excerpts are presented from both *WN* and *TMS*. In contrast to his politically ambitious former student Woodrow Wilson, Ely focuses on Smith's substance and interpretation, rather than his style or eloquence. Regarding *WN*, Ely begins his overview by declaring that "Few books in the world's history have exerted a greater influence on the course of human affairs...."[21] By this point in time, few would argue with this assertion. Specifically, Ely hones in on Smith's close analysis of labor and wages, reminding readers that "He [Smith] wants to make labor central and pivotal."[22] Ely emphatically notes that Smith's oft-misquoted criticism of 18th century labor laws did not refer to trade unions—which did not then exist in the modern sense—but instead to trade apprenticeship and therefore, ultimately, the "interest of the employers" as opposed to the "interests of labor" (see Chapter 13).[23] Writing earlier during the mid–1890s, Ely appears to have been frustrated, as were many other leading thinkers of the day, by the frequent misrepresentation of Smith's views as allegedly being uncritically favorable towards big business monopolies and lack of government regulation.

While American intellectuals like Ely were concerned about the misinterpretation of Smith's ideas, in Great Britain successive Liberal Party prime ministers H.H. Asquith and David Lloyd George were unsuccessfully stumping in favor of one of Smith's most hard-to-misinterpret proposals, namely, a land value (only) tax, or LVT. As British tariff revenue had steadily declined in accordance with implemented free trade policies, resulting budget shortfalls had to be addressed, and the LVT was one proposal for doing this. The concept was directly traceable back to Smith's *WN*, and then later to the American economist Henry George, who had made it a centerpiece of his thinking.[24] By the Edwardian era, a few British politicians began to take a shine to the idea, sometimes producing unlikely coalitions between liberals and conservatives in Parliament. Nevertheless, the LVT never made it into law, and has only found limited worldwide acceptance since Smith first proposed it. One of the Conservative Party Parliamentarians crossing the aisle in favor of an LVT in 1909 had been a young Winston Churchill, soon going on to multiple government roles both prominent and controversial during the war years of 1914–1918, as well as seeing action on the ground as a soldier. By the time Churchill became British Secretary of State for War in 1919, he recognized that unprecedented military spending had wrecked England's finances. Accordingly, he supported immediate implementation of the so-called Ten Year Rule, a decade long (1919–1929) repudiation of all British military spending, now that Germany had been defeated, at least for the time being.[25]

Churchill, like Benjamin Disraeli before him, proved a very literary-minded conservative politician. A prolific writer in many genres, Churchill would be awarded the Nobel Prize for Literature in 1953. His love of reading, which included Smith's *WN*, was traceable back to his days in India during the 1890s, and his familiarity with Smith appeared to manifest itself from the moment he entered public life in the next century.[26] By 1909 Churchill, one of the best orators of the 20th century, was dropping Smith's name during public speeches. At Abernethy on October 7, 1909, while campaigning in favor of an LVT, Churchill declared that "For the principle of a special charge being levied on this class of wealth we can cite economic authority as high as Adam Smith…."[27] Admittedly, at this early point in his political career, Churchill had not yet become the Churchill known to history; in contrast to this image, on the eve of the Great War, he was little more than an aristocratic misfit trying to establish a niche in public life, not unlike his near-contemporary on the other side of the Atlantic, FDR. On the other hand, even at this early stage, Churchill was a very well read politician, and fairly eloquent one at that, both in writing and in person. As World War I rapidly escalated, Churchill was among those few quickly acknowledging the new realities, both in terms of human and financial cost, no doubt partly informed by his previous reading of Smith's similar observations made during an earlier, though not entirely dissimilar time in British history.

With new heights in military spending came novel methods of raising money to pay for it. It was during the era of the Great War that the indelible image of war bond poster art first became fixed in the public mind. Uncle Sam ("I Want You") was used to raise recruits, attractive young women to raise capital. Appearing in *Boston Forbes* as part of the 1917 Third Liberty Loan fundraiser, "Fight or Buy Bonds" and featured a color rendition by American artist Howard Chandler Christy (1873–1952). The erotic image of a young woman—one never to be confused with the Statute of Liberty—waves the Stars and Stripes while cheering doughboys charging into battle, like an American Joan of Arc, except with far less modesty. The implied French connection is subtle and effective. Christy's work is reminiscent of Delacroix's famous painting *Liberty Leading the People*, depicting the symbolic figure of a bare-breasted and musket-wielding Liberty-Marianne leading 1830 French revolutionaries into the breach over their fallen comrades.[28] Unlike Delacroix, Christy created his later work only two years before American wives, mothers, and daughters, all obtained the right to the ballot box. A sense of female empowerment pervades. Political symbolism had thus begun to slowly transform itself into a new American political reality.

The irony—if that is the right word—of the United States lending unparalleled amounts of money to Great Britain for military spending less than a century and a half after Britain had tried to tax the American colonies into submission, is noteworthy. And yet, taking a longer view of history (as Adam Smith surely would have), such revolutions in power are common, if not frequent occurrences. As Smith had written in *WN*, British mercantile special interests of his time were more fearful of market disruptions caused by American independence than by any threatened French or Spanish invasions of the past.[29] After this independence had been achieved, however, it turned out that these disruptions were not so bad (as Smith had tried to assure readers at the time). There was still plenty of money to be made by all interested parties. However, by 1919, national indebtedness—a threat also underscored by Smith in *WN*—had engulfed Great Britain seemingly overnight. As Smith had earlier pointed out many years before, such diminished national credit could turn into a real problem for the country, one far worse than any lost trading monopolies or tax revenues. Now, in the wake of Versailles, perhaps Smith's worse nightmare for England had come to pass, one hardly offset by temporary victory in the field against the Germans.

The Americans, on the other hand, woke up one day to find themselves the largest creditor nation on earth, while in the midst of seemingly unstoppable economic growth. The actual process of this dramatic role reversal had taken decades, if not centuries, to play out. The most obvious, immediate product of the new American ascendancy was a breed never before beheld by the world (and not to be soon forgotten), the affluent American consumer.

12. Ascendant Consumerism (1922–1928)

"All other things I call luxuries; without meaning by this appellation, to throw the smallest degree of reproach upon the temperate use of them. Beer and ale, for example, in Great Britain, and wine, even in the wine countries, I call luxuries. A man of any rank may, without any reproach, abstain totally from tasting such liquors. Nature does not render them necessary for the support of life; and custom nowhere renders it indecent to live without them."—Adam Smith[1]

The swearing in of Warren G. Harding (1865–1923) as 29th President of the United States in 1921 marked, for all practical purposes, the end of the Progressive Era in America that had begun so dynamically under Theodore Roosevelt two decades before. With the Treaty of Versailles finalized, along with other immediate aftershocks of the Great War, the U.S. found itself, for the first time in history, on top of the world both militarily and economically. The entire process, from successful revolution against Great Britain to decisive intervention in favor of Great Britain, had taken exactly 144 years, or less than two full human lifetimes. Its final phase had been marked by a strange combination of unprecedented military build-up, self-righteous legislative reform at home, and unapologetic domination of vulnerable foreign markets. Regarding this last item, traditional American isolationism first came into sharp political conflict with the international demands of American business interests. The same internal, domestic conflict has continued non-stop into the present day. Great Britain had been in a similar though less imposing position after the Seven Years' War, prompting Adam Smith to write *The Wealth of Nations* (*WN*), warning against the economic pitfalls of this perceived advantage. Unfortunately for the world of the 20th century, the Great War of 1914–1918 proved only to be round one in a continuing transcontinental struggle playing out on an even more devastating scale within a few short decades. After that, Americans would find themselves in a position of even greater strength than the one they enjoyed by the early 1920s, one fraught with the very same risks, except on a much grander scale.

The Harding Administration lasted for only two years (1921–1923) before the president's unexpected death, probably brought on by natural causes hastened by anxieties over a growing realization that he was overmatched for the task at hand. Within that short time, Harding's presidency had established itself as one of the most inept in American history. Both a drinker and staunch supporter of Prohibition, Harding possessed matinee idol good-looks, plenty of personal charm, and solid support from a Republican Party previously out of power for a decade. Nevertheless, he was utterly unprepared for the tidal wave of venality greeting him upon his inauguration.[2] Harding genuinely believed the best way to avoid a post-war recession was to remove government from the economic equation, which he spent most of his first year in office putting into practice. Short term results were tangible gains, long term, foreboding weakness. A harsh series of unilateral wage cuts resulted in the Great Railroad Strike of 1922, brutally put down by strikebreakers in tandem with National Guardsmen. This time around there was no strong, even-handed personality like Roosevelt to mediate the dispute.

Then Harding, who had never personally served in the military, vetoed a federal bonus to war veterans because he thought it might imbalance the budget. As if this were not enough, Congress hastily passed the Fordney-McCumber Tariff, raising foreign duties to all-time highs, a move that surely would have been deplored by the author of *WN*. The result was a temporary bubble of prosperity based on protectionism. Meanwhile, in the western states, oil leases on federal lands—the same federal lands so cherished and cordoned off by Roosevelt—were being bought and sold to the highest bidder like commodities. By 1923 the media had caught wind of the dealings, and the Teapot Dome scandal became forever synonymous with corrupted government. Eventually, Harding's Secretary of the Interior, Albert Fall, among other high-ranking, well-compensated collaborators, would go to jail. Indeed, it is difficult to think of another period in national history in which so many harmful things were done so quickly by a single administration, although the full effects of these policies would not be felt for several years.[3]

Upon Harding's death, V.P. Calvin Coolidge (1872–1933) was sworn into office as the 30th President of the United States, later winning his own re-election campaign in 1924. Coolidge, unlike Harding, was a man of some ability, as well as one of the most dedicated opponents of organized labor ever to occupy the White House. Coolidge unapologetically saw himself as an executive instrument of big business, all for the good of the country. The moderating, big bucks philanthropy of the Gilded Age and the proactive government reforms of Roosevelt were nowhere to be found. For that matter, the more balanced approach to international trade and interstate commerce championed a half century previous by the Republican Party (via the economic philosophy of Henry Charles Carey), had by the 1920s given way to a near total *laissez-faire* stance that would have been severely criticized by Adam Smith during his own day.

As the Prohibition American economy rolled along seemingly invincible, there was no immediate reason for the majority of American voters to feel dissatisfied or apprehensive. The election of Republican Commerce Secretary Herbert Hoover (1874–1964) as the 31st U.S. President in 1928 came as a surprise to no one, although in hindsight Hoover was clearly the most moderate and able of his Party's top leaders. Unfortunately for his later reputation, he came into executive office on the eve of the greatest economic catastrophe yet to be experienced by the U.S., and Hoover was no more equipped to deal with the sudden crisis than Harding had been to cope with booming postwar prosperity. In late 1928, however, few Americans could imagine such things.

From 1923 to 1928, there was little for most Americans to complain about, economically speaking, at least in terms of everyday life. Vast fortunes were quickly made and sometimes just as quickly dissipated. Most striking was the manner in which technology had changed mass entertainment. Electronically recorded sound and motion pictures revolutionized the way average people spent their leisure time, and, more importantly, their disposable income.[4] Adam Smith, a devotee of the theatre and performing arts, would have been astonished. Professional spectator sports, led by baseball and thanks to Babe Ruth, fully recovered from the Black Sox scandal of 1919. Prohibition, instead of sobering up the nation, spawned a violent gangster image (and reality) that has perhaps surpassed the American western cowboy in the imagination of worldwide popular culture. Bootlegging and ancillary weapons trafficking became major domestic industries, and the toll on American society was immeasurably high both in terms of innocent and not so innocent lives lost, plus irreparably damaged international opinion. Whatever had been gained during World War I for the United States as a perceived force of benevolence and peace was quickly forfeited. In short, the rest of the world thought that we had lost our minds. There were no noticeable gains in public sobriety; the bootleggers and speakeasies saw to that. In this, Adam Smith would have been far less surprised. The Roaring Twenties were thus off and running for a short but brilliant period in American history.

Recently humbled Great Britain, like most of Europe, stood back and watched events in America with either fear or amazement. In England there was no Prohibition, no Roaring Twenties, no Jazz Age. Though a military "winner" during the late war, it had, like Germany, become a heavy debtor nation. In 1922, Ireland was finally granted free-state status, from which Northern Ireland promptly bolted. With the ascendency in late 1924 of Prime Minister Stanley Baldwin's Conservative government, the ever-restless Winston Churchill found himself appointed as an unlikely Chancellor of the Exchequer for the next five years. Notwithstanding his veneration for Adam Smith, public finance never appears to have been one of Churchill's strengths as a world leader. Churchill's strict initial adherence to a gold monetary standard, a position never advocated by Smith, contributed to a further economic downturn and General Strike in 1926. In mockery, free-lancing John Maynard Keynes that same year produced a short tract, *The Economic Consequences of Mr. Churchill*, lambasting the notion of a tight money policy during times of widespread economic hardship. Churchill, to his credit, was never one to deny that he had made a serious mistake, reminiscent of Thomas Jefferson later regretting his imposed Embargo Act of 1807. The war-crippled British economy would continue to hobble along during the 1920s, so long as that of its creditor and recent ally, the United States, continued to prosper.

Germany under the Weimar Republic was even worse off. Depleted manpower, postwar revolution, hyperinflation, and punishing reparations debt all conspired to keep the German economy a shadow of its former robust self. The election of war hero Paul von Hindenburg as German President in 1925, along with a big influx of American venture capital, brought some semblance of stability and order, but within four years this appearance of normalcy proved illusory. France was hardly better off than its old enemy to the east, and post-revolutionary Russia was certainly in the worst shape of all. British decline also translated into Middle East destabilization and Asian unrest, especially in India. Thus while America partied and brazenly broke its own misguided laws, Europe festered. The unsatisfactory and short-sighted peace of Versailles was, by the late 1920s, manifesting itself in multiple harmful ways that few pundits, with some notable exceptions like Keynes, ever foresaw or acknowledged.

The military and economic distractions being experienced by western nations during this time period allowed some of the stronger Asian societies, particularly Japan, to gain more independence from the West and emerge in its own right as a world power. Japanese Emperor Hirohito ascended to the throne in 1926, and began presiding over a sustained period of military buildup and Pan-Asian expansionism. In the Pacific, only the powerful U.S. Navy stood in Japan's way. Viewing the globe as a whole in the late 1920s, America had thus far been uniquely spared the ravages of foreign invasion and neighboring conflict. American disturbances were mostly limited to the home front: domestic labor unrest, racial tensions, and organized crime, the latter usually inflicting more violence upon itself than from any designated, outside law enforcement officials. In hindsight, the Great World War had never really ended; rather, it had merely gone into a kind of sinister dormancy.

Perhaps the best way to examine Smith's thoughts in relation to distant events in the United States circa mid–1920s is to peruse his writings in *WN* regarding the sale and consumption of alcoholic beverages. These are surprisingly extensive, though infrequently commented upon. As for Smith's own personal habits, though impossible to document with certainty, the circumstantial evidence suggests that he was a light drinker or at least responsible one. Dr. Johnson's notorious descriptor of Smith as "dull" may well be interpreted as a euphemism for "sober," especially given Johnson's own reputation, as well as that of his biographer James Boswell, as being occasionally excessive with drink.[5] The lengthy pages of *WN* devoted to the topic often are in praise of sobriety, or at least strongly imply praise. Smith grew up in a single parent household (that of his mother) where there was no indication of reckless drinking, and his early education informed by the stern moralism of former Presbyterian Francis Hutcheson. His French continental travels of the early 1760s had exposed him to some of the finest wines in the world, and he reputedly developed a lifelong taste for expensive claret.[6] He approvingly remarks in *WN* that France, Italy, and Spain, as wine countries, also appeared to have the lowest rates of alcoholism.[7] With unintentional humor, Smith praises the famous vintages of France while dismissing the popular but less refined and less expensive port wines of the Iberian Peninsula, as being economically illogical in terms of English consumers placing political prejudices over pure trade value.[8] In *WN* Smith also carefully distinguishes between strong "spirituous liquors" versus the "invigorating liquors" of beer and ale having lower alcoholic content.[9] As for the Scotch Whisky of world renown, Smith only makes occasional reference to its malt ingredients, not to the finished product. Historically, Scotch did not achieve widespread international popularity until the 19th century, but it was often over-consumed in Scotland during Smith's time. Taken as a whole, Smith's remarks and biographical data suggest personal temperance more than overindulgence.[10]

This is not to say that Smith condemned drinking; far from it, in fact. In Book IV, Chapter III of *WN*, within the context of import restraints, he defends manufacturers and retailers of alcoholic beverages as legitimate businessmen and not proprietors of a "losing trade" as apparently had been alleged by some his contemporaries.[11] As for consumers, they still had the right to be spendthrifts and drunkards, as far as Smith was concerned, so long as the public was not harmed: "He [the consumer of alcohol] may no doubt buy too much, … as he may of any other dealers in his neighborhood, of the butcher, if he is a glutton, or of the draper, if he affects to be a beau among his companions."[12] Any alleged threat posed by spirits to public finance he appears to have viewed as non-existent: "Though individuals, besides, may sometimes ruin their fortunes by an excessive consumption of fermented liquors, there seems to be no risk that a nation should do so."[13] In short, Smith would have opposed the idea of Prohibition on any economic grounds.[14]

Switching gears, he then launches into a remarkable disquisition on what he believed to be the true economic causes of alcoholism: "It deserves to be remarked too, that, if we consult experience, the cheapness of wine seems to be a cause, not of drunkenness, but of sobriety."[15] In contrast to the temperate Mediterranean countries in which wine is plentiful and the spirit of choice, "drunkenness is a common vice" among unnamed "northern countries" (presumably including Great Britain), as well as "all those who live between the tropics." Underscoring his controversial point, Smith repeats the story of a Northern French regiment traveling south, debauching itself on cheap wine, and then becoming permanently moderate like the locals. He concludes that the best way to help improve sobriety in Great Britain would be to make wine more affordable by the removal of foreign duties.[16]

Way ahead of his time, Smith makes a connection between alcoholic substance abuse and class distinction: "At present drunkenness is by no means the vice of people of fashion, or of those who can easily afford the most expensive liquors. A gentlemen drunk with ale, has scarce ever been seen among us."[17] With respect to passing moral judgment, Smith reserves his condemnation solely for the special business interests unnecessarily driving up the price and scarcity of spirits: "But the mean rapacity, the monopolizing spirit of merchants and manufacturers, who neither are, nor ought to be, the rulers of mankind, though it cannot perhaps be corrected, may very easily be prevented from disturbing the tranquility of any body but themselves."[18] The passage itself is famous among Smithian scholars, but rarely noted that Smith made this remark within the specific context of restrictions on alcoholic beverages.

Later in Book V of *WN*, Smith gets into the nuts and bolts of regulations on alcohol. While being explicitly in favor of taxation on the consumption of all luxury items such as spirits, he vigorously attacks all restraints on importation.

First acknowledging that wine, brandy and rum are then among Great Britain's leading imports, Smith then argues forcefully that the status quo of high tariffs only serves to minimize government revenues and encourage smuggling, not to mention corrupting the temperance of anyone attracted to contraband.[19] Quoting a mock proverb from his favorite satirist Jonathan Swift, Smith asserts that "in the arithmetic of customs two and two, instead of making four, make sometimes only one ..." meaning that restrictions on imports in the final tally only serve to reduce open trade and stifle legitimate demand.[20] Worst of all to Smith, however, was that such restrictions encouraged smuggling, or in the 20th century parlance, bootlegging.[21] Employing his own distinctive brand of satire, he ironically notes that "It has for some time past been the policy of Great Britain to discourage the consumption of spirituous liquors, on account of their supposed tendency to ruin the health and to corrupt the morals of the common people."[22] The only morals affected, according to Smith, are those of the dealers, who often transform from honest businessmen into violent criminals:

> By this indulgence of the public, the smuggler is often encouraged to continue a trade which he is thus taught to consider as in some measure innocent; and when the severity of the revenue laws is ready to fall upon him, he is frequently disposed to defend with violence, what he has been accustomed to regard as his just property. From being at first, perhaps, rather imprudent than criminal, he at last too often becomes one of the hardiest and most determined violators of the laws of society.[23]

The close similarity between Smith's late 18th century British wine smugglers and early 20th century American Prohibition gangsters is not hard to draw. He then goes on to lament the tremendous inefficiency and counterproductivity of such misdirected energy, not unlike his practical arguments in *WN* against the utilization of slave (versus free) labor. For him, slavery and protectionism both represented wasted opportunities, unnecessary costs, and regressive economic policies.

The only personal, first-hand experience this author has had with the regulation and sale of alcoholic beverages came during the mid–1970s while coming of age in the Michiana region near the Indiana-Michigan state line. There, for a brief period of a few years, the legal drinking age in Michigan was 18 years old, while Indiana maintained the traditional minimum of 21. The result was weekend caravans of Indiana teenagers crossing the Michigan line to legally indulge themselves. Southern Michigan taverns on main highways prospered. Gradually, however, Michigan voters and politicians realized that these short-term gains were more than offset by numerous collateral losses, and the legal minimum age was soon changed back to 21.²⁴ Two plus two, as Jonathan Swift and Adam Smith noted long ago, sometimes equaled one. My own observation at the time, living on a state line farm along one of these major corridors, was that teenaged Hoosiers seemed to relish the purchase of alcohol more if it could not be obtained legally on their own side of the state line. Reading Smith's anecdote in *WN* about the Northern French regiment travelling south reminded me in some respects on this strange episode in my own life.²⁵

The 1920s saw the rise of prominent Anglo-American leaders who used, or had previously used, Smith's name and authority in ways best described as improbable. In turbulent Great Britain, the first Labour Party-led government in history came and went in 1924 under Scottish-born Prime Minister James Ramsay MacDonald (1866–1937), before the Labour majority was swept away almost as suddenly as it had begun by a Conservative tide later that same year. The fervent MacDonald had begun his political career back in 1906 by getting himself elected to Parliament, in tandem with having a book published with the provocative title, *Socialism and Society*. This was several years even before another new M.P. on the other side of the aisle, Winston Churchill, began dropping Smith's name during public speeches. At the conclusion of a long and detailed treatise written for public edification, MacDonald declares that "The science of economics and the art of government go hand in hand. In that respect, the Socialist goes back to Adam Smith."²⁶ This was one the first and most prominent instances in which Smith's theories were linked with the British Socialist movement. By that point in history almost every branch of political economic thought, with the notable exception of the Marxists, were attempting to claim Smith as one of their own. Eighteen years and one world war later (in 1924), the same writer of these words would be attempting (unsuccessfully) to politically lead Great Britain out of the deep financial hole that it had by then placed itself into. It must also be considered doubtful whether many of the English voters propelling MacDonald briefly into power that year had ever heard of Adam Smith, let alone read *WN*.

While the same accusation of ignorance could be made against many American voters of the same era, it appears at least that some of the leaders they voted for were in fact better read than their constituents. In 1922, recently appointed Secretary of Commerce Herbert Hoover published his *American Individualism*, which included a somewhat self-congratulatory note on the accomplishments of the Progressive Era regarding recent regulations against the restraint of trade: "This regulation is itself proof that we have gone a long way toward the abandonment of the 'capitalism' of Adam Smith."²⁷

Of course, the mercantilism of Adam Smith's day was not capitalism in any modern sense, but that is perhaps why Hoover put the word in quotes. More troubling is the fact that Hoover, despite all of his public praise for free trade, as Commerce Secretary and, later, as President, appears to have been consistently in favor of the record-high tariff legislation dating from those years. More consistent with behavior was a written comment on Smith from Andrew Mellon, Secretary of Treasury under all three Republican Presidents of the 1920s.[28] In his authoritatively titled *Taxation: The People's Business* (1924), Mellon cites the same passage from *WN* in favor of a progressive income tax quoted by William Jennings Bryan to Congress some 30 years earlier in 1894, no doubt still piqued by Bryan's presumption. Mellon then proceeds to quote a subsequent passage from *WN* in which Smith warned against the potentially counterproductive effects caused by over-taxation, while Mellon himself argues that taxes on Americans should be lowered rather than raised.[29] As a policy advisor, for better and for worse, Mellon was always good on his word, making him a favorite target of criticism for future New Dealers. Just as Bryan had forgotten to mention that *WN* was written on the eve of the American Revolution, Mellon neglected to add that, at the end of day, Smith firmly believed the American colonists should in fact be taxed and pay their fair share of Great Britain's accumulated war expenses against France.

Commercial art of the 1920s reached new heights of sophistication, often incorporating sleek new elements of the Art Deco movement for marketing purposes. Nowhere is this trend better exemplified than in the striking magazine cover illustrations of Anne Harriet Fish (1890–1964), a talented British artist on the payroll of media tycoon Condé Nast, owner of *Vanity Fair*, *Vogue*, and *The New Yorker*. No kind of justice can be done to Fish's prolific work in this short space, but within the context of Prohibition, much of her cover art still has the power to raise eyebrows, if not consciousness. In May of 1925, at the height of alcohol's proscription in America, *Vanity Fair* featured a Fish-designed cover art with a stylized depiction of a speakeasy. Included are an African-American or blackface jazz band, dancing couples, carousing couples sitting at tables, and, very discreetly, at the far bottom right, a seated couple toasting with cocktail glasses. Nineteen twenty-five was the same year that F. Scott Fitzgerald's *The Great Gatsby* hit the bookstalls, condemning or glorifying a society quite different from the one that supporters of Prohibition were trying to promote. By the end of the decade, Fish's cocktail images, as well as commercial art in general, had become more explicit and defiant in this regard. Some people no doubt complained, but based on Fish's clever illustrations, it was clearly the lawbreakers that were having all of the fun. Nor was the value of this controversy lost on Fish's employer Nast, a trendsetting innovator of marketing if there ever was one.[30]

Looking beyond the toxic spillover of organized crime which flowed from the good intentions of the 18th Amendment, some economic positives came out of the Roaring Twenties, many of which are still with us. The ascendant consumerism of an affluent middle class was hardly something Adam Smith would have condemned; in fact, he would have applauded it. *Wealth of Nations* represented, in many respects, a celebration of widespread prosperity, as well as a warning as to how it might be compromised through the greed and machinations of special interests, or as Smith phrased it, their "mean rapacity" and "monopolizing spirit." Unfortunately for the United States, by the late 1920s, things had been pushed well beyond some kind of horrendous breaking point. Just as the U.S. had so recently ascended to the top of the world economic ladder, it would also, seemingly overnight, tumble down to a dysfunctional level, threatening the very democratic foundations of the Republic. Luckily for the country, however, this severe crisis also seemed to produce a bumper crop of great American men and women fully up to challenge of combating it.

13. The Implosion of Laissez-Faire (1929–1939)

> *"When the institutions or public works which are beneficial to the whole society, either cannot be maintained altogether, or are not maintained altogether by the contribution of such particular members of the society as are most immediately benefited by them, the deficiency must in most cases be made up by the general contribution of the whole society. The general revenue of the society, over and above defraying the expence of defending the society, and of supporting the dignity of the chief magistrate, must make up for the deficiency of many particular branches of revenue."*—Adam Smith[1]

In his recent and fair-minded reading of Smith's *Wealth of Nations* (*WN*), humorist P.J. O'Rourke amusingly equates the French, *laissez-faire* Physiocrats known to Smith during his continental travels with modern-day members of the American Republican Party or provincial Tories of the British Empire, with emphasis on the word "provincial."[2] O'Rourke's improbable association of the two groups is apt, as well as funny. The prosperous, consumer-oriented U.S. economy of the 1920s, to whatever extent real or illusory, was mainly driven by almost eight years of Republican sponsored national policies representing a major departure from those of previous Progressive Era administrations, not the least of which was that of Republican icon Theodore Roosevelt. The main architects of American 1920s economic strategy—Presidents Harding, Coolidge, Hoover, and crucially, their Secretary of the Treasury, Andrew Mellon, all shared a firm belief that the proper role of federal government for economic development was simply to get out of the way, or as the French Physiocrats would have phrased it, *laissez-faire* ("leave it alone"). At some imperceptible point during the 19th century, this anti-government stance became somehow synonymous with Smith's own highly nuanced free trade philosophy, much to the puzzlement or chagrin of anyone taking trouble to actually read *WN* for themselves.

13. The Implosion of Laissez-Faire (1929–1939)

On October 29, 1929 ("Black Tuesday"), the Wall Street stock market crashed spectacularly, reducing the Dow Jones Industrial Average by approximately 40 percent in the course of less than one week. Nothing like it had been experienced in recent or distant memory. Thus began a worldwide Great Depression lasting a full decade. The recently inaugurated Hoover administration reacted to the crisis at first with paralysis, then mostly with platitudes and sermons either blaming the victims or urging their patience. The next three years were arguably the most grueling in American history for the average citizen: uninsured bank failures, business insolvency, unemployment, foreclosures, and poverty rates all spiked to unprecedented levels. Absurdly, Congress responded with increased trade protectionism in the form of the Smoot-Hawley Tariff of 1930, resulting only in other countries retaliating against the U.S. with their own tariff legislation, thus making things even worse overall.

In 1932, a few months before the next presidential election, tens of thousands of impoverished World War I veterans, many accompanied by their wives and children, marched on Washington, D.C., to demand early redemption of cash government bonuses. They were driven away by U.S. Army cavalry and tanks under the command of General Douglas MacArthur. Whispers of insurrection could be heard in every corner of the country by anyone not barricading themselves away into seclusion. The sustained fallout caused by the Great Depression was probably nothing like anything witnessed or imagined by Smith during the 18th century; then again, he never witnessed or imagined government nearly abdicating its regulatory role as the U.S. had during the 1920s.

Consequently, the memorable Presidential election of 1932 brought to the White House one of the most enigmatic, inspiring and personally flawed individuals ever to occupy its hallowed premises.[3] Like his fifth cousin Theodore before him (see Chapter 10), Franklin D. Roosevelt was a brilliant public speaker, a fearless advocate of change, and a political genius with little or no fear for the moneyed class from which his family derived. Upon taking the oath of office, FDR wasted no time. Just as the Harding administration had committed an extraordinary number of blunders in less than two years, Roosevelt's "New Deal" probably implemented more impact legislation of lasting consequence within a short time frame than any administration before or since. The first hundred days were a whirlwind of activity, much of which had been carefully premeditated by its "Brain Trust" designers. Commercial banks still standing after the crash were given first a holiday, then reopened under the umbrella of the newly-created Federal Deposit Insurance Corporation

(FDIC), all the while being scrutinized and regulated by a re-energized Federal Reserve System.[4] The next four years (1933–1937) introduced a barrage of legislative alphabet soup, much of which still function (in various evolutions) as safety net programs today taken mostly for granted.

The illustrious centerpiece of the New Deal effort was the Social Security Act (SSA), but lesser known creations such as the U.S. Housing Authority (1937) continue today, in bigger and more diverse forms, to underpin the foundations of the American economy. Other key components included the Resettlement Act (RA) of 1935 and its follow-up, the Farm Security Act (FSA) of 1937, both of which blunted the devastating effects of the Dust Bowl environmental catastrophe of 1934–1936, an event likely caused by lack of regulation in the first place, and one that would have surely incapacitated rural America for years to come had these programs not come into play. Startlingly, rights of organized labor were legally recognized for the first time, and labor immediately ceased to be a disrupting problem for recovery.

Even more controversially, the Works Progress Administration (WPA) of 1935 built massive public works projects throughout the country, most of which are still in use. The WPA also funded countless worthy artistic and cultural activities that otherwise had nowhere to turn for support.[5] In general, New Deal initiatives were characterized by deficit government spending (much to the horror of political conservatives), or in the popular parlance, "priming the pump," i.e., pouring whatever water is left down into a dry well in order to get the well producing water again.[6] The end result was rapid stabilization of a national economy that had long been destabilized into a free fall, followed by measurable, significant improvements in almost all then-known economic indicators, not the least of which was a dramatically reduced rate of unemployment.

Adam Smith would have well recognized forceful government intervention into economic matters, although during his time it would have likely been viewed more as a cause of problems rather than a source of relief. The aspect of the New Deal that probably would have surprised him the most, however, simply because it had never before existed during the course of history, was the proactive, powerful role of women in these affairs on everyday visible display to even the casual observer. Whereas American women had been belatedly granted voting rights during the late Wilson administration in 1919, and had been a continuing force at the polls throughout the Prohibition Era, by 1932 they had, for the first time ever, assumed highly visible positions in the corridors of political power. These prominent roles were as varied and multifaceted as the female personalities themselves involved. Sara Delano

13. The Implosion of Laissez-Faire (1929–1939) 143

Roosevelt, FDR's imposing widowed mother, controlled both his affections and his purse-strings right up until the time of her death in 1941 (three months before Pearl Harbor).

Eleanor Roosevelt, the black sheep favorite niece of Theodore, became the most opinionated, vocal, and mobile First Lady ever known to the American electorate. Like her famous uncle before her, ER was known to sometimes win over the harshest of critics with her limitless courage, energy, and high-mindedness. Her husband FDR carefully listened to her oftentimes relentless advice even long after he had ceased being a conjugal spouse. ER became the extended eyes and ears of FDR, as everyone close to them appreciated all too well. On a day-to-day level, FDR's long-time personal secretary, Missy LeHand, acted as gatekeeper, facilitator, and some would say, common law wife, a close second to ER in the amount of influence exerted over the President's mind and opinions. His distant cousin Daisy Suckley became a designated confidante and valued sounding board, as did fellow aristocrat and old forbidden love interest, Lucy Mercer, the latter being singled out by ER for her sternest disapproval. More overtly and officially, the highly-educated and experienced Frances Perkins became the first female cabinet member in American history as Secretary of Labor, sometimes making organized labor itself feel uncomfortable with the very fact that she was a woman.[7] The supreme irony of this new female political empowerment was that it was enabled by a U.S. President well-known to his inner circle as a multiple personality, completely faithful to no single woman, or person, for that matter.

FDR's re-election in 1936 was a foregone conclusion in which he won more contested electoral and popular votes than any candidate before him. Then he stumbled, but did not fall. At the urging of deficit hawks in Congress and within his own cabinet, especially Secretary of the Treasury Henry Morgenthau, Jr., Roosevelt attempted to balance the federal budget with spending cuts. Spending declined, but then, devastatingly, so did revenue.

Adam Smith would not have been surprised. The impact sent a shock wave through the country, resulting in the "Roosevelt Recession" of 1937–1938, as Republicans dubbed it, even though many had themselves urged spending cuts over the last four years. FDR, however, was never one slow to realize or justify a mistake, and by 1939, deficit spending had not only been reinstated, but ramped up in preparation for the next world war then unfolding in Europe. The economic results were spectacular. By the end of 1939, U.S. unemployment had been virtually eliminated and the economy poised to be even stronger and more robust than it had been during the Roaring Twenties. On September 1, 1939, Germany invaded Poland, and though it would be another two years before the U.S. was forced into the conflict, it was as economically prepared for the prolonged struggle as it could possibly be, thanks to the foresight and finesse of its executive office.

Great Britain, however, continued to struggle. By 1931, partly out of desperation and in recognition of its previous folly, Parliament eased credit by going off the monetary gold standard. The U.S. under FDR wisely followed suit in 1933. As for Winston Churchill, with the fall of the Conservative Party government in 1929, he found himself gradually marginalized by his peers before withdrawing from public affairs in 1931. Thus began Churchill's prolonged "wilderness years" in which he passed his idle time with hobbies such as bricklaying, painting, and writing. Conventional wisdom held that, like FDR during the mid–1920s, he was politically finished. Nevertheless, he was occasionally allowed or invited to speak or write, both activities at which he excelled. Many of these fully displayed his thorough expertise in the growing crisis on the European continent, a grave situation mostly ignored or downplayed by domestically embattled British governments led by Prime Ministers Ramsay MacDonald, Stanley Baldwin, and Neville Chamberlain. Germany, meanwhile, fed up with being impoverished by outside forces beyond its control, politically reinvented itself under the maniacal dictatorship of Adolf Hitler, and began to prosper again largely through military rearmament in brazen defiance of the Versailles Treaty. When total war erupted in 1939, Churchill was recalled to public service, initially, as First Lord of the Admiralty, and then in early 1940, as Prime Minister. He was 65 years old.

Although there is considerable evidence to suggest that Smith's free trade philosophy and anti-mercantilist stance had manifested long before he travelled to France in 1764, it was certainly there that his unfashionable opinions first found respected intellectual confirmation and reinforcement. Smith's two year continental tour must be viewed in hindsight as the pivotal or decisive period in his thought development leading up to the publication of *WN* ten years following his return to Great Britain. During that stint, Smith rubbed elbows with the leading French intelligentsia of that era, culminating in 1766 at Paris and Versailles where he encountered François Quesnay, consulting physician to King Louis XV, as well as the versatile, eccentric leader of the French Physiocrats. Quesnay is closely associated with the policy of *laissez-faire, laissez passer* ("leave it alone, let it pass") within a strict economic context, although the precise origins of the slogan are murky.[8] Smith, despite his knowledge of the French language, never used the same phrase in his writings, possibly underscoring his reservations. Like Smith, Quesnay believed that true economic production derived from agriculture; moreover, both had witnessed firsthand the manner in which over-taxation and restrictive regulation could easily become oppressive, counterproductive forces in society. Quesnay's own theories appear to have been strongly influenced by his expertise in Oriental culture, particularly with respect to Taoist teachings which held that that an ideal sovereign should be hands-off to the greatest extent practicable in policy decision-making.

The distant but tangible connection between Quesnay's Taoist-influenced economic views and the minimalist approach of the Hoover administration in response to the Great Depression is hard to resist. It should be emphasized as well that Smith found himself disagreeing with Quesnay and the French Physiocrats on a number of points, which likely clarified his own thinking in terms of precisely where to draw the line between strict *laissez-faire* economic philosophy and his own theories. For example, Quesnay had a strictly low opinion of banks and bankers, whereas Smith saw modern banking, especially on a nationalized level, as a potentially "great engine of state," capable of bolstering and propelling an economy into prosperous growth, as well as severely damaging it, depending on how it was used.[9]

In Book II, Chapter II, of *WN*, Smith expounds on the virtues and vices of commercial banking institutions, which he views not only as desirable but necessary for modern economic development. He also notes that the English and Scottish banks of his day were regulated by Parliament, without criticizing that government regulation as one might normally expect from him, and further notes that the nation continued to prosper in spite of that regulation, if not because of it.[10] Bank failures, Smith points out, are typically caused by "over-trading" or the "excessive circulation of paper money"—or, in the everyday vernacular, excessive selling of things for more than their true value, along with its close corollary, failing to resell something for which there is insufficient demand.[11] As an example, he makes vivid, specific reference to the "Mississippi scheme" of 1720, in which French investment bankers, facilitated by Scottish economist and entrepreneur John Law (1671–1729), badly overextended themselves in the Louisiana Territory, prompting what Smith described as "the most extravagant project both of banking and stock-jobbing that, perhaps, the world ever saw."[12]

The memory of Law's spectacular banking fiasco was still fresh in the memory of French Physiocrats such as Quesnay, who notoriously dismissed all bankers as a sterile and unproductive class of labor. As for Smith's stated typical cause of bank failures, over-trading, he had earlier in *WN* established that true value of anything "...is adjusted, however, not by any accurate measure, but by the haggling and bargaining of the market, according to that sort of rough equality which, though not exact, is sufficient for carrying on the business of common life."[13] Professional appraisers will immediately recognize in this sentence an early incarnation of the standard definition for market value.[14]

Having laid his theoretical groundwork early in *WN*, Smith proceeds in the final chapters of the work to specify the broad, extensive instances in which a central or local government should properly intervene into private commercial affairs, and moreover be supported by tax dollars while doing so. To Smith, it seems that anything bolstering the general economy but not profitable in and of itself is fair game for government intervention or, as he phrases it, "the Expences of the Sovereign or Commonwealth." These justifiable objects of government intervention and maintenance prominently include "Public Works and Public Institutions," especially those necessary "for facilitating the Commerce of the Society" and "Commerce in general." Smith proceeds to list various essential branches of domestic and international commerce which presumably could not support themselves if privatized based strictly on the forces of supply and demand: the need for transportation infrastructure ("evident without any proof"), coinage, postal, military installations, foreign embassies, and customs duties, the last item soon to supplement Smith's personal income as an appointed inspector.[15]

Given Smith's sweeping framework of definitions, it is difficult not to infer that today's Internet and all other forms of high-speed communication would not be included under his government umbrella of finance and regulation as well. As for alleged exceptions to the general rule, he then famously singles out named joint-stock or regulated companies granted exclusive privileges for foreign trade, which, he acerbically maintains, "...have in the long-run proved, universally, either burdensome or useless, and have either mismanaged or confined the trade."[16] Smith's ultimate response to this problem, however, is not to socialize these companies, but rather to withdraw their monopolistic privileges then being enjoyed under government sanction. In this sense, Smith was a great intellectual forerunner of Theodore Roosevelt's energetic trustbusting activities during the early 1900s.

Before leaving Smith's writings as these might pertain to the Great Depression of the 1930s, it would be remiss not to briefly peruse his great meditation on basic human nature and political leadership from Book VI, Chapter III, of his *Theory of Moral Sentiments* (*TMS*) circa 1759. Many of these comments call to mind the character of FDR himself, though FDR's ancestors were mere New York City businessmen when Smith's words were written. Regarding self-esteem, Smith emphasizes this as an essential prerequisite for successful execution of high office:

Men of no more than ordinary discernment never rate any person higher than he appears to rate himself. He seems doubtful himself, they say, whether he is perfectly fit for such a situation or such an office; and immediately give the preference to some impudent blockhead who entertains no doubt about his own qualifications.[17]

FDR was of course legendary for his limitless self-esteem, or at least his limitless ability to project it, whether this be in the form of contemptuous disregard for his wealthy and powerful political opponents or a confident ability to work either with or against totalitarian dictatorships abroad.[18] Smith's remarks in *TMS* also evoke FDR's less than auspicious early career, in which he oft-times came across as a more dissipated, lightweight version of his famous fifth cousin Roosevelt: "Though your son, under five-and-twenty years of age, should be but a coxcomb; do not, upon that account, despair of his becoming, before he is forty, a very wise and worthy man, and a real proficient in all those talents and virtues to which, at present, he many only be an ostentatious and empty pretender."[19] It is worth remembering that FDR was permanently stricken with polio at age 39, but then elected Governor of New York a mere seven years later at age 46. That he would not have been elected President in 1932 had it not been for polio may be an open question; however, there can be little or no doubt that he would not have been nearly effective as President had it not been for his physically limiting infirmary.

Another famous personage from this era not lacking in self-esteem was British economist John Maynard Keynes, the first great intellectual champion of government deficit spending as an essential remedy for distressed economic stabilization and recovery. The degree to which Keynes was a direct influence on FDR and New Deal policies is debatable and has, for that matter, been more recently shown as indirect and tentative at best; nevertheless, it certainly existed and would become far more pronounced during the postwar period for several decades after Keynes' death.[20] During the 1930s, however, the influence was primarily through the affirmation of new ideas (which are seldom limited to any single individual of an epoch), rather than as any exclusive originator of those principles. Keynes did in fact correspond with, then later meet FDR face-to-face in 1934, and the two appear to have had a high regard for each other, which was not often the case for either strong personality.[21]

Keynes' ideas had been viewed with ambivalence and suspicion in Great Britain ever since he attacked the British establishment in the aftermath of the Great War (see Chapter 11), as well as for his earlier alternative lifestyle, but in the U.S. his bold arguments found fertile ground both in politics and academia. During the early 1930s, Keynes published a tremendous trilogy of works, all still considered required reading for anyone seriously interested in the dismal science: *Treatise on Money* (1930); *The Means to Prosperity* (1933); and his own magnum opus, *General Theory on Employment, Interest, and Money* (1936). Like his Cambridge mentor Alfred Marshall, Keynes was well-versed in Smith's theories. Reading *WN* for the first time in 1910 while on a Greek islands holiday, the philosophically-trained economist simply wrote that "It is a wonderful book."[22] Indeed, it may well be argued that over the course of English-speaking history Keynes runs a close second to Smith in terms of overall fame and influence for innovative economic thought.

Not a household name like Keynes, but perhaps more influential within his own time and place was Keynes' younger American contemporary and counterpart, Marriner Stoddard Eccles (1890–1977), FDR's handpicked Chairman of the Federal Reserve Bank between 1934 and 1951. Eccles was the most unlikely of Keynesians. A Scots-Irish descended banker-millionaire from Utah, Eccles had weathered the early Depression years with a studious avoidance of Smith's dreaded "over-trading" pitfalls. In his spare time he was (somewhat like Churchill) a literary-inclined student of history, and (unlike Churchill) a Mormon.[23]

Upon his retirement from the Fed in 1951, Eccles published a little-read but gripping memoir of the times, *Beckoning Frontiers: Public and Personal Recollections*. In the first sentence of the first paragraph, Eccles makes respectful reference to Smith and *WN*, noting that his father had been born in Glasgow, Scotland, circa 1849, a mere 73 years after Smith's most famous work had been published. This was also only 90 years after Smith had produced *TMS* near the end of his long professorship in the very same city. Eccles goes on to observe that 1849 was the same year that Great Britain repealed its Corn Laws, earlier versions of which were so heavily criticized by Smith in *WN*. Perceptively, he remarks that Great Britain of that era "…was a political economy whose base was formed by a dense mass of slum dwellers." Charles Dickens and Karl Marx are then cited as among the contemporary vocal critics of the Industrial Revolution and its negative social consequences.[24] It was an unattractive world for most of its occupants, mostly unredeemed by conventional religious faith or patriotism, and one from which Eccles' father had wisely fled during youth for a new, far more affluent life in America.

The experiences of Eccles' parents had naturally prejudiced him against more conservative, strictly pro-business interpretations of Smith's theories, and more in favor of a flexible, if not outright liberal reading. On the second page of his memoir, Eccles spells out what he believed to be then-overlooked aspects of Smith's doctrine. First came a more pro-labor sympathy, since Smith wrote that "labor was the sole source of value in commodities." Secondly,

Smith's attack on monopolies applied not only to royal charters but to "those who plundered it [national wealth] in the name of liberating all commercial effort from the trappings of state control." Thirdly, Smith's very title of *WN* implied a more egalitarian "paramount standard" of "*national* welfare" rather than merely "the wealth of *men*."[25] Stunningly, Eccles quotes directly from *WN* one of its least-often quoted, yet sternly unambiguous passages:

> The third and last duty of the sovereign or commonwealth is that of erecting and maintaining those public institutions and those public works, which, though they may be in the highest degree advantageous to a great society, are, however, of such a nature, that the profit could never repay the expence to any individual or small number of individuals, and which it therefore cannot be expected that any individual or small number of individuals should erect or maintain. The performance of this duty requires too very different degrees of expence in the different periods of society.[26]

This tract was clearly used as starting point justification for federal government interventionist programs by a man who was possibly the most powerful financial personage in the country during the New Deal era, after the President himself. Whereas Secretary of Commerce Harry Hopkins was a type of enforcer, and Secretary of the Treasury Henry Morgenthau, Jr., a kind of bean-counter, Federal Reserve Chairman Eccles represented a new kind of force in public financial affairs—non-elected, indefinite tenure, and worldwide impact all rolled into a single office.

Elaborating further on his rationale for radical departure from the past, Eccles strongly implies that without the strong arm protection of federal government, the disaster of 1929–1932 would become a regularly recurring phenomenon:

> This kind of effort has its sanction in humanitarian reasons. But to the hardheaded it also has its sanction in sound economic reasons. For it is the only way by which we can maintain an equilibrium between the goods and services we are able to produce and effective demand for those goods, represented in mass purchasing power. The federal government alone has the taxing power and the borrowing power to redirect unused savings back into channels where they will fan out and provide the mass purchasing power on which an economy in our advanced technological state depends for its health.[27]

Coming from a person of Eccles' successful background and experience, the argument carries considerable force. The line of reasoning is also closely reminiscent of Smith's own earlier double-edged arguments against slavery and protectionism, namely, bad for morals and, more pressingly, bad for business as well. Without strong, central government controls, in the view of Eccles and other New Dealer apologists, modern capitalism, despite all of its other attractive features, ultimately becomes an inefficient, wasteful, and regularly implosive economic system.

In spite of the Great Depression, or perhaps because of it, public art flourished. Many of its themes reflected the times, and much of it was outstanding in quality. In 1930, at arguably the height of national panic and despair, the Empire State Building, an Art Deco masterpiece designed by William Lamb, topped out in New York City as the world's then-highest structure, and quickly became a lasting symbol of its epoch. After the Roosevelt administration assumed power in 1933, artists in all mediums found they were able to occasionally support themselves through federal subsidies. The end results were frequently outstanding and of lasting import. The documentary photographs of Dorothea Lange (1895–1965), funded by the Farm Security Administration, provide only one isolated example in this respect. If the Empire State Building symbolized a grandiose, nostalgic look back at the Roaring Twenties, Lange's ground-level images of Depression-era poverty in rural America continue to epitomize our visualization of that event. They were tax dollars well spent. Not only were New Dealers intent on solving the daunting economic problems overwhelming the country, they prudently sought to memorialize the event for the sake of future generations, or at least those among future generations choosing not to willfully ignore the hard lessons of the past.

One of the earliest and certainly one of the greatest artistic products of the New Deal era was the breathtaking four-wall mural "Detroit Industry" in the courtyard of the Detroit Institute of Art (DIA), fully conceived and executed by Diego Rivera (1886–1957), a Mexican national, outspoken atheist, and political Marxist, but also surely ranking as one of the most talented and prolific painters of the 20th century. Completed in 1933, nine days after FDR had been sworn into office, Rivera's self-acknowledged masterpiece depicts actual and symbolic industrial activity at the legendary Ford Motors River Rouge Plant. It miraculously celebrates and denounces its subject matter, simultaneously. Anyone easily outraged has been outraged ever since. Nevertheless, Rivera enjoyed the full support of his patrons, forward-looking museum director William Valentiner and auto executive patron Edsel Ford, the broad-minded son of tycoon Henry Ford. Controversy filled the DIA with paying spectators, and the astronomical cost of the project was retired without accepting a penny of outside government help.[28] "Detroit Industry" is too big and too complex to discuss within these limited pages; however, it is worth noting that Rivera's distinctly double-edged view of capitalism appears to have owed a debt to German expressionism from the recently-defunct

Weimar Republic. It resembles in some respects Fritz Lang's influential silent film *Metropolis* (1927), it that the future of civilization is portrayed both as exhilarating and frightening. In the year 2015, as the city of Detroit begins the daunting but exciting task of economically re-inventing itself in wake of the American auto industry's long decline, it seems fitting that we should all briefly contemplate Rivera's staggering artistic achievement.[29] Adam Smith, were he alive, would (for one) appreciate the work's dramatically illustrative division of labor, as well as its compassionate view of the common working man.

Former First Lady Eleanor Roosevelt shortly before her death in 1962 complained that the Great Depression had already been forgotten by most American voters.[30] Her observation was accurate and disheartening, yet somewhat explainable, perhaps even excusable. By 1960, and during the short interim since 1939, the United States had produced the biggest, most affluent middle class that the world had ever seen. Unprecedented prosperity had naturally caused many to forget the unpleasant realities of the past, even among those previously compelled to live through it. For younger generations not living through these events, however, the memory of the Great Depression had been mainly reduced to surviving film or photographic images, or if they were fortunate, the oral traditions of eyewitnesses near to them.

Today, of course, the overall situation in terms of public historical memory is much, much worse, notwithstanding many fine attempts in the media to remind its audiences that the U.S. has existed for more than a few decades prior to their own present sense of time. Whether this unsatisfactory state of affairs is the result of systemic failures in the educational system, home environment, or popular culture is an unresolved topic still currently being debated by those having enough leisure to do such things. What matters most in terms of this brief survey is that, beginning in the 1940s, an American leisure middle class began to emerge which, when not busy earning a living, found itself frequently able to indulge its recreational passions, whether these passions be intellectual or otherwise.

14. An Unprecedented Middle Class (1941–1959)

> *"His dexterity at his own particular trade seems, in this manner, to be acquired at the expence of his intellectual, social, and martial virtues. But in every improved and civilized society this is the state into which the laboring poor, that is, the great body of the people, must necessarily fall, unless government takes some pains to prevent it."*—Adam Smith[1]

In his celebrated *Decline and Fall of the Roman Empire*, British historian Edward Gibbon (1737–1794) famously declared that "If a man were called to fix the period in history of the world during which the condition of the human race was most happy and prosperous, he would, without hesitation, name that which elapsed from the death of Domitian to the accession of Commodus," or in terms of strict datelines, from approximately 96 CE to 180 CE.[2] The first volume of Gibbon's classic work was published on February 17, 1776, less than one month before Adam Smith's *The Wealth of Nations* (*WN*) appeared on the same bookstalls of the English-speaking world. Gibbon and Smith, despite their different backgrounds, were mutual admirers of each other's work, and it must be considered a fortunate coincidence or concurrence that both literary masterpieces were generated almost simultaneously. Both authors soon lived to see the Declaration of Independence signed that same year, although neither could be expected to foresee how the American Revolution would play out, let alone the turbulent, explosive, and future economic growth of the United States.

By late 1945, a mere 169 years after Gibbon and Smith wrote, the U.S. had come to dominate the entire world, including what was left of the British Empire, then in the process of rapidly downsizing. If the worldwide Great Depression of the 1930s caused some skeptics to doubt the sustainability of democratic societies, the 1940s and 1950s seemed to triumphantly reaffirm their primacy. Had Gibbon still been alive by 1959, it would have been interesting to see if he would make the same claim of unsurpassed prosperity for Imperial Rome of the Antonines as he had back in early 1776.

The colossal scale of destruction caused by World War II was shockingly unprecedented. In terms of liquidated human lives and sheer dollar-amount damage of property, victorious Russia, then known as the Soviet Union, clearly paid the highest price, although defeated Germany and Japan saw many of their biggest urban centers leveled either through coordinated Allied firebombing or newfangled atomic weaponry.[3] Much of Great Britain's industrial base was reduced to rubble as well, but as in World War I, the U.S. had come to the timely rescue with unparalleled supplies of material and technology, beginning with FDR's brilliantly-conceived, executed, and politically astute Lend-Lease program in early 1941.[4] France was comparatively spared devastation only because it had recognized early that open resistance to the Nazis would be both futile and fatal. Five years later, by the time all of the guns had fallen silent in wake of Hiroshima and Nagasaki, the United States was the only superpower left standing with considerable infrastructure still intact, and until 1949, the only nation with nuclear capability. It also, for a significant length of time, controlled the lion's share of the world's natural resources, either through direct territorial occupation or strong indirect sway over its allies and trading partners. The stage was thus set for arguably the greatest period of prosperity for the greatest number of people in history, or as some historians have dubbed it, the *Pax Americana*, in homage to the *Pax Romana* of a different millennium so praised by Gibbon. Adam Smith would not have recognized the world economic landscape of the mid–20th century, but he long ago had realized that nations with advanced manufacturing bases enjoyed a distinct advantage over their competitors both during times of war and peace. Moreover, he would have recognized the simple fact that any country controlling untapped geographic expanses was most likely to prosper quickly.

The sudden death of FDR in April 1945, mere days before Allied V-Day in Europe, brought Vice President Harry S. Truman (1884–1972) to the White House for final American oversight of the war's conclusion. Upon being informed that the secretive Manhattan Project had developed a viable atomic bomb and delivery system, Truman wasted no time in using it, to the everlasting psychological shock of humankind. In the process he may have spared both the U.S. and Japan the trauma of a conventional military invasion, which would likely have resembled the Eastern Front in horrific scale and scope.[5]

Temporary world peace in late 1945 saw the tentative establishment of Woodrow Wilson's old dream, the United Nations, later given enormous international credibility by Eleanor Roosevelt's active support and involvement. Upon winning a rather unlikely Presidential re-election in 1948, Truman presided over implementation of the European Recovery Program (1948–1952), better known as the Marshall Plan, named after Secretary of State and former U.S. Army Chief of Staff, General George C. Marshall (1880–1959). By then, it had become apparent to most rational Americans that continued U.S. economic prosperity depended considerably upon a stable European recovery.[6] The year 1952 saw the election of Marshall's old friend and comrade in arms (though on the other side of the political aisle), German-American war hero and two-term president Dwight D. Eisenhower (1890–1969). Eisenhower was the last American President born during the 19th century, and despite his many self-acknowledged faults, arguably the last truly impressive chief executive this country has had. It fell to Eisenhower to bring the Korean War (1950–1953) to a close, begun under Truman's watch and instigated by the recently (1949) turned Marxist People's Republic of China, as well as a defiant and now nuclear capable Soviet Union.

These sudden shifts in the balance of world power marked the beginning of a long, grueling Cold War between U.S.–led capitalist nations and non-capitalist countries everywhere else. Another ugly consequence was the aggressive rise of McCarthyism on the American home front, which probably occupied more of Eisenhower's energies than any perceived military threats emanating from the other side of the world.[7] In late 1957, however, the Soviets successfully launched Sputnik, the first orbital satellite, generating yet more American political hysteria, and the astronomically expensive Space Race commenced. The tail end of the Eisenhower presidency was marked in 1959 by the admission of non-contiguous Alaska and Hawaii as the 49th and 50th states in the Union.

The U.S. economic achievements of the Eisenhower years were impressive, especially by today's diminishing standards. Following Adam Smith's dictum of taxpayer-supported transportation infrastructure, a massive and federally-sponsored Interstate Highway System was fully off and running by 1956. Over half a century later, its usage continues to only intensify. Assimilation of African-Americans into the economic mainstream of society proceeded, first with the integration of the military and professional sports, then later in education with the signal U.S. Supreme Court unanimous decision of *Brown v. Board of Education* in 1954. Of all the other domestic triumphs of the postwar era, too numerous to itemize here, perhaps the one now most taken for granted was the G.I. Bill, originally passed in 1944 while the war still raged, then expanded in 1952 in anticipation of the Korean conflict winding down. Another sure sign of FDR's greatness as a political leader had been his ability to conceptualize future needs of the American people, then transform those abstract concepts into timely realities.

The G.I. Bill was perhaps the most visionary of FDR's forward thinking tendencies. In many respects, it represented a goal championed by Vermonter John Dewey (1859–1952), who maintained from the Progressive Era onwards that comprehensive public education was essential to the long-term health and well-being of any democratic society.[8] Dewey's near 98-year life spanned the presidencies of James Buchanan and Harry Truman, during which he established his reputation as America's leading educational philosopher.

Long before Dewey, however, Adam Smith had made a similar link between taxpayer-supported education and the secure political freedom of a nation. Just as the Marshall Plan had jumpstarted economic recovery in Europe, the G.I. Bill succeeded, during less than a decade, in creating an entirely new kind of American work force: professionally skilled, college degreed, internationally travelled, and not deep in financial debt as a result of these things. Lastly, it would be remiss not to mention that my own late father-in-law, Dr. Daniel Buckley, a veteran of both World War II and the Korean War, was among countless recipients of this important government subsidy, one through which he received his medical training, and from which members of his extended family (including myself) continue to benefit directly and daily.

Meanwhile in Great Britain, having survived the Blitz thanks in no small part to Hitler's insane decision to attack the then non-combatant Soviet Union, London proceeded to gradually reassert itself as one of the leading world capitals of finance. Nevertheless, it was painfully apparent to anyone with a sense of reality that England was no longer the center of the economic universe (as it had been in Smith's day), nor ever would be again. King George VI (1895–1952), having ably presided over the war years after the 1936 abdication of his brother Edward VIII (1894–1972), was succeeded by Queen Elizabeth II (b. 1926) in 1952. Winston Churchill, between alternating stints of public favor and disfavor, was forced to witness or preside over the considerable shrinking of the British Empire. The India of Mahatma Gandhi (1869–1948) would finally assert its independence in 1947, while China, upon turning Communist in 1949, would no longer play the role of passive victim to any western power. In the Middle East, Israel, the contentious stepchild of the Holocaust, declared itself an independent state in 1948, much to the chagrin of its displaced Arab neighbors.

On a more positive note, leading British economist John Maynard

Keynes found himself assuming an important moderating role in the American-dominated Bretton Woods (New Hampshire) Conference of 1944, thus avoiding repetition of many economic mistakes made with the Versailles Treaty after World War I. Out of this U.S.–British concord eventually sprang the International Monetary Fund (IMF) and World Bank, although the Bretton Woods System itself would be unilaterally dismantled by the U.S. roughly a quarter century later. The postwar government of Great Britain would be characterized by a resurgence of the Labour Party under the leadership of Prime Minister Clement Attlee (1883–1967). Arguably its greatest achievement, one still standing and considerable exerting influence over British politics, was the National Health Service Act of 1946–1947, the first successful postwar experiment in socialized medicine by a major western capitalist nation.

Any casual reader of Smith's *WN* can hardly miss the strong association that its author seemed to make between a healthy, thriving economy and dynamic institutions of higher education. Where this attitude originated is anyone's guess, but this survey will at least attempt a conjecture. In 1737, an impressionable 14-year-old Smith was sent off to the University of Glasgow to study under, among others, the influential philosopher Francis Hutcheson, doing much to shape Smith's attitudes towards money in general. Over the next three years, Smith not only had his youthful intellect inspired by Hutcheson's enthusiastic idealism, but also his senses assaulted by the explosive growth of Glasgow as a prosperous international trade center.

After Union with Scotland and Great Britain had been politically achieved by 1707, Glasgow, a west coast inland port city on the River Clyde, found itself ideally situated to benefit from the burgeoning commercial traffic between the Old and New Worlds.[9] Under the astute, war-averse management of British Prime Minister Robert Walpole and the hands-off policies of King George II, pro–Unionist Scots looking to break away from the old oppressive feudal order did quite well for themselves. Within a few short years, stupendous private fortunes were being made. Glasgow's rapid population growth curve would proceed unabated throughout the Industrial Revolution, and it eventually surpassed the ancient capital of Edinburgh as Scotland's largest city by the early 19th century, a status still held today. Smith, as a gifted teenage university student coming of age in such an environment, surely made a lasting psychological connection, however real or imagined, between enlightenment of the mind and enrichment of the purse. Some 35 years after leaving Glasgow, Smith would put forth his oft-overlooked proposition that any true democracy puts itself heavily at risk without a strong public investment in educational institutions.

Book V, Chapter I, of *WN* may well represent the least quoted section of that frequently-quoted work, yet certainly deserving higher scrutiny than typically received. Smith's relentlessly dim view of the highly-specialized but undereducated labor force in a modern economy must give considerable pause to any impartial reader. Smith asserts that without proper education, or, more worrisome still, without broader education, modern workers are incapable of making good political choices, essentially retaining the life-long emotional maturity of a 13-year-old, not matter how otherwise occupied:

> The torpor of his mind renders him, not only incapable of relishing or bearing a part in any rational conversation, but of conceiving any generous, noble, or tender sentiment, and consequently of forming any just judgment concerning many even of the ordinary duties of private life. Of the great and extensive interests of his country he is altogether incapable of judging; and unless very particular pains have been taken to render him otherwise, he is equally incapable of defending his country in war....[10]

The last item, that undereducated citizens in a free society, unless intensely trained, make naturally poor soldiers, is especially damning. Then again, coming from a former professional educator such as Smith, such forceful sentiments linking decent education with bravery and patriotism are to be expected. As for this writer, he was quickly reminded of an anecdote from an uncle, a World War II Marine combat veteran, to the effect that better-educated soldiers were quickly given officer commissions, sometimes against their will, because most generals felt that once fighting began, "people with brains" were preferable to lead operations on the ground.

Smith did not place the blame for this situation, at least not entirely, on the shoulders of those "as stupid and ignorant as it is possible for a human creature to become." The problem for them was that, unlike the wealthy and privileged, they had to work for a living. Necessary leisure time and available resources to expand their minds was simply not part of the normal equation for them:

> It is otherwise with the common people. They have little time to spare for education. Their parents can scarce afford to maintain them even in infancy. As soon as they are able to work, they must apply to some trade by which they can earn their subsistence. That trade too is generally so simple and uniform as to give little exercise to the understanding; while, at the same time, their labour is both so constant and so severe, that it leaves them little leisure and less inclination to apply to, or even to think of anything else.[11]

Accordingly, for Smith, the educational needs (among other needs) of "the common people" had to be supported by the uncommon, i.e., affluent, elements of a free society via taxation. Passages such as these resonate when examining the recent history of prosperous postwar America, since it was during this same period that previously all-white institutions (such as the schools) began a long, slow, and painful process towards desegregation. Today, large numbers of Americans have given up on the public school system entirely, if not the very concept of public education itself. Such views, Smith would argue, do not represent those of a truly stable democracy.

Smith concludes this ringing section of *WN* with a long summary reiterating his most important points, one of the few times he seems to repeat himself, as if for the sake of emphasis. Clearly, he was trying to send a message to anyone holding political power in Great Britain that it was in their direct best interests to promote and subsidize the education of ordinary citizens, over and above their highly specialized trades, which the so-called magic of the marketplace had already accomplished quite well:

> The same thing may be said of the gross ignorance and stupidity which, in a civilized society, seem so frequently to benumb the understandings of all the inferior ranks of people. A man without the proper use of the intellectual faculties of a man, is, if possible, more contemptible than even a coward, and seems to be mutilated and deformed in a still more essential part of the character of human nature. Though the state was to derive no advantage from the instruction of the inferior ranks of people, it would still deserve its attention that they should not be altogether uninstructed. The state, however, derives no inconsiderable advantage from their instruction. The more they are instructed, the less liable they are to the delusions of enthusiasm and superstition, which, among ignorant nations, frequently occasion the most dreadful disorders.[12]

Then comes Smith at his best: educated voters in a free society will tend to make better choices than uneducated or undereducated ones.[13] Less self-loathing and more self-esteem would directly translate into better overall citizenry:

> An instructed and intelligent people besides, are always more decent and orderly than an ignorant and stupid one. They feel themselves, each individually more respectable, and more likely to obtain the respect of their lawful superiors. They are more disposed to examine, and more capable of seeing through, the interested complaints of faction and sedition, and they are, upon that account, less apt to be misled into any wanton or unnecessary opposition to the measures of government. In free countries, where the safety of government depends very much upon the favorable judgment which the people may form of its conduct, it must surely be of the highest importance that they should not be disposed to judge rashly or capriciously concerning it.[14]

In Smith's envisioned ideal society of a more broadly and widely educated populace, free citizens will be harder to lead astray through fear or demagoguery.

The argument is compelling, to say the least. It is only surprising that we do not hear it quoted more often in a world which delights in quoting Smith on regular, routine basis.

It is interesting that around the same time that John Maynard Keynes was in New Hampshire helping to hammer out the Bretton Woods agreement for an anticipated postwar world that a serious pushback against more liberal interpretations of Smith's ideas began in England, practically in Keynes' very own backyard. The distinguished economist, philosopher, and academic Friedrich Hayek (1899–1992) had spent the first 30 years of his life surrounded by the dysfunctional chaos of the old Austro-Hungarian Empire. Barely surviving Axis military duty during World War I, he got himself a good education before fleeing the Nazis to the London School of Economics circa 1931.

Hayek's *The Road to Serfdom* appeared in 1944 and has been causing heated debate over its interpretation ever since. Well-versed in Smith's writings, Hayek emphasized the side of Smith that feared tyranny and mostly disfavored government intervention.[15] He knew well from firsthand experience in Europe the mischief that misguided centralized government was capable of committing. The book was, and still is, widely admired. Even Keynes praised it, notwithstanding his publicly exchanged barbs with Hayek shortly after the latter's arrival in London. Hayek went on over the next four decades to become a kind of prominent showpiece for political conservatives both in Great Britain and the United States, solely based on his deep mistrust of all government planning, and despite the fact that he often disagreed with conservative politicians on other specific policies.[16] Keynes, for his part, wrote to Hayek a long letter, addressing him as a colleague, calling *Serfdom* a "grand book" and that he was "in agreement with virtually the whole of it"; yet, also warning against the impracticality of its implementation, since it gave "no guidance whatever as to where to draw it [the line]."[17]

Keynes death in 1946 left a lengthy trail of prominent economic disciples on both sides of the Atlantic going on to influence world leaders for the remainder of the 20th century and beyond. As a kind of footnote to his unexpected admiration for Hayek's work, shortly before his passing Keynes is reported to have made another surprising private remark over lunch to the British academic Henry Clay, not to be confused with the 19th century American Senator who probably never read Smith. Disappointed with continuing American postwar economic ascendency over his native country, Keynes told Clay: "I find myself more and more relying for a solution of our problems on the invisible hand which I tried to eject from economics twenty years ago."[18]

Keynes statement, assuming the reliability of the source, can be taken many different ways, and has. Aside from Keynes' notorious propensity for contrarianism, he was certainly making direct reference to his own controversial article from 1926, *The End of Laissez-Faire*, based on lectures recently given by Keynes in England and Germany. There he had reminded readers and audiences that Smith chose never to use the phrase *laissez-faire* and that his sole reference to the invisible hand in *WN* had often been misinterpreted. Was Keynes repudiating his long-held beliefs in the face of death? Very unlikely. More likely he was acknowledging the British government's by-then limited ability to closely control international events within the context of a global economy, or possibly that undesirable American policies were leading the United States down a path of unintended consequences. Perhaps, like William Pitt the Younger two centuries before, Keynes felt that the best way for England to deal with America was simply to out-trade them to whatever extent possible. Keynes spoke to Clay on April 11, 1946. Ten days later he died at home. The day after his death, a *Times* obituary for Keynes asserted that "To find an economist of comparable influence, one would have to go back to Adam Smith."[19]

In 1949, following Hayek's surprisingly well-received book, amidst stateside hysteria over China's Marxist conversion combined with sudden Soviet nuclear parity, *The Return of Adam Smith* by New York attorney George S. Montgomery was published. The title incorrectly implied that Smith had been away from the academic eye for any length of time, but still asserted that Smith's true legacy had in fact been disregarded by a younger generation of radicalized students coming of age after the war. Moreover, like Hayek, it underscored the tangible anti-government facets of *WN*, but then added a surprising, almost McCarthy-like attack against alleged subversion within the American educational system. "The task of overthrowing the ideals of liberty and independence of the individual American commences with the seduction of the minds of youth" thundered Montgomery.[20] A hostile, dismissive review of this now obscure book by *Library Journal* was almost immediately countered with a glowing review plus lengthy essay in the *ABA Journal* by Seattle attorney William Gardner McLaren ("Some Thoughts on Collectivism and Democracy").[21] Whereas Smith had warned that free societies were likely to fail without the government aid of publicly supported education, Montgomery and McLaren more feared a public educational system indoctrinating impressionable students with unconventional ideas which, in some cases, might go against the personal political beliefs of their elders.

A more measured response to Hayek came from the Scots-Canadian born American economist (and occasional novelist) John Kenneth Galbraith (1908–2006), whose first important work, *American Capitalism: The Concept of Countervailing Power* (1952) appeared the same year that Eisenhower was elected President. Dividing his time between teaching in the Ivy League and working for the Neal Deal during the 1930s, Galbraith first fell under the intellectual spell of Keynes while visiting Cambridge in 1937, then fell in love with and married the American languages scholar Catherine Atwater (1913–2008), becoming an American citizen in the process. One of their sons, James K. Galbraith (b. 1952), went to become a noted academic as well, and continues in his father's tradition as a prominent economics commentator.

Disillusioned with the xenophobia of postwar American politics, Galbraith turned to his real talent, writing about dollars and cents topics for the general reading public. Following his respectably received *The Great Crash, 1929* (1954), Galbraith produced the work for which he is probably still best known, *The Affluent Society* (1958), in which he took the old phrase "conventional wisdom" and coined it in the more modern, negative sense. Despite America's prosperity, Galbraith saw trouble on the horizon, and he proved to be right. Early in the book, he acknowledges Adam Smith as "the first great figure in the central economic tradition," noting that a common thread between the 18th and 20th centuries was a disparity in bargaining power between labor and capital—as had Lord Acton during the Victorian era—except that the late 1950s represented the height of organized labor's political influence in the U.S.[22] Like Smith before him, Galbraith stressed the inseparable link between economic prosperity and prioritization of public education. He would go on to exert notable influence in the political sphere for the remainder of the century and beyond. Fear of improper student indoctrination by the public school system did not seem to particularly concern him.

One individual that could never be accused of having been indoctrinated by anybody was the Scottish-born, multi-media artist Sir Eduardo Paolozzi (1924–2005). Born near Adam Smith's birthplace of Kirkaldy to an embattled family of Southern Italian immigrants, the phenomenally talented, impossible-to-pin-down Paolozzi has probably done more than anyone over the last century to integrate art and commerce. As a teenager, the same age at which Adam Smith was taking in lectures by Francis Hutcheson, Paolozzi found himself detained as an Italian-Scotsman by the British government after Mussolini declared war on England.[23] The mild fascist and national socialist sympathies of his parents had only instilled the young artist with a love of uniforms and deep mistrust of all politicians.

Instead of turning to a life of crime, Paolozzi turned to art. Attracted as an artist to the prewar outlandishness of Dadaism and Surrealism, Paolozzi divided his time immediately after the war mostly between Paris and London, carving out his own original niche. Between 1947 and 1952 he produced, among other wonders, a series of 45 collages, composed mostly of commercial magazine clippings given to him by American servicemen. These formed the cornerstone of the historic 1952 Independent Group Exhibition in London, which in turn proved to be the wellspring from which all subsequent commercial Pop Art sprang, including the work of Andy Warhol during the 1960s. Taken as a whole, these irreverent images were clearly a reaction by Paolozzi and other European artists (especially in Great Britain) against the ascendant American Abstract Expressionism of the period, the latter remaining relatively free of prevailing censorship by not being overtly political or controversial in content.

Paolozzi's memorable collage series for the London Exhibition, enthusiastically entitled *Bunk!*, forced the new consumer middle class, especially in America, to take a good hard, unpleasant look at itself.[24] Individual titles typically consist of real marketing slogans shrilly proclaimed with ironic relish. For example, "You'll soon be congratulating yourself" (1949) from a distance appears like just another innocent fashion advert until closer inspection reveals a labyrinth of Byzantine fine print causing remorseful purchasers to slap themselves on the head. "You can't beat the real thing" (1951) juxtaposes the promise of a tabloid cover girl tell-all with a detailed Firestone tire sales pitch. Human beings are themselves reduced to commodities in "I was a rich man's plaything" (1947), throwing in Coca-Cola and war bonds, among other items, as bonuses. "It's daring it's audacious" (1949) hawks Van Heusen men's neckties with full endorsement from the frozen ancient statue of a Greco-Italian warrior. The list goes on. Taken as a whole, any product or widget related to modern science, aerospace, science fiction, mass production, or any form of advanced technology, receives scathing treatment from Paolozzi's rough sense of street humor. After the furor over the *Bunk!* Exhibition had died down, Paolozzi spent the next half century exploring other artistic mediums, mostly related to public sculpture, with similarly bracing and thought-provoking results. Never was a knighthood more aptly bestowed by the British government than in his case.

The American consumer's paradise of the 1950s was, of course, not all glamour and fantasy, or, as one of Paolozzi's collages disturbingly proclaimed, "a baby's life is not all sunshine."[25] By the close of the decade, economic warning signals had certainly begun to appear. Repeated Keynesian deficit spending during relative peacetime (some 13 years after the Keynes' death) had placed the United States on a permanent wartime footing against Communism or any other perceived outside threat. Military contractors had certainly been enriched, and if one was a white male adult or attached to a white male adult, everything seemed to be going fine, at least on the home front. The American middle class, despite all of its vices and follies, had become the envy of the world. The last of the U.S. Presidents helping the nation in a prominent leadership role to beat European Fascism and the Great Depression was in poor physical health, and preparing to step down.

Exactly 200 years earlier, in 1759, as he had watched Glasgow merchants grow incredibly wealthy from international trade, Adam Smith in *The Theory of Moral Sentiments* warned how great success can often breed great presumption even in the best of leaders. Smith observed that "Success, however, joined to great popular favour, has often so far turned the heads of the greatest of them, as to make them ascribe to themselves both an importance and an ability much beyond what they really possessed...."[26] Smith thus held that it was basic human nature to strive and succeed because of high self-esteem, but then immediately to stumble and fall because of it as well. He finishes the same sentence with "...and, by this presumption, to participate themselves into many rash and sometimes ruinous adventures."[27] A stern warning indeed. By 1959, the *Pax Americana* had lured many of its leaders and voters into a similar sense of false confidence and security.

15. Military-Industrial Complex (1960–1975)

"It seldom happens, however, that a great proprietor is a great improver."—Adam Smith[1]

On January 17, 1961, outgoing U.S. President Dwight D. Eisenhower, in many respects the individual embodiment of "the greatest generation," gave his farewell address to the country on national television. In that noteworthy speech, Eisenhower warned many American voters that "In the councils of government, we must guard against the acquisition of unwarranted influence, whether sought or unsought, by the military–industrial complex."[2] This from the man who coordinated the monumental and successful Allied War effort against Fascism some two decades earlier.

Eisenhower was referring to the tight connections between government, private industry, and military spending that had intensified more or less unabated in the U.S. for the previous 20 years, and would continue strong into the foreseeable future. It surely galled one of the most prominent heroes of World War II that socioeconomic forces similar to ones supporting Nazi dominance in Germany—the homeland of Eisenhower's ancestors—now seemed to be taking hold in the U.S. as well. Moreover, the growing American middle class, which had done so much to support Eisenhower's administration over the last decade, seemed to have little objection to the status quo, as long as it continued to economically prosper. The very idea that government sponsored military spending was gradually comprising a bigger percentage of the domestic economy had probably never even occurred to most of them, nor ever would, as subsequent political events demonstrated. Three days after Eisenhower's eerie and unconventional public warning, John F. Kennedy (1917–1963) was sworn in as 35th President of the United States.

Having barely won a closely contested national election in 1960, Kennedy was in some respects reminiscent of Republican President Warren G. Harding from an earlier era: handsome, well-spoken, genuinely sympathetic to oppressed minorities, and unfortunately, also like Harding, having a penchant for making big mistakes in rapid succession, especially with respect to foreign policy.[3] Within a year of taking office, the same Cuba so boisterously overrun by Theodore Roosevelt's Rough Riders two generations earlier was balkanized into a hostile Marxist enclave, in turn becoming a flashpoint for the terrifying and barely defused Cuban Missile Crisis of 1962.[4] In Europe, 1961 witnessed the ominous construction of the Berlin Wall, driving a physical and symbolic wedge between East and West, poisoning relations between the two blocs for the next quarter century.

The worst reaction to Kennedy's presidency, however, came from southeastern Asia, where a dormant and simmering civil war in Vietnam between a growing Marxist majority and U.S.-supported elites began a gradual but relentless escalation. Kennedy reacted with conventional but outmoded wisdom of the times by authorizing a prolonged and disastrous American commitment to that region. On the home front, and far more on the positive side, he strongly supported the heroic efforts of the Civil Rights movement and created the Peace Corps as an outlet for youthful idealism.[5] The American Camelot of the early 1960s was long on misconceptions and short on practicality. Adam Smith would have deplored its pronounced military aspect.

After Kennedy's horrific murder in late 1963, Lyndon B. Johnson (1908–1973) of Texas assumed executive power for most of the remaining decade. Johnson's prodigious political and legislative skills were eventually betrayed by his fatal blind spot in regards to Vietnam, but not before signing into law the landmark Civil Rights Act of 1964.[6] The rest of the Johnson administration was a tumultuous, embattled holding action. As the unpopular Vietnam conflict reached unanticipated levels of fury and controversy, the twin assassinations of Martin Luther King, Jr. (1929–1968) and JFK's brother, Presidential candidate Senator Robert F. Kennedy (1925–1968), within months of each other, all combined to effectively end Johnson's credibility with voters. Johnson then mercifully announced his intention not to run for re-election, and a badly divided Democratic Party was swept away in the 1968 election by Eisenhower's politically resurrected former Vice President, Richard M. Nixon (1913–1994). In retrospect, the surprisingly ineffectual JFK–LBJ presidencies of 1961–1969 must be viewed as one of the more disappointing episodes in American history.[7] The U.S. has seemingly been recovering from these setbacks ever since.

Nixon authoritatively presided over a traumatized nation for a little over five years, easily winning re-election in 1972, but at the cost of being forced to resign midterm as a result of the Watergate scandal, not so much over what was actually done as for what was publicly denied being done. Earlier in 1969, unable to solve problems on earth, the United States won a ghastly expensive Space Race by putting a man on the moon. This pyrrhic victory was in many respects a fulfillment of Eisenhower's worst fears regarding too closely aligned special interests, Eisenhower himself having passed away roughly four months earlier. Closer to home, the postwar Bretton Woods System was unilaterally abandoned in 1971 by the U.S., the first open acknowledgment that it may have financially over-extended itself during the 1960s with new military adventures and social initiatives.

In 1972, Nixon made the important move of initiating normalized trade relations with China, but then OPEC embargoed oil in 1973. Thus for nearly the first time since the 1930s, America was starting to receive serious economic pushback from foreign powers. The result was stagflation, the unpleasant one-two punch of rising costs in tandem with flattening revenues, which the now shrinking middle class continued to battle over the next four decades. The process of globalization, foretold by American pundits for so long, had finally begun in earnest, with the formerly robust American manufacturing sector being outsourced to non-union foreign countries, then gradually converted to a service and technology sector, which did not even begin to replace the number of jobs being lost. This also marked the true beginning of the implied, longstanding social contract between corporate America and its workforce being first re-negotiated, then shredded. After Nixon's timely resignation in 1974, his second term was filled out by the colorless Gerald R. Ford (1913–2006), seemingly overmatched by escalating events and capable of doing little to stem the ongoing tide of discontent, except to officially pardon the ex-President who had so recently elevated him to power.

Nixon-Ford also presided over the end of the Vietnam War, putting as a good a face on the defeat as was plausible. After a gradual and incredibly destructive scorched earth retreat by the U.S., Saigon finally surrendered to the Viet Cong in early 1975. Of all the American lives that were lost or irreparably damaged as a result of the conflict, the biggest loss was surely that these wasted lives and talents were not channeled into more productive, useful outlets for the country and domestic economy. Moreover, incalculable amounts of capital were squandered. Another big mistake of the era, perhaps the biggest mistake of all, had been the political and financial neglect of the once-vaunted American public educational system, in wake of the Civil Rights movement and racial integration, as precious resources, energies, and lives were diverted into other less productive and more short-sighted directions.

Not since Prohibition had the U.S. lost so much international prestige so fast. It was as if the nation's lawmakers, along with their voting constituents, were intentionally flaunting or inverting the priorities of national defense and public education so vigorously expounded by Adam Smith in *Wealth of Nations* (*WN*) some two centuries earlier.[8] The delayed harmful effects of these expensive policy errors would proceed to hit the country full force throughout the late 1970s and early 1980s. One of the few positives to come out of the Vietnam fiasco was a strong influx of Hmong refugees into the U.S., especially the upper Midwest, adding to the country's ethnic diversity and range of potentially untapped talent.[9]

During this same approximate time frame, the homeland of Adam Smith, Great Britain, seemed to make the most of its recent reduction to second class status as a world power. With the death of a long-retired Winston Churchill in 1965, the old generation that had come of age during the old British Empire now seemed to be passing away. Inspired or driven by the American example, Britain began to export culture and mass entertainment to the rest of the globe (including the U.S.), and discovered a huge pent-up demand for this commodity. The Brits also learned that while they could never compete with the U.S. in terms of mass production, they could still often offer higher quality of products in return. The Labour Party continued to dominate British politics, particularly under off-and-on Prime Minister Harold Wilson (1916–1995), although a crucial interlude occurred between 1970 and 1974. During this brief period, concurrent with the tail end of the Nixon presidency, the British Conservative Party under Prime Minister Edward Heath (1916–2005) held the reigns of government, but more importantly, introduced to the international community as one of its cabinet members, the 45-year-old M.P. Margaret Thatcher (1925–2013).[10] By 1975, after Heath's premature fall from power (again, like Nixon), the energetic Thatcher had replaced him as Leader of the Conservative Opposition in Parliament.[11] She was known, among many other things, for carrying a copy of Smith's *WN* in her purse.

Winding the clock back to 1767, Adam Smith returned from France to his home town of Kirkaldy, north of Edinburgh, and began to write the work which over 200 years later an ambitious Margaret Thatcher would always keep close at hand. In 1767, however, British political concerns were quite different than in 1975. British military involvement in American colonies began to escalate in the aftermath of the highly unpopular Townsend Revenue Act, named after the very same man sponsoring Smith's recent continental tour. By 1770, occupying British troops were shooting unarmed Bostonians for throwing snowballs at them ("the Boston Massacre"). The colonial situation was clearly getting out of hand, not unlike Vietnam during the Kennedy administration. For many British subjects, especially Scotsmen such as Smith, a strict definition of "national defense" did not include paying for overseas troop deployment in response to snowballs and verbal abuse.[12] As for Smith's own travel experiences on the continent, undertaken when he was in his early 40s, everyone seems to have considered it private money well spent. Taking trouble in *WN* to comment upon such things, Smith noted that English continental grand tours are often undertaken far too young in the teen years for the student traveler to truly benefit from the experience, and frequently has the opposite effect in damaging character and morals. This is frequently done, Smith acidly remarks, to avoid exposure to the then prevailing mediocrity within the English university system.[13] The comment tied into his larger theme of an urgent need for educational reform within Great Britain, even as he watched deteriorating political events in America from afar.

Smith hated feudalism, particularly the unnecessary concentration of wealth that always seemed to attend it. He was consistently hostile towards all forms of monopoly, conglomeration, consolidation, exclusivity, and commercial bigness in general. To him, all of these undesirable qualities characterized the Dark Ages, a time in which wealth or "opulence" was highly isolated and progress in the modern sense of the word was nowhere to be found—bigger was not better. The precise context of his remark about "great proprietors" specifically refers to the decline of agriculture during the Dark Ages, but could easily be applied to any sector, given that Smith viewed agriculture as the starting point for all economic prosperity. In the same paragraph, Smith elaborates as why a "great proprietor" is seldom a "great improver"—namely, lack of motivation combined with a lack of expertise:

> In the disorderly times which gave birth to those barbarous institutions, the great proprietor was sufficiently employed in defending his own territories, or in extending his jurisdiction and authority over those of his neighbors.... When the establishment of law and order afforded him this leisure, he often wanted the inclination, and almost always the requisite abilities.[14]

The very same extension of "jurisdiction and authority" which preoccupied European feudal lords, thus causing them to neglect their own back yards, or at best, leaving these to stagnate, has resonance with respect to modern colonialism. The first British Empire was considerably downsized after a failed attempt to bring its American colonies to heel, while the second British Empire (of the 19th century) overextended itself globally in the face of intensifying international competition. As for the U.S., its economic fortunes and expectations began to roll back almost from the moment it tried to unsuccessfully assert its political and military will in southeastern Asia. Under these circumstances, for both the United States and Great Britain, great improvement and great proprietorship, in a very real sense, had become mutually exclusive concepts.

Rarely commented upon is Smith's strong suggestion in the concluding chapters of *WN* that proper taxpayer investment in public education may represent a way forward through the seemingly insurmountable economic problems of modern free nations. In the England of Smith's day, as he wrote from his home in Kirkaldy, several universities—presumably including Oxford—had become "sanctuaries in which exploded systems and obsolete prejudices found shelter and protection, after they had been hunted out of every other corner of the world."[15] It was comments like this that later so infuriated James Boswell and other members of Samuel Johnson's London literary circle.

One immediate, controversial reform that Smith put forward was to give teachers greater performance incentives by allowing them to accept privately funded bonuses from students, in addition to publicly funded base salaries. Another was encouragement (rather than discouragement) of student competitiveness through standardized examinations and prizes.[16] Although such specifics may represent a liberal's nightmare with respect to educational theory, the underlying assumptions behind all of Smith's proposals (as he makes clear from the get-go), is prioritized public funding for these endeavors, at the expense of almost everything else, with a few detailed exceptions. The unpleasant alternative, as Smith spells out in the same chapter, is intensified division of labor making most workers, even highly-skilled ones, "as stupid and ignorant as it is possible for a human creature to become."[17] As if to underscore this combative argument, Smith reiterates it in the lengthy concluding paragraph of Article 2d.[18]

Much earlier in *WN*, in Chapter I, Book X, Smith had gone to some length in emphasizing that farmers tended to be more adaptable, flexible, and attuned to reality than their neighboring village tradesmen. As Smith explained, farmers were constantly required by their livelihood to perform multiple tasks outside their normal comfort zones and beyond any strict division of labor. Thus, despite their reputation "as the pattern of stupidity and ignorance," farmers were in fact "seldom defective in ... judgment and discretion."[19] Because of this, farmers tended to make better citizens in the political arena and, for that matter, better soldiers as well. Though lacking in formal education and book learning, they had at least not been subjected to the potentially debilitating and destructive mental effects of highly specialized labor skills so afflicting to tradesmen. In lieu of Smith's stated opinions on education, is it any wonder that these passages from *WN* are rarely ever quoted?

As for the military establishment, Smith more famously declared that "Fleets and armies are maintained, not with gold and silver, but with consumable goods."[20] Apart from his consistently dubious attitude towards precious metals (see Chapter 9), Smith believed that astronomical military spending for overseas fighting could only be sustained by a robust domestic economy. Thus he continues: "The nation which, from the annual produce of its domestic industry, from the revenue arising out of its lands, labour, and consumable stock, has wherewithal to purchase those consumable goods in distant countries, can maintain foreign wars there."[21]

Unfortunately for the United States, by the late 1960s and 1970s, domestic industry was in the process of being globalized, its manufacturing labor force outsourced, control of natural resources beyond its borders reduced, its agricultural base conglomerated, and the purchasing power of its consumer middle class gradually diminished. Hence its financial ability to fight conventional world wars or even a limited conventional war on say, the Korean or Indochina Peninsulas, had become far more restricted. In the celebrated final chapter of *WN* ("Of Public Debts"), Smith accurately outlined how this problem would eventually play out for the British Empire in a projected, lengthy military struggle against the American colonies. Almost two centuries later, the same humbling dynamic was leading to a major but inevitable U.S. foreign policy setback in southeastern Asia, or as Smith would have derisively described it, "not an empire, but the project of an empire."[22]

Truth be told, Anglo-American reactions to Smith's theories had been comparatively muted since the Great War had traumatically ushered in the 20th century with international upheaval back in 1914. All that began to change, however, during the early 1960s when University of Chicago economist Milton Friedman (1912–2006) first published his best-selling polemic, *Capitalism and Freedom* (1962), then hard on its heels, the imposing cornerstone of Monetarist thought, *A Monetary History of the United States, 1867–1960* (1963), co-authored with Anna J. Schwartz. The two books demonstrated a repeating dichotomy in Friedman's mature work: on one hand, original analysis of empirical data, winning him academic recognition and later (in 1976), a Nobel Prize; and on the other hand, stridently conservative political views which would eventually help to turn Friedman into the most politically influential economist since Keynes.

Friedman had begun his professional life in the 1930s as a federal government employee and supporter of the New Deal, but later recoiled from many of its more aggressive regulatory aspects. Married to the Ukrainian-born Rose Director (1910–2009), Friedman and his wife eventually joined the faculty at the University of Chicago after World War II. The two frequently collaborated in their subsequently published political-economic work, while their son David Friedman (1945–) has since become closely associated with the modern Libertarian movement. Friedman's intense rivalry with near-contemporary John Kenneth Galbraith over political and popular influence was unremitting and not particularly cordial over the course of the late 20th and early 21st centuries.

The text of *Capitalism and Freedom*, over half a century after its publication, still has the power to startle and provoke, particularly for any reader indoctrinated into the myth of Camelot. Clearly reacting to the recent, controversial election of JFK and multiple missteps of his early administration, Friedman begins by quoting Kennedy's famous inaugural address "Ask not what your country can do for you...." Outraged, Friedman muses what kind of American could ask such a selfish question in the first place. In fact, Friedman's reputation for sharp, brilliant repartee with interviewers and debating opponents would soon become legendary. Later in his book, Friedman quotes Smith's "invisible hand" passage from *WN* within the context of "Social Responsibility of Business and Labor," emphasizing "a framework of law" establishment that would promote freedom and fairness, as opposed to political or bureaucratic autocracy, and unlike the Kennedy administration had been recently been doing with respect to the steel industry, Friedman quickly added.[23] In the last chapter, Friedman makes another reference to the sanctity of Smith's "invisible hand" and concludes his work with a quote attributed to Smith outside of *WN*: "There is much ruin in a nation," strongly implying, like Galbraith had some four years earlier, that the U.S. was on the wrong economic policy course, but for seemingly opposite reasons.[24] Smith allegedly made the enigmatic comment in late 1777, upon receiving news that the British Army had been defeated by the Americans at the battle of Saratoga.[25]

In 1967, five years after Friedman dropped his bombshell on Camelot, just as the escalating Vietnam War was about to reach an irretrievable tipping point, Galbraith published *The New Industrial State*, seemingly echoing Eisenhower's public warning made upon his exit from office. During the Kennedy administration, Galbraith had flourished as a foreign ambassador to India and informal advisor to the President. Kennedy had once been Galbraith's student at Harvard, but also preferred to keep his old professor "at a suitable distance."²⁶ When Galbraith later broke with LBJ over the war, he delivered a well-received series of lectures on the BBC, these later becoming the foundation for *New Industrial State*. Adam Smith was cited a number of times therein, though inexplicably, not his opposition to monopolies, even though by then the American military-industrial complex had become, in the eyes of many, a monopolistic oligarchy.²⁷ Galbraith's latest work was widely quoted but also permanently linked him with leftist politics (fairly enough); hence, he spent the rest of his long life and career writing from the outside of political power centers. His books continued to find a steady reading audience, but not necessarily a growing one. In 1973, on the eve of the Watergate scandal, Galbraith followed up with *Economics and the Public Purpose*, in which he advocated novelties such as socialized medicine, a system then benefitting the citizens of his Canadian homeland. The concept of universal health care would have been foreign to Smith; however, a good argument can be made that he would have favored any central government intervention for any activity benefiting commerce but not sufficiently profitable in and of itself (see Chapter 13). Two years later, Friedman countered almost tauntingly with his popular essay collection *There's No Such Thing as a Free Lunch* (1975).

Meanwhile, within the British Empire, socialized medicine continued to thrive as Margaret Thatcher began her impressive rise to political power. No sooner had she become leader of the Conservative Opposition in Parliament than she was invited to Roosevelt University in Chicago, Illinois, to deliver a keynote address on September 22, 1975.²⁸ Standing before a group of curious but admiring Midwestern corporate leaders, Thatcher began by reminding them that the upcoming New Year (1976) would mark the 200th anniversary for both the Declaration of Independence and Adam Smith's *WN*. She then proclaimed that "Adam Smith in fact heralded the end of the strait-jacket of feudalism and released all the innate energy of private initiative and enterprise which enabled wealth to be created on a scale never before contemplated."²⁹ Also making favorable reference to Keynes and Hayek (both associated with Great Britain), Thatcher proceeded to place Smith's economic theories firmly within the sphere of conservative political beliefs, whether those be American or British. Like Milton Friedman the previous decade, Thatcher had effectively reclaimed Smith's theories for big business. Delighted, these same corporate interests could now point to one of the world's great books for justification of its low-tax, non-regulatory agendas, sometimes distorting Smith's teachings through selective quotation and outright invention of things that he never wrote or stood for, or stood firmly against.

By this point in the long, interactive history of commerce and art, diverse examples demonstrate the rise of the American military-industrial complex so feared by Eisenhower. The same downtown Chicago area visited by Thatcher in 1975 features some outstanding displays in the form of public architecture. German-born Bauhaus architect Ludwig Mies van der Rohe (1886–1969) fled Hitler's Germany during the early 1930s, found a new home in the American Midwest, and eventually became a central figure in establishment of the International Style, which today continues, to varying degrees, extending its dominant influence on global building design, especially in the ever-burgeoning world of commercial high-rises. Mies took cost-effective technological breakthroughs in modern construction and beautified them ("Less is more").[30] Myriad imitators have often been unable to recreate his subtlety or sense of proportion. His philosophy was frequently compared to that which created the great European Gothic cathedrals, which also utilized the latest technologies and materials for artistic effect within large communal spaces. During Smith's own day, one of the most celebrated tourist destinations of this kind could in fact be found at Glasgow Cathedral, a classic exemplar of the Scottish Gothic style dating from the late 12th century, and the highest, most prominent building in Glasgow when Smith taught at the nearby university. While Smith had nothing to say about architecture in his surviving works, he surely would have made the connection between the Gothic masterpieces of his own time and the Gothic-inspired public buildings of Mies van der Rohe some two centuries later.

The modern skyscrapers include the massive Chicago Federal Center and Plaza, consisting of the Dirksen and Kluczynski Federal Buildings, along with the jewel box–like Loop Station Post Office, constructed between 1964 and 1974, and widely considered to be one of Mies' most successful designs.[31] One might object that Adam Smith would never advocate such large-scale federal public works, until realizing that these facilities have always been used for courts of justice, military recruiting, postal services, and other necessary government functions expressly justified in *WN* as "Expences of the Sovereign or Commonwealth." Smith would also have approved of the imposing *Flamingo* mobile designed by Scots-descended American sculptor Alexander Calder (1898–1976) which graces the outdoor Federal Plaza.[32] Mies van der Rohe's most acclaimed work, however, is surely the IBM Plaza in Chicago (today known as the AMA Plaza), completed in 1973 and often held forth as the apotheosis of the International Style. It seems fitting that the former world headquarters for this ubiquitous American corporation was largely financed, either directly or indirectly, by huge profits made as a prominent U.S. military contractor during that troubled era. It continues to stand as an impressive, appropriate symbol of that time and place, both for better and for worse.

The chaotic fall of Saigon on April 30, 1975, marked the official end of the Vietnam War, although U.S. policy-makers had wisely but secretly elected to cut its losses long before then. Strategically misconceived from the very beginning, based on faulty intelligence and vain pretense, it took American leaders over 14 years for some (but not all) of them to even admit that a mistake had been made. Many American voters had reached the same conclusion by the mid-1960s. Voters and politicians alike seemed surprised when the financial toll, in addition to the human one, became apparent.

The only really surprising thing, however, was that so many people were surprised. It was not as if this sort of thing had never happened—Adam Smith would have attested to that. Psychologically, it was well that Vietnam should be put behind the national consciousness before the American bicentenary. Now American business could focus on making money and trying to break out of the financial doldrums gripping the U.S. economy since the early 1970s, and only appeared to be getting worse day by day. Instead of paying for a futile and an endlessly expensive military struggle, investors could look to new opportunities on the home front. To facilitate this exciting objective, however, big business would insist upon a boost from big government to maintain or restore its former profit margins.

16. Tax Credit Utopia (1976–1988)

> "Every tax, however, is to the person who pays it a badge, not of slavery, but of liberty. It denotes that he is subject to government, indeed, but that, as he has some property, he cannot himself be the property of a master."—Adam Smith[1]

In 1987, at the high noon of President Ronald Reagan's "Morning in America," the best-selling and critically-acclaimed novel by Tom Wolfe *Bonfire of the Vanities* appeared.[2] Like any commercially successful book, it represented many things to many different people; however, fair to say that it definitely represented, on various interpretive levels, an indictment of unbridled materialist values then seemingly rampant in American society. Moreover, America's true war-zone no longer seemed to be somewhere on the other side of the world, but right at home—in the case of *Bonfire*, the South Bronx of New York City.

The source was also interesting. Wolfe has never been anyone's idea of a bleeding heart. An unapologetic, nay, enthusiastic supporter of conservative political causes throughout his long career, Wolfe wrote about these things with the authority of an insider. Coming from any liberal-leaning novelist, the story would have been much less convincing. *Bonfire* spawned a host of imitators or benefitted similar concurrent fictions (as well as non-fictions) over the next few years. Lost in all of the hoopla was the distant historical background of Wolfe's clever title conceit, to be found in 15th century Tuscany where religious fanaticism often prompted literal bonfires of luxury goods then starting to proliferate in prosperous parts of Europe. A few years later in 1516, the English Catholic, future knight, Chancellor of England, martyr and saint, Thomas More (1478–1535), published a book titled *Utopia*, in which he appears to hold up as an ideal society that which, among other things, places least emphasis on materialism and private ownership of property. It may well be said that in the United States of the late 20th century a quite opposite notion of Utopia was being held out by American captains of industry and the elected officials whose political careers had been largely financed through those same special interests.

American income taxes, moderate in comparison with those of other developed countries, had been steadily rising for over a century since Abraham Lincoln had first introduced them during the Civil War. Tangible relief first came under the presidency of JFK (of all people) with the Revenue Act of 1962, including the introduction of a previously obscure device known as the investment tax credit (ITC). The ITC was, simply put, a dollar for dollar subtraction from income taxes due for certain qualified investments. The idea was to encourage taxpayers to invest in productive things, as opposed to the opposite. It was, and still is, a good concept.[3]

Three decades later, after much economic disruption caused by the war in southeastern Asia and accelerating globalization, the newly elected Congress and administration of Ronald Reagan implemented the Economic Recovery Tax Act of 1981 (ERTA), providing significant relief for most tax brackets, as well as tax breaks for wealthier capital gains. The ERTA unleashed a flurry of economic activity not seen in the U.S. since the early 1960s. It also unleashed a tidal wave of criminal greed at the highest levels of corporate and governmental decision-making not seen since the Roaring Twenties, frequently cloaked in the guise of patriotism or religious fervor. Contrary to what Reagan had always preached, government and government spending grew by leaps and bounds.

Upon Reagan's landslide re-election in 1984 came the Tax Reform Act of 1986, one of its most distinctive features being an unprecedented, expanded usage of the ITC for those who could afford to benefit from it, particularly with respect to the real estate industry. Wealthy U.S. taxpayers, especially corporations—either directly or indirectly—now possessed the utopian tax shelters they had been seeking ever since the American military-industrial complex began to overstep its capacity during the late 1960s.

How would Adam Smith have reacted to all of this? It is difficult to say. On one hand, he would have probably lauded the deregulatory posture and many of the tax reductions of the Reagan administration, and indeed Smith's name was frequently evoked in favor of these policies. On the other hand, it is unlikely that the criteria for equitable taxation so specifically laid out by Smith in Book V, Chapter II (Part II), of *Wealth of Nations* (*WN*) would have been met anywhere close to his satisfaction. Nor would he likely have approved of the manner in which powerful special interests seemed to expand and tighten their control over big government in the process.

16. Tax Credit Utopia (1976–1988)

The late 1970s began promisingly enough with the election of former Georgia Governor and peanut farmer James Earl "Jimmy" Carter (1924–) as president in 1976. Judging the best way to stabilize to U.S. economy was to stabilize the Middle East oil market, Carter proceeded to broker a tremendously difficult but lasting peace between Israel and Egypt with the Camp David Accord of 1978.[4] Carter's historic initiative, however, was then immediately overshadowed by the Iranian Revolution and Hostage Crisis of 1979–1981, in which America's previously closest ally in that region transformed nearly overnight into its most vocal and dangerous opponent. Far worse for Carter's approval ratings, the U.S. domestic economy continued rapidly to lose ground, aggravated in no small part by the controversial decision of newly-appointed Federal Reserve Chairman Paul Volcker to crush inflation with unprecedented interest rate levels in the high teens. Inflation was defeated, and so was Carter in the 1980 election. Carter's one-term presidency must be viewed in retrospect as representing the final days of the Keynesian orthodoxy which had held sway in economic circles for over 40 years, while simultaneously ushering in a new and aggressive breed of anti–Keynesian politicians and academic thinkers, even while Carter was still President.

The main beneficiary of these upheavals was former California Governor and Hollywood actor Ronald Reagan (1911–2004), elected as 40th President of the United States, narrowly surviving a crazed assassination attempt shortly thereafter, and easily winning re-election in 1984. Lower interest rates, combined with contained inflation, deregulation, major tax breaks (especially for the rich), and a temporary calm in the Middle East, all translated into an economic surge during the Reagan years. Those lacking resources and wherewithal to take full advantage of these things, however, continued to fall further behind, and disparities in U.S. wealth distribution began to surge as well. Paradoxically (or not), government spending, both federal and state, also reached record levels.

By the late 1980s, other malfunctions began to appear. In October 1987, the stock market had its worst crash since 1929 but was quickly stabilized by all of the old safety valves implemented by the New Deal. Worse still was the Savings & Loan Crisis of 1986–1987, a byproduct of deregulation, and eventually resulting in the passage of Financial Institutions Reform, Recovery, and Enforcement Act (FIRREA) of 1989.[5] Critics of the new strategy variously dubbed these policies as "supply-side," "trickle-down," and "Reaganomics," although Reagan's 1980 Republican primary opponent and soon-to-be Vice President, George H.W. Bush (b. 1924), at one point disparagingly referred to the mixed bag as "voodoo economic policy."[6]

None of these upheavals would have surprised Adam Smith, whose fresh memories of John Law's speculative escapades in French Louisiana were reiterated at length in *WN*. Unscrupulous businessmen and politicians had been bilking innocent investors and shareholders in the Old World long before they ever did so in the new one. During the 1980s in Great Britain, the British economy also enjoyed a significant rebound while simultaneously appearing less prone to the negative side effects hitting stateside so visibly later in the decade. With the historic election of Margaret Thatcher as Prime Minister in 1979, postwar dominance of British politics by the Labour Party came to a temporary halt as the Anglo-American world chose its first female major head of state.[7]

Thatcher may well be described, without too much hyperbole, as the first modern world leader who was also an outspoken preacher of Adam Smith's economic gospel, at least from a politically conservative point of view. Concurrent with the American example, Great Britain implemented aggressive policies of lower taxes, deregulation, chastisement of organized labor, and privatization of former state industries. The imposing British welfare state previously constructed by the Labour Party was scaled back but mainly left intact as an effective buffer against the ravages of unrestrained capitalism—unlike the U.S. which had a much more water-downed version, descended mainly from Roosevelt's New Deal, and more recently LBJ's Great Society, which was in effect the final extension of the New Deal.

Thatcher and her ministers, to their credit, did not forget that Smith in *WN* (Book V, Chapter I) had been a strong proponent of active government intervention into some designated matters, though an opponent of its intervention into others. In America, on the other hand, the new interpretation and emphasis of Smith's "Invisible Hand" seemed to be suddenly equated with the old French Physiocrat notion of *laissez-faire*, or in other words, just let everything take care of itself. What may have saved the U.S. economy from severe collapse during the late 1980s was that there were still simply too many long-established government regulatory and welfare apparatuses to be completely dismantled over the course of a single decade. Voters may have been ready to eagerly punish "welfare queens" and other designated scapegoats, but they were not about to relinquish their Social Security checks or Medicare payments.

One of the biggest failures of the Reagan administration was its complete inability or unwillingness to tame the burgeoning military-industrial complex so dreaded by Eisenhower. Then again, one arguable rationale for this deliberate expansion was to break the under-capitalized Soviet Union once and for all with an arms race in which the latter could not financially afford to engage. A 1979 Soviet invasion of Afghanistan had so outraged the U.S. that it elected to boycott the 1980 Summer Olympics in Moscow, further decreasing then–President Carter's popularity. Soon after Reagan became President in 1981, the Soviet era of Leonid Brezhnev (1906–1982) came to an end, followed in rapid succession by the lackluster premierships of Yuri Andropov (1914–1984) and Konstantin Chernenko (1911–1985). Finally in 1985, the selection of Mikhail Gorbachev as the new Russian head of state, combined with Reagan's recent decisive re-election, brought the Soviets to the bargaining table, even as their short-lived postwar control of Eastern Europe began to unravel. The enormous military spending prompted by the American Strategic Defense Initiative ("Star Wars"), though little more than a peacetime boondoggle, also served to bankrupt the Soviet state as it vainly strove to keep pace. Adam Smith would have recognized the folly of both sides involved, but probably surprised that this spending was achieved with barely a shot fired in anger, not counting distant skirmishes between Soviet army regulars and U.S.-supplied Afghan rebels.

The real U.S. offensive of that era, however, was against heavy taxation of the wealthy, often pointing to the writings of Smith for justification. These writings tend to speak for themselves, but their impetus must remain somewhat conjectural. Nevertheless, there can be little doubt that the pending American Revolution of 1776 shaped and sharpened Smith's ideas. Specifically, his last encounters with Benjamin Franklin in London during the early 1770s, though clouded in speculation, had to have been pivotal. Smith's biographer John Rae agreed: "Much of the book [*WN*] as we know it must have been written in London."[8] Moreover, Rae fully subscribed to the old tradition that Smith and Franklin frequently or intensively interacted with exchanges of views and ideas.[9] Most everyone agrees that Smith displays in *WN* an unusually detailed knowledge of American colonial affairs, including those of Franklin's home state, Pennsylvania. Writing to Smith from Edinburgh in 1774, David Hume queried: "Pray what strange accounts are these we hear of Franklyn's conduct?"—a clear reference to Franklin's recent dressing down by Scottish nobleman Alexander Wedderburn before the British Privy Council.[10] As for Smith, his ability to see both sides of the American issue would be aptly demonstrated with the publication of *WN* in early 1776.

The flip side to Smith's advocacy of Parliamentarian representation and moderate taxation was hope for continued unity of the British Empire and, yes, his firm belief in the Americans paying taxes. In addition to his last conversations with Franklin, Smith also had the example of the Scottish Jacobite

Rebellion. After the British army delivered Scottish loyalists such as Smith from the frightening prospect of a Jacobite insurgency at Culloden in 1746, the prosperous merchants of Glasgow and Edinburgh were likely more than happy to pay taxes for protection while receiving Parliamentary representation in the process. It may well have been Franklin who reminded Smith that the Scots received Parliamentary representation whereas the American colonists did not. Smith proceeded to advocate in *WN* American representation in Parliament, and that they should then be taxed accordingly. The final chapter of *WN* includes a startling vision in which the first British Empire was maintained with the American colonies intact and expanded even further. Evoking the famous work of Thomas More, Smith writes: "Such a speculation can at worst be regarded but as a new Utopia, less amusing certainly, but not more useless and chimerical than the old one."[11] The problem was that Smith imagined a Utopia in which taxes were fairly paid by everyone, as opposed to one in which individual taxes were defrayed based on political clout. Smith's remark also betrays his lingering pessimism whenever it came to the ability or limitations of human beings to lay aside personal interests in favor of any perceived common good.

Writing in reference to the taxation of ground rents, but having broader implications, Smith in *WN* asserts: "Nothing can be more reasonable than that of a fund which owes its existence to the good government of the state, should be taxed peculiarly, or should contribute something more than the greater part of other funds, towards the support of that government."[12] In other words, if a business owes its profitability to the protection of the state, then that protection should be paid for by the business like any other necessary line item expense. Moreover, these taxes should be moderated only to the extent in which these might impact productivity.[13]

Regarding the forces of supply and demand, Smith declared that "Consumption is the sole end and purpose of all production; and the interest of the producer ought to be attended to, only so far as it may be necessary for promoting that of the consumer."[14] The sentence reads not too ambiguously as a repudiation of supply-side economic theory, of which 1980s world leaders were so enamored. On the other hand, Smith was no apologist for the proletariat. For him, wherever there was accumulated wealth of any consequence, there would also always be someone else trying to steal it, whether they be rich or poor. To him, this harsh reality necessitated courts of law, and taxpayer support thereof: "But avarice and ambition in the rich, in the poor the hatred of labour and the love of present ease and enjoyment, are the passions which prompt to invade property, passions much more steady in their operation, and much more universal in their influence. Wherever there is great property, there is great inequality."[15]

Conversely, and hardly desirable outside of Thomas More's fictional Utopia, Smith noted that "Where there is no property, or at least none that exceeds the value of two or three days labour, civil government is not so necessary."[16] Perhaps naively (ideally at least), Smith viewed the judicial system as a sovereign apparatus protecting rich and poor from each other's rapacity, rather than protecting one exclusively from the other.

The late 1970s and 1980s were bad times for liberals, even as some of their bank accounts swelled with help from double digit interest rates. The ever loquacious John Kenneth Galbraith in 1977 published *The Age of Uncertainty*, based on a BBC television series produced that same year. He lamented the upheavals of the post–Watergate era then beginning to take their toll on major western economies. In 1979 came Galbraith's unapologetic *Annals of an Abiding Liberal*, which included a full chapter essay, "The Founding Faith: Adam Smith's *Wealth of Nations*." Galbraith dryly observed that Smith's *WN* "enjoys the distinction of being one of the three books that people may refer to at will without feeling they should have to read them"—the other two being Marx's *Das Kapital* and The Bible.[17] Praising Smith for his "gift of language" and penchant for "curious facts," Galbraith then betrays a lack of deeper understanding for "Scotland's finest son" by asserting that "Smith's system was destroyed by its own success," having among other perceived shortcomings not foreseen the political dominance of modern corporations.[18] He complains that Smith badly underestimated humankind's "capacity ... for cooperation," or perhaps it was Galbraith who overestimated it.[19] Returning to his usual level of keen perception, Galbraith then acerbically notes that "With his contempt for theoretical pretense and his intense interest in practical questions, he [Smith] might have had trouble getting tenure in a first-rate modern university."[20] Disappointingly, Galbraith's "Founding Faith" essay seems to sidestep the pending full appropriation of Smith's economic philosophy that conservative politicians and academics would decisively achieve over the next two years.

Almost right on cue, a spotlight-loving Milton Friedman was there to object strenuously to anything that Galbraith had to say. Energized by his recent Nobel Prize and right on the cusp of the 1980 Reagan Revolution, Friedman launched his unattractively glib but astoundingly successful *Free to Choose: A Personal Statement*, both as a book and as a PBS television series. Latching on to Smith's "invisible hand"—a phrase used a grand total of once in *WN*—Friedman transformed this into a stern credo of pursuing self-interest for the sake of the public welfare. If we were just allowed to make our own choices without government interference—as if the African-American residents of the South Bronx had that many choices to begin with—then everything would work out for the best. This was almost the same French Physiocrat *laissez-faire* argument so mercilessly lampooned hundreds of years earlier by Voltaire in *Candide*.[21]

With respect to the supply-side economic theory so enthusiastically embraced by conservative politicians of the era, the idea itself originally harked back to another French theorist and disciple of Smith, Jean Baptiste Say (1767–1832), who maintained (with a limited degree of plausibility) that manufacture of a product creates demand for the product. In other words, build it and they will come, as real estate developers of the 1980s often proclaimed.[22] As an informal advisor to the Reagan administration, Friedman's media pronouncements assumed the proportions of secular oracles for public consumption. It was now entirely possible to quote and interpret Smith's *WN* in any preferred fashion, without too much concern that anyone who actually had read the book might object to the manner in which it was being spun, as long as the message in question was amplified loudly and broadly enough.

Far away from the world of media entertainment, however, at street level where the average citizen was being directly impacted by daily bread and butter issues, the person surely exerting the most influence, though his name remained widely unknown to the general public, was recently-appointed Federal Reserve Chairman Paul Volcker. Volcker's eight-year term was interesting on several levels. A Democrat appointed by a Democrat, reappointed by a Republican, and then forced out by the same Republican, he proved the most independent-minded Fed Chairman since Marriner Stoddard Eccles. In 1984, breaking with the secretive traditions of the Fed, Volcker appeared on the Emmy Award–winning PBS television show, *Adam Smith's Money World*, hosted by the late George Goodman under his well known pseudonym, Adam Smith.[23]

By this time, Smith's name seemed to be everywhere at once, although how many people were in fact reading his books was highly questionable. While earnest White House staffers wore "Adam Smith" neckties and praised his legacy to the skies, had any of them been asked to explain Smith's "vile maxim," it is doubtful whether any would have been familiar with that particular passage from *WN*, let alone anything Smith had written earlier in *The Theory of Moral Sentiments* (*TMS*).[24] As for Volcker's grim defeat of systemic inflation with high interest rates during the early 1980s, it must be viewed as a historic achievement, although in hindsight some of us who actually lived through the event are still conducting a cost-benefit analysis of the manner in which it was accomplished.[25] Like hundreds of thousands of other bewildered job seekers, this author unhappily found himself an unemployed postgraduate degree holder circa 1981–1983. He was fortunate, however, unlike many others and probably because his relative youth, naiveté, and desperation, in that he did eventually find a job.

To gain a better appreciation for the survival-of-the fittest mindset dominating Reagan and Thatcher's ministers of state during this period, one can do no better than to peruse a speech given in the not-too-distant past by Thatcher's former Chancellor of the Exchequer from the crucial period between 1983 and 1989, Nigel Lawson. Titled for later publication as "Five Myths and a Menace," Lawson's address was delivered in late 2010 at Cambridge University, right on the home turf of a long-deceased John Maynard Keynes.[26] Making an unapologetic connection between Smith's alleged economic philosophy of *laissez-faire* and the allegedly brutal scientific teachings of Charles Darwin, Lawson only succeeded in distorting both.

Explaining away the extensive human wreckage caused by the 2007–2008 economic downturn, Lawson's numbingly pedantic article did admit that the author was not an Adam Smith scholar, nor "was [I] brought up on him."[27] After outrageously implying that Smith's *"The Theory of Moral Sentiments*—[was] of no interest at all," Lawson quotes Smith's famous assertion that "consumption is the sole end and purpose of production"—not to deny supply-side theory, but rather to attack job creation as a misguided policy priority, claiming in the process that Smith would have agreed with this sad and cynical proposition. Lawson's "Five Myths and a Menace" article does, however, serve to further illustrate our main criticism of the modern conservative political claim for exclusive ownership of Smith's teachings, namely, that its fervent admiration of Smith often seems capable of only focusing on one isolated aspect of his genius at a time while ignoring all the rest.

Reflecting the popular culture of the 1980s, one can do no better than to screen Oliver Stone's acclaimed 1987 film *Wall Street*, featuring a riveting lead performance by Michael Douglas as junk bond tycoon Gordon Gekko, loosely based on the real-life shenanigans of inside trader Ivan F. Boesky. In probably the most infamous sequence from the movie, Gekko proclaims to his enraptured audience: "Greed, for lack of a better word, is good. Greed is right. Greed works." This speech was in turn reduced for all time, in the common vernacular, to the oft-repeated slogan of "Greed is good." Thus by 1987, the morally-based economic teachings of Adam Smith had been completely inverted in the name of deregulated capitalism. Douglas, despite winning an

Oscar as best actor for his disturbing portrayal, has since found himself repeatedly explaining to audiences, particularly American audiences, that Gekko is not intended to be a good guy or a hero, nor does Douglas endorse the heinous philosophy espoused by Gekko in the film. John Kenneth Galbraith, for his part, had seen it all coming back in 1973, bitterly observing that "amateur defenders of the market, enchanted to discover, as did Adam Smith two centuries ago, that good seems to proceed from evil, have often gone on to conclude that avarice is an original virtue."[28] Galbraith wrote these words near the tail end of the Nixon presidency intending to be outrageous, but by the end of Reagan's second term, it had arguably been transformed into the popular conventional wisdom, to use another favorite phrase frequently employed by Galbraith.

Despite all of the economic warning signals from the previous year (and, indeed, the previous administration), the Democrats never stood a chance in the 1988 Presidential election, with Vice President George H.W. Bush easily defeating Massachusetts Governor Michael Dukakis to become the 41st President of the United States. In what should have been a vigorous public debate about the potential downside of *laissez-faire* policies, the Republicans succeeded spectacularly in tapping into public anxieties over the widening gap in wealth distribution or, to put it more bluntly, festering racial tensions. These were the same tensions that were helping to make Wolfe's *Bonfire* a national bestseller around the same time period. Displaying the devious brilliance for which he was sometimes noted, Bush's campaign manager Lee Atwater turned the entire election into a single referendum over one Willie Horton, a convicted murderer and rapist granted furlough under Dukakis' watch as governor, who proceeded to commit more violent crimes. The perceived soft-on-crime Dukakis was effectively beaten the same day the attack ads began to air.

Meanwhile, at the 1988 Republican convention—held at the same New Orleans Superdome that would become a P.R. problem for Bush's son and the Republican Party some 16 years later—Bush Senior declared: "I want a kinder, and gentler nation." Little would in fact really change over the next three presidential terms (at least in terms of the now dominant, corporate-friendly, tax credit utopia), except that the widespread image of cruelty and harshness unintentionally cultivated by the previous administration was due for a makeover.

17. A Kinder, Gentler Corporate Mandate (1989–2000)

"The government of an exclusive company of merchants is, perhaps, the worst of all governments for any country whatever."—Adam Smith[1]

Like Jimmy Carter before him, George H.W. Bush proved to be a one-term president. This was surprising given the trouncing the Democrats had taken from Republicans during the last three White House elections, plus the fact that Republicans had won five of the last six presidential contests. The problem for Bush Senior was, in the words of Democratic campaign manager James Carville, "the economy, stupid."[2] Domestic social fallout from the deregulatory trends of the 1980s was, by the early 1990s, reaching unmanageable proportions, blunted only in part by isolated and halfhearted legislative attempts at reform. The American middle class, at least by 1950s definitions, was still contracting, and wealth distribution continuing to skew. The Republican "thousand points of light" never materialized; what did materialize in 1992 was the worst urban rioting seen by the country since the 1960s. Moreover, the short, successful Gulf or First Iraq War (1990–1991), notwithstanding Bush Senior's able oversight of that conflict, only provided a temporary boost in his flagging popularity.[3] Ultimately, he was unable to maintain the allegiance of the numerous "Reagan Democrats" who supported his avuncular predecessor. The tax credit utopia created by the Reagan Revolution was, for the first time, in real danger of losing its longstanding electoral mandate.

Corporate America clearly needed a better salesman for its tax break agenda and hit the jackpot in 1992 with Arkansas Governor William Jefferson "Bill" Clinton. It is safe to say that Adam Smith never beheld the likes of Bill Clinton, or if he did, could hardly imagine such an individual as the two-term leader of the free world. Like Carter, Clinton was a congenial Southerner possessing folksy charm and a skillfully projected lack of pretense; there the similarity ended. A younger, Democrat-version of Ronald Reagan, Clinton always had his ear planted firmly to the ground of public opinion, while carefully serving the same big-moneyed interests that brought both he and Reagan into power. Like Reagan, Clinton studiously avoided lengthy, expensive foreign entanglements, while focusing on domestic economic expansion, combined with (unlike Reagan) budget deficit reduction. The multiple sex scandals that his hero JFK had always managed to keep hidden from public view were, in Clinton's case, routinely paraded by mass media before a squirming or fascinated international audience. His popularity with voters only increased, as did that of his long-suffering wife and political partner Hillary Rodham Clinton.[4]

The sole legislative hiccup during the Clinton years was a failed public health care reform initiative in 1993–1994, faltering mainly because a jittery insurance industry retreated from supporting it after some initial enthusiasm. As for congressional Republicans, it would be difficult to say which they objected more to, the very concept of government-sponsored health care, or the fact that the initiative was being spearheaded by the First Lady. Thus ended in defeat the first tentative American attempt to imitate the successful British example of socialized or publicly-subsidized medicine. The only other Republican victory (of sorts) on a national political level was the symbolic 1998 impeachment of the President in the House of Representatives, widely viewed as an outlandish move at the time but now rather benign by today's low Beltway standards.[5]

Among other things, the 1990s saw a continued expansion of the American service sector economy, driven by the rapidly advancing computer technology that began in earnest during the 1980s, accelerated by commercialization of the Internet in the mid–90s. Meanwhile, U.S. manufacturing continued to be outsourced to wherever unskilled or semi-skilled labor was cheapest—to be more precise, wherever there were no labor unions. Foreign manufacturers entered the U.S. (for the most part) only in states with weak organized labor or massive subsidies for companies, which often found themselves being courted by more than one state vying for a new plant location.

The economic centerpiece of the Clinton years was the North American Free Trade Agreement (NAFTA), passage of which in 1994 did not prevent some critics from noting that enrichment of a few special interests did not necessarily translate into tangible benefits for the rest of society. Adam Smith most certainly would have favored the free trade principles championed by NAFTA advocates; whether he would have supported the flawed nuts and bolts of the legislation itself is an open question. Use of the Investment Tax Credit, pioneered by the Reagan administration, was also ramped up and further embellished by the Clinton presidency. The real estate industry boomed, but this illusion of middle class expansion was offset by bigger, more long-term trends less prominently touted, namely, that American wages were simply not keeping pace with relentless cost of living increases. The real expansion was in the number of working poor. Budgets were balanced, but overall standards of living were imperceptibly slipping. Nevertheless, the Clinton administration displayed unsurpassed virtuosity when it came to rewarding big business with unparalleled tax breaks while blunting this negative image with mostly symbolic entitlements for the poor.

In Europe, the big news was the final breakup of the Soviet Union and fall of the Berlin Wall in 1989, leading in turn to the historic reunification of Germany. Great Britain now faced the dreaded prospect of playing economic second fiddle in the Eurozone to the Germans, a valid fear contributing earlier in the century to World Wars I and II. No sooner had the Berlin Wall come crashing down than Margaret Thatcher, never defeated in a popular election, was ousted as British Prime Minister in 1990, not by voters, but by her own Conservative Party constituents. New party leader and Prime Minister John Major, over the next seven years (from 1990 to 1997), and despite unconvincing attempts to imitate his dynamic predecessor, more or less presided over England's steady loss of economic ground to a newly-energized and boldly assertive German nation. British voters eventually acknowledged this handicap (and new normal) in 1997 by bringing the Labour Party back into political power, along with Scottish-born Anthony Charles Lynton "Tony" Blair as Prime Minister. To begin with, Blair moved quickly to mend political fences with Ireland, no doubt recognizing that, unlike Great Britain, the Irish would be adopting the newly official Euro currency on January 1, 1999. Blair recognized, if nothing else, that Great Britain's continued status as a first tier world power depended upon maintaining good foreign trade relations, beginning with its immediate geographic neighbors.

Although the United Kingdom (Great Britain and Northern Ireland) had been a charter member of the European Union since 1973, Soviet collapse, German reunification and the Euro currency had suddenly made the E.U. far more than a mere symbol or idea. Frankfurt quickly became headquarters for the recently christened European Central Bank representing 18 nation-states (today 19), and Ireland, as one of these, in turn became very prosperous.[6] The long memory of the Irish people in regards to the Great Famine of the 19th century and other indignities suffered at the hands of the British had caused them keep Great Britain at permanent arm's length in most of their dealings. Adam Smith's old proposal in favor of full Irish union with Great Britain (like Scotland), despite becoming a 19th century reality in legal form, and similar to his urgent proposal for full union with the American colonies, never really found true cultural or political traction. This rollback had occurred in no small part because of the long-term failure of the British-Irish union to deliver widespread economic prosperity for Ireland in a similar manner earlier achieved for Scotland, including for the likes of Adam Smith's very own family and personal career. As for Germany, it now began to enter a new phase of dramatic growth, technological prowess and world political influence not seen in that geographic sphere since the ancient fall of the Roman Empire so eloquently recounted by Smith's British colleague Edward Gibbon.

Americans irrationally reacted to the breakup of the Soviet Union as if worldwide Communism had been vanquished once and for all. Most of them forgot about the Peoples Republic of China (PRC), even as recurring media images of the suppressed 1989 Tiananmen Square protests provided convenient sound bites for self-congratulatory western censures of Chinese political oppression. The unpleasant truth was that ever since President Nixon had semi-normalized American relations with the PRC back in 1972, China had been slowly closing the vertiginous economic gap between East and West— a gap so big at first that it could hardly do anything but contract, then by the 1980s began gaining strong momentum as its manufacturing sector asserted inherent ability to uncut foreign competition with seemingly limitless reservoirs of cheap and unskilled labor.

After Tiananmen temporarily provided western critics with another poor excuse to underrate the Chinese, a new PRC government led by Jiang Zemin and his economic point man, former Shanghai mayor Zhu Rongji, refined and improved the pro-growth policies of Zemin's predecessor Deng Xiaoping (1904–1997). Metaphorically speaking, these policies effectively borrowed large pages from the capitalist playbook while maintaining an overall Marxist political and social stance. For the first time in modern economic history, both in reality and the popular imagination, China began to seriously challenge Japan as a national economy in terms of Gross Domestic Product (GDP). The pivotal moment probably came in 1997 when Great Britain was obliged to return its leasehold interest in Hong Kong to the Chinese mainland; thus one of the great four "Asian Tigers" formally joined forces with the PRC.[7] By the end of the 20th century, Adam Smith would have been perhaps astonished at the more recent economic achievements of China, given that his writings consistently criticize that populous nation's longstanding disinterest and ineptitude in regards to foreign trade.

Returning to the 18th century world better known to Smith, this is perhaps a good place to delve more into his personal life, given that the 1990s seemed to expose nearly everyone else's personal life for more public scrutiny. Smith's biographers, beginning with Stewart and Rae, agree that while visiting France Smith probably for the first time in his life received something that he had never received before: a fair amount attention from the fairer sex. Smith's well-received *The Theory of Moral Sentiments* (*TMS*) from 1759 not only secured him a small pension from the nobility, but a chance to travel the European continent as well. As a Scots-British literary celebrity and acknowledged friend of David Hume, Smith found himself suddenly exposed to the most prestigious literary salons of France, including some of the best-educated (and free-spirited) women of that pre–Revolutionary time and place. It would have represented quite a change from the relatively quiet and secluded bachelor's life of a former Glasgow academic. By this time, he was in his early 40s with a steady income and good prospects ahead of him, but always self-deprecatory regarding his physical appearance and notably eccentric in his personal habits.

No scandals involving Smith have ever been reported, although some interesting, even endearing, anecdotes have come down to us. Among several, his most famous female acquaintance (and booster) in France was the former actress and popular romance novelist Marie-Jean Riccoboni (1714–1792), known by literary critics as the French Samuel Richardson. Riccoboni, nine years Smith's senior, was married, though separated from her husband, and a friendly hostess to most of the great French intellectuals with whom Smith regularly mixed. She does not appear, however, to have been the main focus of Smith's attention. Both of Smith's earliest biographers, Stewart and Rae, repeat an intriguing story told by fellow Scotsman and eyewitness Dr. James Currie (1756–1805), regarding Smith's short excursion to Abbeville from Paris in late 1765 and early 1766.[8] According to Currie, Smith wanted there to court a visiting, attractive Scotswoman whom he had known for some time, and who in fact never married afterwards. Quixotically, but in perfect keeping with his noted single minded tendencies, Smith tried, failed, and never tried again, even though at least one other French woman was clamoring for his attention.[9] Currie scrupulously (and frustratingly) preserved the anonymity of Smith's fixated Scottish love interest.

Within the context of intimate human relationships, Smith maintained that it was generally more sympathetic to have an excess of natural affection for another rather than the opposite extreme. In writing of the supremacy of emotions over reason in most of these situations, Smith had observed in *TMS* that "The poets and romance writers, who best paint the refinements and delicacies of love and friendship, and of all other private and domestic affections, Racine and Voltaire; Richardson, Maurivaux, and Riccoboni; are in such cases better instructors than Zeno, Chrysippus, or Epictetus."[10] This is a far cry from the more modern interpretation of Adam Smith as a philosopher allegedly advocating a strict type of Darwinian self-interest as the best means to achieve the general welfare of society, or even the general welfare of two people interacting with each other. Regarding lovers, families, or friends, for Smith there is no invisible hand or vile maxim, only sympathy or lack thereof, with the former being a desirable thing and the latter, a detestable one. It also provided a good reason for contemporary French writers such as Voltaire and Riccoboni to graciously welcome Smith when he later toured their homeland in wake of British victory following the Seven Years War.

Regarding China of the 18th century, Smith several times held that country forth as a negative economic exemplar not to be emulated, notwithstanding his considerable respect for its venerable and ancient culture. In *Wealth of Nations* (*WN*), Book IV, Chapters II–III, Smith expounds his celebrated views on the misguided futility of official restraints on foreign trade by any nation, repeatedly referring to China as a classic case in which such restraints had a terrible retarding effect on national development and international influence. "The Chinese have little respect for foreign trade," declared Smith, in stark dramatic contrast to the PRC of today's world.[11]

Moreover, Smith strongly implied, there was a direct link between this regressive attitude and the feudal concentration of wealth then characteristic of Chinese society, leading in turn to widespread social injustice: "oppression of the poor must establish the monopoly of the rich."[12] Smith was similarly contemptuous of all British or Chinese policy arguments favoring balance of trade between countries: "Nothing can be more absurd than this whole doctrine of the balance of trade, upon which, not only these restraints, but almost all the other regulations of commerce are founded."[13] For the author of *WN*, balance of trade was irrelevant; what mattered was who was raising their standard of living and who was not. Foreign trade itself was not something to be feared or over-regulated or discouraged, but rather the final desirable stage of fiscal development for any civilized society.[14] These passages in *WN* could well be reduced to single maxim: let us not be like China.

However, Smith was writing of 18th century China, not the PRC of the 21st century. Another example of Smith's extremely different perspective and historical context could be found earlier in *TMS*, where he reassured readers that "National prejudices and hatreds seldom extend beyond neighbouring nations."[15] How things have changed! In Smith's world on the eve of the American Revolution, Great Britain's chief rival was France; today, economic rivalries are worldwide and transcontinental—some would say even transnational—and certainly becoming more so as time passes.

As to the policy architects themselves, Smith leveled withering criticism, or as he himself later described *WN*, made a "very violent attack" upon them. Derogatorily and repetitiously describing England as a "nation of shopkeepers" acting as "principle advisors" to the British government, Smith unfavorably accuses the merchants of "groundless jealousy" regarding any real or perceived commercial competition.[16] He does not stop there. Official or unofficial representatives of merchants and shopkeepers—or as Ulysses S. Grant later dubbed them, "lobbyists"—make the worst possible policy architects. The rarely cited concluding paragraph of Book I, Chapter XI, Part II, deserves to be quoted here: "To widen the market and to narrow the competition, is always the interest of the dealers, however, in any particular branch of trade or manufactures, is always in some respects different from, and even opposite to, that of the public."[17] Then comes the final condemnation:

> The proposal of any new law or regulation of commerce which comes from this order, ought always to be listened to with great precaution, and ought never to be adopted till after having been long and carefully examined, not only with the most scrupulous, but with the most suspicious attention. It comes from an order of men, whose interest is never exactly the same with that of the public, who have generally an interest to deceive and even oppress the public, and who accordingly have, upon many occasions, both deceived and oppressed it.[18]

It is hard to imagine such words ever being quoted by a Margaret Thatcher or a Milton Friedman, even though both always claimed intimate familiarity with *WN*. One might argue that those members of the general public deceived or oppressed in such instances were more than happy to be so; on the other hand, we cannot help but wonder whether their reactions would have been any different had anyone actually read and comprehended Smith's warning in the first place.

By the 1990s, the old ideological spat between Milton Friedman and John Kenneth Galbraith (after more than three decades) was beginning to slow a bit, not due to any fence-mending, but because the participants were becoming older and surpassed in media attention by younger, more energetic, more strident voices. Just before Clinton's election in 1992, John Kenneth Galbraith released *Culture of Contentment*, an indictment of the remaining American middle class which seemed to have insensibly turned its back on social justice, as well as good political common sense, in return for a certain guaranteed stream of consumer goods and entertainment. With respect to the irrepressible wave of 1980s Conservatism claiming to worship the father of modern economics, Galbraith complained that "It is perhaps unfortunate that few, perhaps none, who so cited Adam Smith had read his great book."[19]

Smith himself would have never presumed the average consumer had much social conscience, let alone common sense, though he would have preached both. Six years after Galbraith's lament, a serene Milton Friedman in his memoir *Two Lucky People* (1998), fully conscious of conservatism's triumph, basically ignored his old rival, but made a veiled illusion to him by quoting *WN*. Drawing upon Smith's express criticism for "The man of system" in legislative matters, Friedman reiterated Smith's observation that central economic planning is not like moving chess pieces on a chessboard, because in real life each of the chess pieces has an independent will of its own or, in Friedman's favorite expression, were "free to choose."[20] Within this framed context deviously provided by Friedman, it was difficult not to associate Smith's critique of worldly naïveté with Galbraith himself.

A far more forceful liberal voice protesting the misinterpretation of *WN* was provided by Clinton's handpicked Secretary of Labor and fellow Rhodes Scholar, Robert Reich. Rather than fret over the manner in which Smith's views had been widely distorted, Reich penned his own best-selling treatise, *The Work of Nations* (1991), laying out in detail how Smith's theories should be specifically applied by modern governments, namely, with a strong emphasis upon human rather than monetary capital. By the end of the 20th century, after a successful stint at his government post and resuming his academic career, Reich wrote a new introduction to *WN* for the 2000 Modern Library edition. He begins (like so many others before him) by noting book's curiously revered but unread status: "Adam Smith's masterpiece is one of those rare classics that almost everyone knows about, many people quote from, but a very few have actually read."[21] The last sentence of the same intro underscores the oft-ignored humanist aspect of Smith's economic philosophy, as well as its continued relevance:

> In these times, as when Adam Smith wrote, it is important to remind ourselves of the revolutionary notion at the heart of Smith's opus—that the wealth of a nation is measured not by its accumulated riches, but by the productivity and living standards of all its people.[22]

The "living standards" reference was especially appropriate given that *WN* did in fact place such a high priority on this factor, and because the tail end of the century witnessed such a noticeable decline in living standards for so many U.S. citizens. Reich would go on to produce more noteworthy works, including the 2013 film documentary *Inequality for All*, directed by Jacob Kornbluth.

At the other end of the political spectrum in Great Britain, Prime Minister John Major largely continued the policies of his predecessor, including the privatization of former British state industries. The culmination and centerpiece of this effort came with the 1993 Railways Act and privatization of British Rail, which remains in effect to this day. A driving think-tank advocate of this trend had been the Adam Smith Institute (ASI), in existence since the late 1970s but exerting tangible political influence first under Thatcher, then under her successor. Speaking before the ASI at Whitehall in late 1992 on the eve of the Railways Act, Major repeatedly and not too surprisingly dropped Smith's name as alleged traditional support for the sweeping changes then afoot:

> Adam Smith believed that the State had a responsibility for reform, to remove impediments to natural liberty and to facilitate the development of services like basic education for all. I agree with Adam Smith.... For an increasing number of public services the State should be an enabler and facilitator. Adam Smith believed that in providing services, the State should simulate market conditions wherever possible.[23]

In essence, conservatives took passages from *WN* in favor of privatization for some industries and interpreted these as support for privatization of most if not all of them.[24] While not quoting from *WN* directly, Major repeatedly used the phrase "Adam Smith believed," by now a standard rhetorical device employed by all sides in political debate. As for Smith, he did not live to see (and likely could not imagine) mass rail transit, although he was personally acquainted with the famed steam engine inventor, fellow Scotsman and Glasgow resident James Watt.[25] All in all, there is a reasonable chance that Smith would have supported the British Railways Act so long as it did not represent a commercial monopoly or negatively impact national defense, two big "ifs" it must be conceded by any reasonable observer.

In terms of private versus public commercial enterprises, Smith would have been amazed by late 20th-century Los Angeles County, where some of world's largest (and richest) art museums voraciously competed for funding and customers as they grew to unprecedented scale and scope. Among numerous outstanding institutions, perhaps the two most prominent are the privately endowed J. Paul Getty Museum and the more publicly supported Los Angeles County Museum of Art (LACMA). Individually, each is considered an industry leader; combined, along with other L.A. County fixtures such as the Huntington, MOCA, and the Natural History Museum, they comprise perhaps the most imposing cultural conglomeration ever witnessed on a concentrated local level.[26] The peak of this frenzy occurred in 1997, when the sprawling, newly-constructed Getty Center campus in Brentwood was unveiled to astonished visitors.

Meanwhile, along the Wilshire Miracle Mile, LACMA responded by announcing its own ambitious expansion plans, much of which came to fruition during the following decade. Amidst all of publicity and fanfare, the lines between public, for-profit, and not-for-profit enterprise often became blurred or indistinguishable, even as paying art lovers flocked to these prestigious facilities and billionaires competed to outdo each other with highly-visible philanthropic gestures. These relatively recent developments appear even more dramatic in hindsight when one considers that most of these institutions barely existed before the 1960s and 1970s. Within a few short decades, however, their magnificence had far exceeded anything ever conceived by the Renaissance Florentine Medici in their wildest dreams or imaginations.

During Smith's day there was certainly no such thing. The first great Anglo cultural institution, the British Museum of London, was founded in 1753 (while Smith was teaching in Glasgow), when the Scots-Irish royal physician Hans Sloane bequeathed his spectacular private collection of artifacts and manuscripts to King George II. Then, through a royally-approved Act of Parliament, a publicly accessible facility was created and established in the Bloomsbury district. The British Museum swiftly grew by leaps and bounds as other collections were added. A mere 14 years after its initial foundation, Smith utilized the museum library (in 1767) upon his return journey to Scotland from France, while beginning his research work on *WN*.[27] Smith was also an enthusiastic connoisseur of the arts, and during his Glasgow tenure had written a preserved essay on "The Imitative Arts" of painting, sculpture, music, poetry, and dance.[28]

Living during an age in which these disciplines were supported almost exclusively through the largess of the European nobility, Smith focused his thoughts on precisely why these things appeal to us, as opposed to any notion that major commercial enterprises could revolve around the same activities. As noted by subsequent commentators, it is a shame that Smith's later projected works never came to fruition, especially since he may have delved into this fascinating subject matter. Confronted with the physical, growing reality of the British Museum circa 1767, Smith could easily have pondered the direction in which cultural and commercial trends were headed, and how they might intertwine, although (to repeat), the culmination of these trends during the late 20th century would have probably left him astounded, as well as personally pleased.

Politically, the American 20th century ended with a whimper. Clinton's anointed, would-be successor, Vice President Al Gore, instead of achieving an expected easy victory, ran straight into a hail storm of media criticism and voter resistance, led mainly by the growing masses failing to economically benefit from the two previous decades or (worse) falling further behind. Texas Governor George W. Bush, son of Bush Senior, to the delight or consternation of most Americans, achieved a stunning but undeniable stalemate in the Electoral College (despite losing the popular vote), a stalemate soon broken by the U.S. Supreme Court and Gore's unselfish decision to not throw the country into further turmoil.[29] As Bush Junior prepared to become the president of the United States, a lingering sense of foreboding seemed to grip the national consciousness, driven by a growing awareness that all was not well within the body politic, despite all of the perceived accomplishments of the Reagan and Clinton administrations. Not the least of these problems was the stark fact that the greater world at large was noticeably and rapidly becoming smaller. In short, North American sovereign borders, inviolate since the War of 1812, were no longer impervious to asymmetrical foreign attacks.[30]

18. Post 9-11 (2001–2015)

"For it may be observed, that in all Polytheistic religions, among savages, as well as in the early ages of Heathen antiquity, it is the irregular events of nature only that are ascribed to the agency and power of their gods. Fire burns, and water refreshes; heavy bodies descend, and lighter substances fly upwards, by the necessity of their own nature; nor was the invisible hand of Jupiter ever apprehended to be employed in those matters."—Adam Smith[1]

In early 2002, shortly before her health began to fail, former British Prime Minister Margaret Thatcher published her swan song treatise on good government, *Statecraft: Strategies for a Changing World*, dedicated to her American political counterpart Ronald Reagan, then also in failing health. The book was widely ignored or given condescending acknowledgement, a rather surprising response given that Thatcher had been one of the most influential world leaders of the postwar era. Toward the end of *Statecraft*, Thatcher revisits her old reverence for Adam Smith, cautioning readers (or justifying to them) that policies of deregulation and privatization—championed during her tenure of leadership—though healthy in the long run, frequently result in severe bumps and missteps along the way. Evoking the infallible "invisible hand" from *The Wealth of Nations* (*WN*), Thatcher warned that no one, not even Smith, ever said things were going to be easy. As she figuratively put it, "Adam Smith's 'invisible hand' is not above sudden, disturbing movements."[2] In other words, to Thatcher and other proponents of *laissez-faire*-like policies, business cycles were inevitable, however unpleasant these might be. A few pages later, Thatcher lets the cat out of the bag completely: "It is through this propensity that what Smith calls an 'invisible hand' operates to shape an economic order, whereby the individual pursuit of profit leads to the material benefit of society as a whole."[3] "Economic order," "pursuit of profit," "material benefit"—perhaps no one better than Thatcher could have captured in so few words the conventional wisdom (to borrow a favorite phrase from J.K. Galbraith) of late 20th century Anglo-American economic policies.

The presidency of George W. Bush began innocuously enough in 2001 as he surrounded himself with mostly older cabinet members drawn from the ranks of previous Republican administrations; many of these advisors, however, would be resigning before the end of Bush's first term. Then on September 11 of that year, the country and the world changed with the attack on the World Trade Center and the Pentagon. Mass murder and destruction on American soil were bad enough; what possibly hit the nation hardest over the long term was a paralyzing wave of fear and xenophobia felt by a struggling American middle class, one still being felt to this day. The subsequent "War on Terror," along with expensive U.S. military invasions of Iraq and Afghanistan, proceeded to consume immeasurable billions, perhaps trillions, of dollars while achieving mixed results at best. In the process, traditional civil liberties were willingly traded away and cooperating private contractors, enthusiastically enriched. Any European NATO ally daring to question American judgment and decision-making was either ignored or mocked.[4] France, still a major power with whom the U.S. has never been at war and often allied with during wartime, was particularly vilified, so much so that Bush's weak challenger for re-election in 2004, Senator John Kerry, was ridiculed on national television for looking "French."[5] Adam Smith, a Scottish Francophile inspired while in France to write *WN*, would have been scandalized by the rampant Francophobia in a country that partially owed its successful revolution against Great Britain to timely and committed French military intervention.

In addition to the wasteful and damaging aftershock of 9-11, the worldwide economic downturn of 2007–2008, or "Great Recession" as it came to be popularly known, for many people saw the tenuous or illusory financial gains of the 1980s and 1990s completely erased, in some instances within a matter of months. The dogmatic and extreme deregulatory posture of the second Bush administration led to a general implosion of assets reminiscent of 1929, beginning in the financial, service and manufacturing sectors on which millions depended for a middle class or minimum livelihood.

The unpleasant climax came in September 2008, more or less derailing what should have been an easy Republican retention of the White House. Instead, Democrat Senator Barak Hussein Obama seemed to come out of nowhere within the space of two years to become the first elected African-American President, taking the oath of office in early 2009. Obama, despite his superb education and manifest good intentions, was curiously ineffective at dealing with energized and recalcitrant congressional opposition which, notwithstanding media portrayals, has in fact accomplished its main goal by simply blocking or stalling most of the new administration's legislative agenda.

The great exception—and a battle still being waged as this is written—was the Patient Protection and Affordable Care Act of 2010, a highly diluted and imperfect attempt by the U.S. to catch up with the rest of the civilized world by offering some form of minimal, universal health insurance. Rather than focus on replacing the staggering (and growing) number of jobs lost, Obama spent what little political capital he had available on reforming the American health care system, surely representing (at least in part) a memorial to his late mother who had suffered at the hands of a dysfunctional and unjust status quo. FDR was frequently held up as a role model, but hardly emulated in practice. Meanwhile in the U.S., the two things which Adam Smith had deplored the most, lower standards of living combined with higher concentrations of wealth, have continued to play out on a wider, unprecedented scale in more recent years.

Though less significant in the overall scheme of things, Scotland's popular vote on September 18, 2014, to retain its membership within the United Kingdom (versus independent statehood), is interesting within the context of Smith's Scottish legacy. Despite widespread punditry offering various explanations for the decisive outcome of that memorable referendum, the driving force behind the average Scotsman's desire to remain a British subject was relatively simple. Reduced to its essence, the vote ultimately came down to how many Scots still wanted to take advantage of the British social welfare system, particularly with respect to health care, and the answer still was (and still is), the majority (over 55 percent), especially those over 30 years of age. It had been a cherished and well-tested system that even Margaret Thatcher in her heyday had dared not over-tamper with. Adam Smith would have been in favor of continued union as well, even though universal health care was an unknown concept in his day. Smith liked being a British subject because it advanced his career, provided him with a decent livelihood, and allowed him some spare time to do other things besides work-work, as it had done for his father before him. Smith also liked the old feudal Scottish nobility being held in check by British union. Nevertheless, in the weeks leading up to the vote, Adam Smith's name was publicly dropped by both sides as being either in favor or being against union, even though he had been dead for 224 years by this point in time.[6] Speculations over where the Scottish economic icon would have hypothetically stood on the issue in fact received more media exposure than how independence may have affected the national sport of golf (in terms of making it more affordable for the booming tourist trade).[7]

Many a commentator across the entire spectrum of political opinion has noted that Adam Smith was far more than a founding founder of modern economic thought; he was first and foremost—and this can never be dismissed or discounted—a moral philosopher. The origins of Smith's individual moral or religious beliefs are anyone's guess, but this is as convenient a place as any to briefly examine how his early childhood may have shaped these defining traits. As noted in chapter 4, Smith was briefly abducted as an infant by gypsies, and this could possibly explain the psychological affinity he displays for smugglers in *WN*, particularly Book V, Chapter II, Part I. Even before this close encounter with fate, however, Smith had been born a posthumous child, whose father, Adam Smith Senior, had passed away approximately two months before the birth of his famous son. Thus Smith came of age in Kirkaldy without a father figure and, not too surprisingly, became very attached throughout life to his attentive widowed mother. Moreover, the reality of a "fatherless world" would continue to haunt him, spilling over into his adult philosophical musings, at least in the broader religious sense. It may well have been this deep-rooted insecurity which, as a university student at Oxford, eventually led him to the unorthodox writings of fellow Scotsman David Hume, and likely as well into the Deist camp of religious thought so prevalent among prominent thinkers of that era. Nevertheless, taken as whole, Smith's limited, recorded expressions in regard to personal religious beliefs are difficult to precisely gauge, and have indeed proven subsequent fodder for substantial debate among scholars and specialists.

The closest Smith ever came to publicly expressing personal religious beliefs was in *The Theory of Moral Sentiments* (*TMS*), with a famous series of paragraphs in Chapter VI, Section II, Part III ("Of Universal Benevolence"). In contrasting religious faith with philosophic principles, he underscores the latter as being no adequate substitute in terms of offering personal happiness or peace of mind:

> This universal benevolence, how noble and generous soever, can be the source of no solid happiness, to any man who is not thoroughly convinced that all the inhabitants of the universe, the meanest as well as the greatest, are under the immediate care and protection of that great, benevolent, and all-wise Being, who directs all the movements of nature; and who is determined, by his own unalterable perfections, to maintain it, at all times, the greatest possible quantity of happiness. To this universal benevolence, on the contrary, the very suspicion of a fatherless world, must be the most melancholy of all reflections; from the thought that all the unknown regions of infinite and incomprehensible space may be filled with nothing but endless misery and wretchedness.[8]

These hardly appear to be the sentiments of an anti-religious "infidel"—as some of Smith's critics such as James Boswell characterized him; and yet, a close read reveals the author to be ultimately noncommittal on the topic of faith.[9]

Smith's caution was understandable, given that his friend David Hume had not too long previous incurred sharp institutional wrath (which probably damaged his career) by writing on the same subject matter more freely. More firmly documented is that Smith, during his unhappy student days at Oxford University, was censured for being caught reading one of Hume's works. This unpleasant experience, one so unjust in its motivation and consequences, surely provided negative reinforcement towards the young Smith's already suspicious attitude towards institutionalized religion, as well as giving him a lifelong affinity with another famous Scottish philosopher.

Sometime before Smith released the first edition of *TMS* in 1759, he made another murky reference to humankind's propensity for religious faith in the unseen, if not monotheist belief, in his lecture and essay posthumously published as *The History of Astronomy*. Strikingly, he made this same reference in tandem with one of his three known written expressions of the celebrated phrase "invisible hand." To make the context even more noteworthy, *History of Astronomy* belongs to a very small group of early lecture-essays that Smith saw fit for preservation and publication under his own name, as opposed to the destruction and oblivion which he ordered his executors to carry out for many other unpublished papers after his death. The essay itself is a lengthy meditation on the various psychological and emotional impulses causing intelligent beings to contemplate the visible universe over the course of recorded history, especially in the innovative, groundbreaking wake of proto-Enlightenment English scientist Isaac Newton (1642–1727).[10] More specifically in this case, Smith dwells upon the natural human tendency to ascribe any natural phenomena otherwise seemingly inexplicable to the inscrutable will of divinity.

Unlike his later isolated references to an "invisible hand" in *WN* and *TMS*, Smith's *History of Astronomy* uses the phrase in a fairly unambiguous, pagan religious sense, but not necessarily in a reverential tone. Smith's "invisible hand of Jupiter"—not God or Jehovah or Yahweh—is the alleged force of an ancient, polytheistic chief deity coming into play only when human intellect is puzzled or, to be more precise, taken off guard. Once someone the caliber of a Newton came along to explain the previously inexplicable, however, there was no more invisible hand, only the immutable laws of nature and science.[11] Students in Smith's classrooms must have been delighted; Scottish clergymen less so. In the same essay, Smith later reverently mentions "the Creator of all things," but the usage is more in the classic Deist sense of the term, that is to say, a far cry from the Presbyterian image of God adopted by the Church of Scotland, the same institution which had then of late seriously considered declaring David Hume a religious heretic.[12] Smith's citation of Jupiter's invisible hand in this particular instance mainly comes across as ironic or tongue in cheek at best; at worst, subtle sarcasm.

In terms of ongoing Smithian scholarship, the 21st century began with a challenging reassessment of Smith's intentions by a leading academic. On the eve of the 9-11 attacks, British-born historian Emma Georgina Rothschild, closely associated with both Harvard and Cambridge universities, published an elegant treatise titled *Economic Sentiments: Adam Smith, Condorcet and the Enlightenment* (2001). The second moniker in the title referred to Smith's younger contemporary, the French philosopher Nicolas de Caritat, Marquis de Condorcet (1743–1794), who late in life had assisted with the translation of *WN* into French.[13] Rothschild's central thesis, or at least her most controversial point, is developed in Chapter 5 of her work, subtitled "The Bloody and Invisible Hand"—a near direct quotation from Shakespeare's *Macbeth* (III.ii.48), a play written and performed well over a century before Smith was even born.[14] Smith's work, Rothschild maintained—like any work of any important writer—should be studied within the context of the time and place in which that writer wrote. Within the ever-changing field of political economy, the suggestion seems especially pertinent.

Rothschild also posited that, lacking this essential contextualization, many past interpretations of Smith, especially with respect to his vaunted "invisible hand," are either too shallow, completely wrong, or both. Like a growing minority of commentators, she felt that Smith's use of the phrase was probably intended to be ironic. The book in effect sought to address the old lament made by Beatrice Webb during the 19th century that Smith's humanist philosophy had been somehow hijacked and twisted. As for Smith himself, there can be little doubt that he knew Shakespeare's "Scottish Play" quite well, not only as a classics scholar and lover of the theatre, but as a Scotsman as well. *Economic Sentiments* was widely reviewed upon its released; numerous critics reacted with energetic outrage while those who dared to praise it were often in turn attacked themselves. Rothschild is not a politician or even a politically influential academic, but her fresh interpretation of *WN* did manage to create a huge ripple effect within the world of book-chat, and this in turn soon spilled over into the realm of British politics. More recent commentators such as Nobel Prize-winning economist Joseph Stiglitz have gone even further, maintaining that "Adam Smith's invisible hand ... is invisible ... because it is not there."[15]

The year 2006 saw the passing of both John Kenneth Galbraith and Milton Friedman. Friedman outlived his old rival by less than seven months.

The American economy, despite the re-election of W. Bush and ongoing, astronomical expenditures in the Middle East, seemed to be stabilizing, if not occasionally prospering. Mercifully, neither Galbraith nor Friedman lived to see the cruel downturn soon to transpire. Both would have had plenty to say about it, one can be sure. The same period saw a flurry of new Adam Smith biographies or studies, including *Adam Smith's Lost Legacy* (2005) by Gavin Kennedy, *The Authentic Adam Smith* (2006) by James Buchan, and P.J. O'Rourke's silly yet profound *On The Wealth of Nations* (2007). More serious and lengthy works soon appeared after the world economy tanked. These included the second edition of Ian Simpson Ross's *Life of Adam Smith* (2010), a significant update of his first edition from 1995, and then soon afterwards, Nicholas Phillipson's imposing *Adam Smith: An Enlightened Life* (2012). Despite an apparent market glut for these books, they continue to be written, purchased, and read (witness this own modest effort). In short, it appears that as the 300th anniversary of Smith's birth approaches in 2023 (now less than a decade away), his legacy only seems to grow in importance and contemporary relevance, despite the fact that the pre-capitalist world he personally knew has since completely transformed into nearly unrecognizable dimensions and permutations.

Although W. Bush was the first President to hold an MBA degree (from Harvard), and despite world-class educational opportunities throughout life, he never professed much concern for historical business precedents, let alone the past works of major economists. W.'s apparent lack of interest, however, may have been feigned for perceived political purposes.[16] This was far less the case with his successor. Upon taking office, Obama immediately sought outside help for containing the economic downturn, an endeavor for which he clearly lacked personal experience and training. One of the first people he brought into the fold was former Federal Reserve Chairman Paul Volcker as part of his Economic Recovery Advisory Board. Surprisingly, Volcker began by citing Adam Smith as authority for his opinion that banks should not be too big to fail and that smaller banks were more desirable in general. This philosophy was in turn incorporated into the "Volcker Rule" of the 2010 Dodd-Frank Act forbidding various kinds of speculative investments for government-insured lending institutions.[17] Volcker's proposal, or perhaps his unexpected citation of Smith, ruffled many feathers within the banking industry, despite his longstanding reputation as an honest (if sometimes heavy-handed) regulator. It took nearly another four years for Congress to work out the details of a relatively straightforward plan which simply disallowed irresponsible behavior largely causing the financial crisis in the first place. Rather than being sent to jail for their crimes, perpetrators were allowed to push back.[18] To analogize, it was if the infamous John Law of Smith's youth had been asked by Parliament to shape legislation in wake of the economic panic he personally instigated. Smith would have likely been left speechless at such a thing.

Obama's Republican Presidential challengers in 2012 were former Massachusetts Governor Mitt Romney and Wisconsin Congressman Paul Ryan, both of whom saw fit to drop Adam Smith's name while on the campaign trail. In response to a general question about good versus bad capitalism, Romney quipped "I think Adam Smith was right," praising the "invisible hand" of the market place versus the "heavy hand of government"—even though modern capitalism did not exist during Smith's time, and Smith expressly advocated government intervention in many specific instances.[19] This was noteworthy as an instance in which a U.S. presidential candidate felt a need to agree with Adam Smith while seeking election.

Republican V.P. nominee Ryan was a bit more scholarly (nowadays a startling trait in any candidate for public office), producing a P.R. tract titled *Roadmap to America's Future*, in which he made reference not only to Smith's *WN*, but to *TMS* as well, possibly a first ever for the latter within the American political sphere.[20] Although Ryan's *Roadmap* received a fair amount of media attention, his mention of Smith's *TMS* drew nothing but bewildered silence in terms of public response, even from his many critics. This was not too surprisingly in and of itself; however, the very fact that he or his ghost writers took the trouble to link Smith's economic theories with his moral philosophy was a refreshing change. It would be interesting to see if anyone had pressed Ryan (which no one did), on what exactly that precise link happened to be, how he would have responded. Nevertheless, this incident, which took the form of a carefully planned and edited document for public consumption during a contemporary presidential campaign, probably reflected modest progress of sorts, though with a very low bar to begin with.

British politics of the 21st century have been similarly turbulent with Adam Smith's legacy evoked just as often, if not more frequently, as in the United States. While the Labour Party-led government of Tony Blair passed the torch along to new Prime Minister Gordon Brown in 2007, Great Britain found itself with a Scottish-born leader coming of age in Smith's very own hometown of Kirkaldy, Scotland.[21] As one might expect, Brown like to tout Smith as the "hero of the Scottish Enlightenment" while attempting to reclaim *WN* as an economic manifesto for the British political left.[22] Three years later in 2010, however, the Conservative Party regained power under its comparatively young Prime Minister David Cameron, currently still holding the office. During the recent loud debate over Scottish Independence, Cameron's party came under fire from Scotland's pro-independence First Minister Alex Salmond, accusing the British Conservative government of what it has often been accused of over the centuries, namely, favoring the interests of the few over those of the many:

> It was Adam Smith who said that no society can flourish and be happy if too many of its people do not benefit from its wealth. We need to heed those words—and the message from Scotland's job and wealth creators today is that the land of Adam Smith will flourish as an independent country.[23]

Alas (as previously noted), the great majority of Scottish voters preferred British socialized medicine and other safety net provisions over any promises or reassurances from Scotland's "job and wealth creators." This majority attitude is not likely to change anytime soon, unless Great Britain's welfare state, an impressive creation of the postwar Labour Party, should suddenly and unexpectedly collapse.

Political bombast aside, today the name of Adam Smith is most closely associated with the vicissitudes of international trade. It was the contradictions and abuses flowing from international commerce across several continents which triggered the central historical event of Smith's own era, the American Revolution. In the year 2015, arguably the most visible, physical symbol of modern, borderless commerce can be seen at Ground Zero in New York City with the recently-completed One World Trade Center. At 104 standard stories high, the new WTC is currently the tallest building in the western hemisphere.[24] Following the 9-11 attacks, the original 2002 design concept provided by celebrity architect Daniel Lebeskind was later revised by David Childs of Skidmore, Owings & Merrill, with construction topping out 2012 and the building open for business by late 2014. Although critics of the end result are plentiful and easy to find, no one can deny that the finished product does anything less than completely dwarf all which preceded it, including the destroyed twin towers formerly located on the same site.[25] For better or worse, the entire process, from start to finish, took a little over 13 rather symbolic years.[26] In this lengthy, drawn-out respect, the development of One World Trade Center has been not unlike the ever-evolving War on Terror itself.

Casual observers may well attribute a quasi-religious or spiritual aspect to the second WTC development, perhaps appropriate since devotees of practically every major world religion died during the attack. Adam Smith, had he witnessed the tragedy, would have provided clear explanations from *TMS* as to why the United States (and the victims) received so much worldwide sympathy immediately after the event, as well as why and how that international sympathy was so quickly squandered afterwards. Smith would have also recognized the public impetus creating the memorial and edifice after the fact. Tall buildings and monumental structures tend to reflect true social priorities. Only the size and scale of these have grown larger over time. Whereas Glasgow Cathedral towered over the same city during Adam Smith's academic days there during the 1750s, One World Trade Center now dominates the skyline of America's largest city while bearing a name instantly calling to mind the secular commercial forces first causing it to come into being, then targeted by criminal malcontents for that very same reason, and finally rebuilt to even more colossal proportions, all the while retaining its original namesake and designated function.

America and the world in 2015, to put it mildly, have become quite different places from those known to Smith some three centuries ago. In different senses, they are both much larger and much smaller than they used to be, even compared to only a century ago when the Great War sent a similar unpleasant shock wave through the modern consciousness. Now we are immeasurably bigger in terms of population, infrastructure, production, trade, and the very accumulation of wealth itself. On the other hand, previously unimaginable advances in communication, transport, and artificial intelligence have transformed the world into a smaller, more competitive, and more volatile planet.

Counterintuitively, this closer interconnectedness has caused many people across the globe, at least those possessing the resources, to retreat further away from fellow beings via the Internet and other forms of electronic, virtual media, both for purposes of work and leisure. As technology continues to advance at a dazzling pace—the same advanced technology so respected by Smith as a benchmark for military and economic supremacy—new questions arise. For example, with our ability to now purchase almost anything from anywhere utilizing portable laptop computers, what exactly is "foreign" trade? If a product we purchase is partially constructed in half a dozen different countries, including our own, what is "domestic" manufacturing? If capital can now move globally across national borders at will, then are nation-states even relevant anymore, except as regional police forces for the moneyed interests which they appear to serve? And so forth. Meanwhile, Smith's authority is quoted or paraphrased more than ever as being for against this economic policy or another, although the actual number of readers perusing his texts is doubtful. As to what the near or distant economic future may hold for humanity, no one can really say. If Adam Smith were still alive, however, it is a safe bet that he would have an opinion on the matter worth consulting.

Summary

"But the rate of profit does not, like rent and wages, rise with the prosperity, and fall with the declension, of the society. On the contrary, it is naturally low in rich, and high in poor countries, and it is always highest in the countries which are going fastest to ruin."—Adam Smith[1]

What would Adam Smith make of today's complex and highly interconnected global economy? Hard to say, since our world is so utterly different from that which he knew. And yet there are similarities. It is likely that he would continue to espouse the core ideals articulated in *The Wealth of Nations* (*WN*) and *The Theory of Moral Sentiments* (*TMS*)—namely, freedom of trade in tandem with ethical obligations of humankind towards each other, the latter far superseding any individual motivations of monetary profit or political liberty. More intriguing still is the unknown side of Adam Smith, the philosophical part of him which probably went up in flames after his death by his express direction to his executors to burn his unpublished writings. Bits and pieces, however, come down to us through legend and anecdote. Indeed, this unknown aspect of Smith's thought, possibly never resolved in his own mind, may hold the key to how he would have reacted to the perplexities of modern life.

In essence, *TMS* was about abstract moral issues (as well as how these are formulated and put into practice), while *WN* dealt with real world economic realities outside the walls of academia. Smith certainly had plenty of personal experience with both. Is it possible that his projected, never-completed works would have attempted some great fusion or extension of the first two? We will obviously never know. This writer will venture speculation that had Smith witnessed the horrors of 9–11 or fallout of the Great Recession, as well as various responses to these events, he would have explanations, as well as recommendations, based largely upon what he had already written and published. In other words, much of *WN* and *TMS* still seem surprisingly applicable to us in the 21th century.

Contextualization, on the other hand (and despite its literary importance), can also have severe limits. In his recent perceptive study of *WN*, humorist P.J. O'Rourke summarizes a list of big issues from Smith's time that still find wide resonance today: "law and order, political pork, failures of the educational system, religion in politics, burgeoning national debt, runaway defense spending."[2] Nevertheless, in spite of these similarities, Smith wrote in a completely different time period during which Great Britain and the United States had not yet formally split apart over trade issues and parliamentary representation. The Industrial Revolution was still in its infancy. Truly modern capitalism, the type of which Marx and Dickens later wrote about so critically, did not yet exist. Complete dominance of the political process by business corporations and wealthy robber barons, becoming so prevalent by the end of the 19th century, had yet to transpire. The English language itself (in which Smith wrote), though ascendant in world affairs, had not yet become the undisputed language of international trade and commerce. Anglo-American dominance of the New World, though widely acknowledged after British victory in the French and Indian War, was still relatively recent and far from being taken for granted by anyone.[3] As for today's global economy, the differences between now and then are too numerous and profound to catalogue within this limited space, even were it necessary to do so. One hypothetical question naturally presenting itself, however, is what if the United States and Great Britain had not separated in 1776? What if, say, Great Britain had avoided the American Revolution, not by force of arms, but rather by granting colonial representation in Parliament and reigning in the greed of its own mercantile special interests?[4] Would a united Anglo-American political entity, no matter how diffuse, face the identical and seemingly intractable problems that these separate cultures face today? These questions would appear worth asking, given that nowadays every regional state or local principality frequently claims the inalienable right to independent political sovereignty, in addition to freedom of international trade.[5]

Having recently queried both politically liberal and conservative acquaintances on what they first and foremost associated with Adam Smith, both groups and everyone in between responded with "The Invisible Hand"; yet, all seemed to share the same misconceptions as to what Smith precisely meant by the phrase, at least for the single instance of its usage within *WN*. Most appeared to think of the concept as a defense of *laissez-faire* economic policy, or "leave it alone and everything will take of itself." A few thought of it as the invisible or unseen hand of divinity which would in turn cause all things to work out for the best in the final scheme of things—the sort of notion that Voltaire mocked so ruthlessly during Smith's time. No one saw the phrase as being ironic in any sense, or as an economic principle of unintended consequences, or applicable only to a very narrow set of circumstances. Then again, none of the individuals queried admitted to having read Smith within the last 20 years, if at all, nor did anyone express interest in revisiting or consulting the text itself. Nothing is more difficult to change (or fix), it would seem, than a faulty education or, for that matter, a thorough indoctrination. If nothing else, this questionable state of affairs within the American body politic underscores Smith's lengthy, passionate emphasis in *WN* on public education at taxpayers' expense. Regarding his own political categorization, if that is at all relevant or even possible with contemporary terminology, "hardheaded liberal" would seem to be just as accurate a descriptor for Smith as the "compassionate conservative" label so frequently applied to him.[6] After all, Smith, as a teacher and loyal British subject, exalted personal education, moral fairness, and duty to society far more than individual liberty or accumulation of wealth, however so much he often praised the latter two items.

Smith's liveliest prose gives some indication as to why he was such a popular teacher among his students. Many a modern reader, including some politicians, have been more impressed with Smith's considerable skill at written expression than the rather imposing substance of his works. Nowhere are Smith's writing talents better on display than in Book I, Chapter II, of *WN* ("Origin of Division of Labour") in which he asserts that "the propensity to truck, barter, and exchange" is the main essential quality setting humankind apart from the animal kingdom.[7] With respect to specialized human skills, he notes that true differences between, say, a philosopher and a street porter relate mainly to "habit, custom, and education," and that these differences are otherwise far less extreme than those between different breeds of dogs.[8] So much for the miraculous division of labor, according to Smith. Nor does he stop there. By Book V he warns what division of labor can lead to if taken to its logical, unmoderated extreme, namely, the breakdown of democratic political process.

As for 18th century technologies (primitive by modern standards), Smith acknowledges its essentiality in warfare, and implicitly links it to efficient production, but goes no further than that. Today, two and a half centuries later, staggering technological advancements have surely changed many if not most of the underlying economic assumptions Smith was working with during the late 1760s and early 1770s. If globalization has proven anything over the last generation or two, it has demonstrated that product affordability usually trumps product quality in the marketplace. In this strategic sense, with respect to technological innovation, it would seem usually better for an entrepreneur to be slightly behind the cutting edge of progress rather than right upon the edge itself, particularly in terms of patents and copyrights. Worst of all, there is now a widespread (and far from imagined) sense of anxiety that technology generally kills more jobs than it creates.[9] If all of this is true, then it bodes ill for the traditional Anglo-American workforce, typically in the past trained (if at all) for highly specialized tasks which may well come and go within a single lifetime. Moreover (and more dire for society), large segments of this workforce appear unable or unwilling to adapt to these rapid changes in terms of job retention.

Much has been written in recent years about the distribution or redistribution of wealth, its growing inequality and, far more worrisome, growing inequity based on merit. This was another big contemporary issue barely on Smith's radar, but a close read of *WN* makes it clear what he would have said on the topic. Smith was not impressed by high profit margins. For that matter, sprinkled throughout *WN* are remarks normally disconcerting for anyone trying to confine Smith's thinking to within their own narrow confines. His contempt or hatred of feudalism, with its inherent appropriation of huge resources by a small number of individuals ("the vile maxim"), is hard to miss for any reader paying half attention. Smith does not comment upon minimum wage law, except to mischievously observe that "We have no acts of parliament against combining to lower the price of work; but many against combining to raise it."[10] Prospects for meaningful change in this regard are unrealistic, he suggests, because "Civil government ... is in reality instituted for the defence of the rich against the poor, or of those who have some property against those who have none at all."[11]

Perhaps most significant of all, contemporary economists addressing current affairs frequently dispense with "What would Adam Smith say?" altogether. Noteworthy books in recent years such as Enrico Moretti's *The New Geography of Jobs* (2012) and Thomas Piketty's *Capital in the Twenty-First Century* (2014) make little or no mention of Smith.[12] This is perhaps just as well. It is definitely time to break new ground in the field of economics. Nevertheless, as one reads these pathfinding works, one repeatedly hears echoes of Smith's thought, acknowledgment of which is probably unnecessary, yet reassuringly there regardless, especially if the author has any kind of background in moral philosophy, as most economists once did.

As many would hopefully agree, the most disturbing socioeconomic development over the last generation has been a sharp rise in political extremism worldwide. The best place to begin any truthful examination of this alarming trend is within the United States itself. While considerable amounts of media attention have been directed towards racial and religious minorities, illegal immigrants, welfare cheats, inner-city crime, and various imaginary threats to middle class well-being, the real (and mainly unreported) story in the U.S. during the last half century has been the startling proliferation of an entirely new underclass, especially in rural areas, many of whom are surprisingly numerous and politically active. The profile is familiar: mostly white, formerly middle class, formerly employed in construction, manufacturing, or "turbulent" (in the words of Margaret Thatcher) sectors of the service economy, heavily-armed, not particularly well-educated, unwilling to retrain or do menial tasks, and completely frightened, with some good reason, of the outside world since the new global economy has little to offer them. The more fortunate ones have female members of the household holding steady employment for less pay than the male formerly earned at a since-downsized job. Insensible of the hidden forces reducing their standards of living and quality of life, they tend to be angry in general, viewing anything visibly alien as a convenient scapegoat. To them, any recent arrival in their native land, whether it be good or bad, simply represents more competition. Entertainment, especially spectator sports, talk radio, network television, internet social media, and inexpensive alcoholic beverages are all crucially important to this demographic. They do not read Adam Smith.

Smith's reaction to this new underclass, if he were still around, would likely be similar to his attitude towards the feudalistic Highlanders defeated at Culloden by the British Army in 1746 (see Chapter 3). Many Jacobites who died in the rebel ranks were, in Smith's view, little more than serfs to the powerful feudal lords whom they served under, notwithstanding their own defiant self-image as free men. Though many nowadays cloak their beliefs under the Tea Party banner or whatever label happens to be fashionable at the moment, most could not in fact be more indentured to the moneyed special interests paying them a menial wage and subsidizing their political activities. Unlike the original American colonists, the modern-day Tea Party (or however one chooses to characterize the extreme political right), including their wealthy financiers, already has plenty of legislative representation. More stunningly, and contrary to common media portrayals, a good part of this representation has been legitimately achieved without any district gerrymandering or disenfranchisement of potential voters. Elected federal and local government officials merely reflect an accurate image of their voter constituents, however unpleasant or unflattering that image may happen to be.[13]

Despite this fearful situation, it seems more than likely that from the same aforementioned, disaffected group will eventually arise a few voices of reason, possibly even good leaders, to counteract all of the bad ones currently dominating public discourse. Some will in fact come to their senses eventually—the real question is whether their numbers will be significant enough to save the country. A few of these may even pick up a text by Adam Smith, actually read it, and be surprised, enlightened, or inspired in the process. Old books can still sometimes make a difference. One of America's leading historians, the Scots-Irish descended David McCullough, author of the Pulitzer Prize-winning biography of Founding Father John Adams, once quipped that "I've gotten so fascinated with the eighteenth century, I'm going to stay there ... I may never come back."[14] McCullough published his inspirational portrayal of Adams in 2001, just as world history was about to alter its course. His expressed sentiments still resonate. While Adam Smith lived, thought, and wrote within an entirely different historical context, much of his work is (to repeat) still highly relevant to our times, and if nothing else, that same historical context is crucial to understanding the beginnings of our republic. After all, in the paraphrased words of a great poet-philosopher from the 20th century, those who forget history are condemned to repeat it.[15]

Chapter Notes

Introduction

1. Taken from speech by Twain given in 1900, "The Disappearance of Literature." See http://www.twainquotes.com/Classic.html.
2. Regarding Great Britain and the American colonies, Smith concluded that "total separation ... seems very likely." See *WN*, V.III, 1205.
3. For example, Smith's admiration for an unnamed but unmistakable David Hume can be found in *TMS*, IV.I.2, among other places.
4. Smith wrote mostly from Scotland during the years leading up to the American Revolution of 1776; (nearly) complete Scottish union with Great Britain had been formalized much earlier in 1707, at which point the "United Kingdom" or "first" British Empire came into existence. For purposes of this study, the term "Great Britain" will be used to describe the official British government working initially in opposition to the United States and then much later as a close military and economic ally.
5. Buchan, 127.
6. Galbraith, *The Affluent Society* (Houghton Mifflin, 1958), 26.
7. Buchan, 2.
8. Phrase attributed to Scottish philosopher Thomas Carlyle (1795–1881), who at one point was a teacher in Smith's hometown of Kirkaldy.
9. O'Rourke, 26.
10. *TMS*, VI.III.54.
11. For example, Plutarch was clearly one of Smith's favorite classical authors. The updated English translation of Plutarch by John Dryden had been published in 1683. *TMS* also opens with multiple references to Shakespeare. See *TMS*, I.1.4 & I.I.11.
12. *TMS*, IV.I.10.
13. *Ibid*.
14. Buchan, 136.
15. Chomsky, Noah, *Power Systems: Conversations on Global Democratic Uprisings and the New Challenges to U.S. Empire*, Interviews with David Barsamian (Metropolitan Books, 2013), 8. Like many others, I am indebted to Professor Chomsky's insistent emphasis on this theme over the course of many decades, first encountered by myself over 30 years ago, during the height of the 1980s and Smith's American political elevation to iconic stature. It then occurred to be for the first time that some of Smith's most intriguing passages were rarely or never quoted. The very title of this study was suggested by Chomsky's longstanding quotation of Smith's original and powerful turn of phrase.
16. O'Rourke, 47.
17. Buchan, 91.
18. For an exhaustive if somewhat tedious study of this topic, see William D. Grampp's "What Did Smith Mean by the Invisible Hand?" from the *Journal of Political Economy*, 2000, Vol. 108. No. 3. Smith's first usage of the phrase, though the last one published chronologically, was from his early essay *The History of Astronomy* (see Chapter 18).
19. See Swift's poem *A Ballad, to the Tune of the Cut-Purse* (1702). One reading is that Swift's "invisible hand" refers to a ghost writer.
20. *WN*, III.IV, 525. Note: all page number references to *WN* within this text will use the Bantam Books/Random House edition from 2003.
21. *WN*, IV.II, 572.
22. *Ibid*.
23. The very first biographical sketch of Smith was by his younger Scottish contemporary Dugald Stewart in 1793 (see Chapter 3).
24. For example, in 2011, Oxford University Press published two fairly well-received books on this topic: *The Moral Foundation of Economic Behavior* by David Rose and *Economics of Good and Evil: The Quest for Economic Meaning from Gilgamesh to Wall Street* by Tomas Sedlacek.
25. Borrowing a subtitle from Lewis Carroll's second-most famous book seems appropriate in this case. Special thanks to our good friend Charmian Akins (1922–2015) for long ago suggesting

this idea in reference to widespread, passive acceptance of misinformation by the American body politic.

Chapter 1

1. Smith, *TMS* VI.II.46.
2. Native Americans, correctly surmising that the colonists represented bad news to their long-term interests and safety, generally sided with the French during this conflict, hence the popular name of the war.
3. Smith ruefully records the astonishing and unprecedented combined financial cost of these wars to the British Empire. Then he provocatively points out that the interest payments alone on the newly incurred national debt incurred was less than the total profits gained from American trade that the war itself was supposed to protect. See Smith, *WN* IV.VIII, 841. See also VI.III, 1207.
4. *WN* (Krueger intro), xiv–xv.
5. *WN* (Krueger intro), xxii.
6. To be more precise, Smith probably owed his government appointment to a recommendation from his former traveling pupil, the Duke of Buccleuch. The time demands of the appointment also effectively prevented Smith from writing any more books, which may have also been a motivation for his benefactors.
7. Smith's annuity income of £300 was now supplemented by an annual salary of £600. See Rae, 321.
8. As has been well documented, the young George Washington's fighting skills were influenced by and honed during the earlier French and Indian conflict, particularly with respect to the asymmetrical tactics often successfully employed by Native Americans against the British Army.
9. Artistic representations of Valley Forge typically include the French Marquis de Lafayette standing faithfully at General Washington's side during the harsh winter. Since the French were official American allies by this point, the symbolism becomes quite literal.
10. *WN* IV.VII, Part III, 791.
11. Smith in fact never uses the phrase *laissez-faire* in *WN*, another indication that he did not accept the idea wholesale, as is sometimes claimed.
12. *WN* IV.VII, Part III, 782. See also V.III, 1204.
13. *WN* IV.VII, Part III, 782–783.
14. *WN* IV.VII, Part III, 789–790.
15. *WN* V.III, 1208.
16. *WN* IV.VIII, Part III, 727.
17. *WN* IV.VII, Part III, 729.
18. *WN* IV.VIII, 839.
19. *WN* (Krueger intro), 22.
20. A brief summary of these influences can be found in Chapter 5 of *Adam Smith and the Origins of American Enterprise* by Roy C. Smith (St. Martin's Press, 2004).
21. Franklin was arguably the greatest self-made man in modern history. Not only did he make himself wealthy, famous, and a respected intellectual worldwide, he also was instrumental in recreating his own native country.
22. Good discussions of the known facts behind this crucial interaction between Franklin and Smith can be found in "The Relations between Adam Smith and Benjamin Franklin before 1776" by Thomas D. Eliot, *Political Science Quarterly*, Vol. 39, No. 1 (March 1924), 67–96, and *Benjamin Franklin and the University of Pennsylvania*, Issue 2, by Francis Newton Thorpe (U.S. Government Printing Office, 1893).
23. See *Adam Smith: Critical Assessments*, edited by John Cunningham Wood, Vol. I, "The Life of Adam Smith and Perspectives on His Thought" (Routledge, 1984), 784.
24. Rae, 287.
25. Smith in fact owed his new appointment to none other than Lord North, who by late 1777 appears to have been borrowing ideas from *WN* for implementing new domestic taxes. See Rae, XVIII.15. North may have also shrewdly believed that the best way to keep a man of Smith's caliber under close control was to employ him, rather than persecute him.
26. This important case is currently headed for a federal court decision. See http://www.pbs.org/newshour/bb/health/july-dec13/drugs_12-31.html.
27. In a very real sense, the Far East tea trade helped to build the British Empire, then spark the American Revolution. As for the modern-day Tea Party, it has little to do with tea per se.
28. The entire series of mezzotints may be conveniently perused, along with exhaustive commentary, in *The Boston Port Bill as Pictured by a Contemporary London Cartoonist*, published by R.T.H. Halsey (Grolier Club, 1904).
29. The overall effect is similar to recent media portrayals of unruly protests by the modern-day Tea Party in favor of the 2013 federal government shutdown in Washington, D.C.
30. This is an English paraphrase from *The Leopard* by Italian novelist Giuseppe Tomasi di Lampedusa.
31. See the concluding sentence to *WN*, V.III, 1208.

Chapter 2

1. *WN*, V.III, 1193–1194. Smith included most alcoholic beverages as luxuries. See *WN*, V.II, Part II, Article 4th, 1103–1104.

2. See Smith, Roy C., *Adam Smith and the Origins of American Enterprise* (St. Martin's Press, 2004), 188, 190–191.

3. This was from Jefferson's letter to Thomas Mann Randolph. See http://www.monticello.org/site/research-and-collections/wealth-nations.

4. Smith, Roy C., 188.

5. Washington was a reader, though; for example, he was known to be fond of quoting Shakespeare.

6. Buchan, 128.

7. Smith, Roy C., 50, 97–98.

8. Rae, XVIII.15.

9. According to Dugald Stewart, Petty told him that Smith had converted him to his free trade theory via conversation as early as 1761. This was not only long before *WN* had been published, but also before Smith's tour of France during which he is believed to have begun writing *WN*. If true, this would lend support to the speculative view that Smith's opinions on free trade had been formulated much earlier on, perhaps as early as his student days at the University of Glasgow under Francis Hutcheson. It would also help to explain theoretical affinities between *WN* and *TMS*.

10. Rae, XVIII.10.

11. Amazed and disgusted, Smith later wrote: "A single, and as, I thought a very harmless Sheet of paper, which I happened to Write concerning the death of our late friend Mr. Hume, brought upon me ten times more abuse than the very violent attack I had made upon the whole commercial system of great Britain." See Buchan, 127.

12. Buchan, 127. For example, the original draft of Smith's letter favorably contrasted Hume's demeanor in the face of death with that of a "Whining Christian." The phrase was sensibly edited out of the published version of the letter.

13. For starters, Johnson as an impoverished young man had been repeatedly denied academic posts due in part to his own incomplete formal education.

14. *WN*, V.I, Part 2, 965.

15. Boswell previously had written: "Smith too is now of our club. It has lost its select merit." See Rae, XVII.5.

16. Ross, 251.

17. Buchan, 171*n*23.

18. Rae, 156.

19. Buchan, 129–130. See also Smith, *Correspondence*, Appendix D. Later in 1779, near the same waters (off the northeast English coast), Jones commanded the French-built *Bonhomme Richard* as it won a dramatic naval victory over HMS *Serapis* ("I have not yet begun to fight!"). The French had named the *Bonhomme Richard* as a tribute to the popular *Poor Richard's Almanac* written by American French ambassador Benjamin Franklin. Less gloriously, in 1778 Jones had raided western Scotland attempting to kidnap the Earl of Selkirk for ransom, but succeeded only in stealing the Earl's household silverware, which he later returned in response to bad publicity.

20. Buchan, 133.

21. Buchan, 134.

22. Buchan, 138.

23. It was also during this last period that Walter Scott later remarked (rather snipingly) about Edinburgh housewives believing Smith to be mentally deranged. See Buchan, 131, 137.

24. Buchan, 143.

25. Buchan, 137.

26. Buchan, 140.

27. This was David Douglas, the future Lord Reston and noted Scottish jurist. See Buchan, 143–144.

28. Buchan, 144–145.

29. *WN*, V.II, 1043.

30. *WN*, V.II, 1094.

31. For example, in a now little-remembered incident from 1769, Jefferson the state representative and his cousin Richard Bland had suffered humiliation before the Virginia royal government much in the same manner that Benjamin Franklin would five years later before the British Privy Council. The issue, ironically enough, was whether prerogatives for slave emancipation ultimately rested with the Crown's official designate or local planters.

32. See *WN*, I.IV, 34 and V.III, 1200–1201.

33. *WN*, V.III, 1201.

34. See http://www.theguardian.com/society/2013/jun/01/thinktanks-big-tobacco-funds-smoking.

Chapter 3

1. *WN*, V.I, 899.

2. Paine, the famed and influential author of *Common Sense* during the American Revolution, accused Burke of lacking Smith's talent and misinterpreting his work. Thus within one year of Smith's death, liberals and conservatives were battling for possession of Smith's intellectual legacy on an international level.

3. See "Hamilton and Adam Smith" by Edward G. Bourne, *The Quarterly Journal of Economics*, Vol. 8, No. 3 (April 1894), 328–344.

4. Washington politically breaking ranks with his fellow Virginians likely stemmed in part from his father-like personal attachment to

Hamilton (see Chapter 2), as well as unpleasant recollections of deprivations suffered by his Continental Army during the Revolution, thanks in no small part to the ineffectiveness of a weak central government.

5. For a balanced discussion of these complex events, see "The Aftermath of Hamilton's 'Report on Manufactures'" by Douglas A. Irwin, *The Journal of Economic History*, Vol. 64, No. 3 (September 2004).

6. Abagail Adams also referred to Hamilton as a "Cassius" (i.e., traitor), which proved to be an accurate descriptor for Hamilton's political relationship with her husband. See *John Adams*, by David McCullough (Simon & Schuster, 2001), 480, 518, 549.

7. Upon learning of Washington's death, Bonaparte reportedly bowed his head in respect, a rare gesture for him. By contrast, Hamilton's death was little mourned at home or abroad. His crucial contributions were not widely or fully appreciated until over half a century later, when the American Civil War necessitated unparalleled financial innovations by the U.S. federal government.

8. Hamilton was eulogized shortly after his death by James Kent specifically for resisting the "fuzzy philosophy" of Adam Smith. See J.K. Galbraith, *The Affluent Society* (Houghton Mifflin, 1958), 12.

9. Some modern estimates for the acquisition cost equate to less than 50 cents per acre, making the Louisiana Purchase arguable the great real estate bargain in history, that is, one achieved without military force or intimidation.

10. The Jay Treaty of 1794, supported by both Hamilton and Washington, normalized trade relations with Great Britain for nearly a decade, before British diplomacy with the U.S. again began to deteriorate during the Jefferson presidency.

11. The sad fact of the matter is that Jefferson himself was far from self-sufficient. His main financial assets consisted of slave labor (see Chapter 4); even so he died insolvent.

12. Thus for the second time in less than four decades, the United States attempted to take Canada by military conquest and failed.

13. There were of course glorious American naval exceptions to British dominance, the most famous being the exploits of the U.S.S. *Constitution* ("*Old Ironsides*"). Still to this day, most of the public buildings in D.C., including the Executive Mansion, are whitewashed in memory of the widely forgotten event that the U.S. capital was once sacked by a British invading force.

14. Aside from Andrew Jackson himself, arguable the most successful American general in this regard was another future President, William Henry Harrison, who defeated and killed Chief Tecumseh on Canadian soil (in southwestern Ontario) in 1813; "The Star-Spangled Banner" was composed by Francis Scott Key after witnessing the British bombardment of Fort McHenry in 1814.

15. DeMille directed the 1938 film and later produced the 1958 film directed by his then son-in-law Anthony Quinn. Fredric March and Yul Brenner each played the role of Lafitte, respectively.

16. Culloden was also the last major battle of any sort fought on Anglo-Scots soil.

17. To Smith, a progressive British loyalist, the Jacobites represented an outmoded system of feudalism. See O'Rourke, 88–89.

18. *WN*, V.I.I, 898–899.
19. *WN*, V.I.I, 899.
20. *WN*, V.I.I., 900.
21. Smith, Roy, 188–190.
22. *WN*, I.XI.I, 202. See also Bourne (Note 2 above), 344.
23. Smith, Roy, 123.
24. Davila's *Istoria* had first been translated into English in 1647.
25. *TMS*, I.III.22. See also John Adams, *The Works of John Adams*, Charles Francis Adams, Editor, Vol. 6 (Boston: Charles C. Little & James Brown, 1851).
26. The Jacobite Rebellion of 1745–1746 had threatened Smith's original hometown of Kirkcaldy, temporarily gained control of his future home, Edinburgh, and extorted money from Glasgow, the city of his alma mater and future professorship. See O'Rourke, 88.
27. This group of Smith's guests included Henry Addington, Pitt's immediate successor as British Prime Minister. See Rae, 405.
28. Buchan, 138.
29. It is interesting that Stewart, an academic, focuses on Smith's credentials as a former academic, rather than his final occupation of 12 years as an appointed customs commissioner in the real world of international commerce.
30. The younger Stewart had also, like Smith, been a former student, and later, philosophy professor at the University of Glasgow.
31. The presumed British trading vessel moored in the background flies the Union Jack.

Chapter 4

1. *WN*, III.II, 493.
2. Whitney must be viewed in hindsight as one of the most unlikely inventors in American history. A northerner (Massachusetts) by birth,

Whitney temporarily landed in Georgia by accident and through invitation from Catherine Greene, widow of Revolutionary War hero General Nathanael Greene. According to tradition, it was at Mulberry Plantation near Savannah where Whitney first developed his cotton gin design. He never personally profited from the venture, went bankrupt, and eventually returned north to earn a living as an arms manufacturer.

3. The fabled Mason-Dixon Line, first establishing the boundary between southern Pennsylvania and northern Maryland, had been established during the colonial mid-1760s through a commissioned team led by British astronomer Charles Mason and British surveyor Jeremiah Dixon. Both were rough contemporaries of Smith, who around that same time period was receiving his own second education of sorts while touring France (see Chapter 1).

4. Former President James Madison had preceded Burr in death earlier that same year; infrequently remarked upon is the documented fact that Burr, a popular ladies man throughout his life, had many years previous introduced the shy Madison, supposedly a confirmed bachelor, to his future wife, the celebrated Dolly Madison.

5. Jackson also appears to have belonged to a long line of prominent Southern slave owners having great reservations about slavery as he grew older.

6. For example, *The Slave's Lament*, a famous poem by Smith's admirer and fellow Scotsman Robert Burns, was published in 1792.

7. *WN*, I.VIII, 113.

8. The basic premise to Smith's insight was that extracting labor from an unwilling worker was itself a major line item expense, though admittedly hard if not impossible to precisely measure on a ledger sheet.

9. *WN*, I.VIII, 113. Smith repeats this statement, nearly verbatim, in *WN*, III.II, 493.

10. *WN*, III.II, 491, 493.

11. See *Lectures on Jurisprudence*, 175–199.

12. *TMS*, V.I.19.

13. *WN*, I.V, 43.

14. *WN*, I.V. 46–47

15. *WN*, III.IV (Conclusion of Book III), 525. According to Smith, the medieval aristocracy was able to indulge their own venality because short periods of peaceful prosperity during the Middle Ages gradually provided surplus goods not readily available since the fall of the Roman Empire.

16. *WN*, III.I, 486–487.

17. *WN*, II.II, 408.

18. Madison, though subscribing to many of Smith's other theories, had previously opposed the Hamiltonian ideal of state-sponsored central banking as early as the 1780s while co-authoring the Federalist Papers with Hamilton and John Jay under the pseudonym of "Publius."

19. For example, French observer Alexis de Tocqueville in 1831 ridiculed the semi-literacy of American frontier Congressmen Davy Crockett as being more typical.

20. Van Buren had replaced John C. Calhoun as Vice President after the latter had been ousted by Jackson following the Nullification Crisis of 1828–1832 (see Chapter 3).

21. "Of course, he was neither" Clay's enemies were known to have replied.

22. See *Monument to the Memory of Henry Clay*, edited by A.H. Carrier (W.A. Clarke, 1857), 475. "Adam Smith's book" refers to *The Wealth of Nations*.

23. Webster, Daniel, *Private Correspondence*, Vol. I (Little Brown, 1857), 501. The second reference is to Thomas Roderick Dew (1802–1846), professor of political economy and noted pro-slavery apologist at the Virginia College of William & Mary.

24. The origins of the British abolition movement, curiously enough, are found during the American Revolutionary period (see Chapters 1 & 2), culminating in the landmark legal decision of *Gregson v.Gilbert* in 1783. These events, along with the remarkable biography of Dido Elizabeth Belle (1761-1804), the African-British niece of the Lord Chief Justice William Murray, Earl of Mansfield, who ruled on the *Gregson* decision, were recently retold in the acclaimed film *Belle* (2013), directed by Amma Asante.

25. Brougham noted in the text that some of his writings on Smith dated from over half a century before the 1855 publication. He had access to correspondence not earlier utilized by Stewart, but later cited by Rae (see Chapter 9).

26. Brougham's political career appears to have been a casualty of his abolition crusade, having made many powerful enemies in the process, which many historians also generally believe led to the fall of the British Whig Party administration in 1834.

27. Tocqueville, Alexis de, *Democracy in America*, translated by Arthur Goldhammer (Library of America, 2004), 642.

28. *WN*, V.I, Part III, Article 2nd, 987.

29. Tocqueville, Alexis de, *Democracy in America*, translated by Arthur Goldhammer (Library of America, 2004), 400.

30. *Ibid.*, 398.

31. *Ibid.*

32. *Ibid.*, 399, 401.

33. *Ibid.*, 397.

34. Abraham Lincoln was born 1809 in

Hardin County, KY; Ulysses S. Grant, 1822 in Point Pleasant, OH; William Tecumseh Sherman, 1820 in Lancaster, OH.

Chapter 5

1. *WN*, IV.V, 663.
2. Dickens, Charles, *American Notes* and *Pictures from Italy* (Oxford University Press, 1842/1989), 246.
3. *Ibid.*, 241–243.
4. Harrison was the last American President born a British citizen (in 1773).
5. The now nearly-forgotten Treaty of Wang Hia was signed in 1844 and ratified in 1845.
6. Scroggie's mother was the maternal niece of Smith.
7. *WN*, IV.V, 665. This commentator retains an open mind on the subject. The Scots are well known for plain speaking, as well as parsimony. That Scroggie's tombstone was either defaced and/or uncomplimentary must be considered a possibility absent concrete evidence to the contrary.
8. Scrooge's traumatic confrontation with his own tombstone in *A Christmas Carol* is one of the most dramatic scenes in all of English literature and film.
9. Noted economist, Royal Society of Edinburgh member, Exeter College (University of Oxford) Rector, and recent editor for *The Economist*, Frances Cairncross (b. 1944), was recently quoted (not too surprisingly) naming Adam Smith as her favorite historical personage. See http://www.gla.ac.uk/schools/business/newsandevents/aspire/issue10autumnwinter2011/confessionsofaneconomist/.
10. *WN*, IV.V, 663.
11. *Ibid.* Some argue that the Great Irish Famine of the mid–19th century was a genocidal "starving" implemented by the British government through active policies or lack thereof, as opposed to merely a "famine" primarily caused by natural forces.
12. *WN*, IV.V, 674, 682.
13. *WN*, IV.V, 687. Smith's citation of Plutarch's *Life of Solon* was another good example of his training in classical literature.
14. Smith refers to the 1740 famine in *WN*, I.VIII, 120.
15. One of the more bizarre episodes of the Mexican War involved the defection the Irish-born "San Patricios" regiment to the Mexican side of the conflict, an offense for which some of them were later captured and executed by the American Army.

16. Mexico had effectively won its political independence from Spain by the 1820s, but official recognition was slow in coming.
17. The Oregon Country Treaty of 1846 between the United States and Great Britain had secured the Pacific Northwest for the U.S., establishing today's boundary with Canada. A young Ulysses S. Grant, an army lieutenant and combat veteran during the Mexican War, later spared no words regarding American complicity in that conflict, adding that the bloody and expensive American Civil War was a later direct and deserved consequence. Soon afterwards, Grant was stationed in the Pacific Northwest, before being forced to resign his commission, reputedly because of drinking while on duty. Finally, Grant wrote in his memoirs, perhaps with intended bitterness, that earlier while attending West Point he became addicted to tobacco (which would eventually kill him), a product produced by the same Southern planter interests later provoking both the war between the states and the Mexican conflict. The Mexican War produced three veterans later becoming U.S. Presidents: Grant (1822–1885), Zachary Taylor (1784–1850), and Franklin Pierce (1804–1869).
18. *WN*, IV.VII, Part II, 725.
19. *WN*, IV.V, Part Second, 715.
20. *WN*, IV.VII, Part II, 738.
21. See *The Speeches of Sir Robert Peel, Delivered in the House of Commons*, Vol. IV from 1842 to 1850 (George Routledge and Co., 1853), 5.
22. Cobden also single-handedly spearheaded the Cobden-Chevalier Treaty of 1860, liberalizing trade relations between England and France after decades of hostility in wake of the Napoleonic Wars.
23. *WN*, I.X, Part II, 168. See also *Speeches on Questions of Public Policy by Richard Cobden*, Vol. I (MacMillan and Co., 1870), 89.
24. Not surprisingly as a result of lacking oversight, Walker was accused of using government funds for personal gain during his tenure as Secretary of the Treasury.
25. See *Speech of the Hon. Robert J. Walker at the Banquet Given by the Mayor & Municipal Authorities of Southampton* (London: Waterlow & Sons, 1851), 16.
26. See http://www.clarelibrary.ie/eolas/coclare/history/condition_of_ireland/condition_of_ireland_iln_dec22_1849.htm.
27. By 1850, Clay only had two years left to live. His old rival Daniel Webster would outlive Clay by only four months.
28. From *Christian Non-Resistance: In All Its Important Bearings, Illustrated and Defended*. The expression itself is ancient and uncertain in origin, possibly traceable to the Greeks.

Chapter 6

1. *WN*, I.I, 13.
2. The Northern-born (upstate New York) Fillmore would be mainly remembered for signing into law the odious Fugitive Slave Act, part of the 1850 Compromise.
3. Alexander would also later sell the Alaska territory to the United States, mainly to spite the British. Like his contemporary Abraham Lincoln, he would eventually, for his trouble, be assassinated by marginal discontents at home.
4. Russia would in fact be torn apart by its own civil war a little over half a century later, the result of military defeat in World War I (see Chapter 11).
5. Eleven Confederate states officially seceded from the Union; four slave-states remained with the Union, at least in strict legal terms, these including Missouri, Kentucky, Maryland, and Delaware.
6. Expression originally attributed to Senator James Henry Hammond of South Carolina in 1858.
7. Also made into a 1984 PBS television film, *Solomon Northup's Odyssey*.
8. Northrup, Solomon, *Twelve Years a Slave*, Introduction by Ira Berlin, Foreword by Steve McQueen (Penguin, 1853/2013), xxvii–xxviii.
9. *Ibid.*, 31.
10. *Ibid.*, 217.
11. *TMS*, VI.I.14. The statement recalls Grant's famous assertion that the best public service is to be expected from those who are summoned to it, rather than from those who seek it for themselves.
12. See my earlier study on this same subject, *Ulysses S. Grant, 1861–1864: His Rise from Obscurity to Military Glory* (McFarland, 2007).
13. Sam R. Watkins, *Co. Aytch: A Confederate Memoir of the Civil War* (Simon & Schuster, 1882/2003), 28, 31. Watkins also wrote that "We [the South] are an agricultural people; they [the North] are a manufacturing people." See 6.
14. Smith makes reference to this burgeoning trade in *WN*, III.IV, 529–530. Smith spent most of his professional career, both as academic and civil servant, in Glasgow and Edinburgh.
15. *WN*, III.IV, 520.
16. *WN*, III.IV, 525.
17. *WN*, IV.VII, Part III, 744–745.
18. *WN*, IV.IX, 869–872.
19. *WN*, III.I, 481. See also *WN*, IV.IX, 872.
20. *Diary of Charles Francis Adams*, Volume 6, November 1834 to June 1836, edited by Marc Friedlaender and L.H. Butterfield (Harvard University Press, 1974), 25.
21. *The Salmon Chase Papers*, Volume 1, Journals 1829–1872, edited by John Niven (Kent State University Press, 1993), 57.
22. Carey reminded Lincoln that, among other factors, perceived economic factors were driving Southern states to secession, particularly Republican protectionist and pro-tariff policies.
23. See letter from Herndon to publisher Jesse Weik, dated January 1, 1886, from *The Hidden Lincoln* by Emanuel Hertz (Viking, 1938), 117.
24. These included the Revenue Acts of 1861, 1862, and 1864.
25. See Douglass' speech *A Friendly World to Maryland: An Address Delivered in Baltimore, Maryland on 17 November 1864*.
26. See http://pastispresent.org/2014/goodsources/twelve-years-a-slave-the-book-dramatizations-illustrations-editions/.
27. Many Irish-Americans of course also fought for the Confederacy, such as this writer's great-great grandfather. These tended more typically, however, to have arrived on American soil before the Great Famine of the late 1840s.

Chapter 7

1. *TMS*, IV.I.10.
2. For example, the burning cross had long been a Scottish military symbol, one in fact used by the Jacobite rebels in 1745, among many others.
3. Surely the most famous example of this defense or romanticizing was the 1915 film *Birth of a Nation* by D.W. Griffith, based on the 1905 novel *The Clansman* by Thomas F. Dixon, Jr. The film essentially celebrated the 50th anniversary of the Klan's foundation.
4. Sharecropping is usually defined as a form of tenant farming in which the tenants do not own their own equipment or livestock, and hence receive a lower share of the produce in relation to the landowner. It has a long history throughout western civilization and beyond.
5. The first American labor union, the National Labor Union (1866–1872), was founded in the immediate wake of the Civil War. The longer lived Order of the Knights of St. Crispin was founded in 1867.
6. *WN*, V.III, 1204.
7. *WN*, III.IV, 523–524.
8. *WN*, I.VIII, 91.
9. *WN*, I.VIII, 94.
10. The legalized trade apprenticeships criticized by Smith in *WN* are sometimes confused with modern labor unions. The similarities between the two are slight at best.

11. *WN*, I.VIII, 94–95.
12. *WN*, I.VIII, 95.
13. *WN*, I.VIII, 97, 110–111.
14. *TMS*, IV.I.10.
15. The Shakespearean-like phrase in English is first recorded in *Euphues and His England* (1580), by John Lyly, thus predating the King James Bible.
16. It can never be forgotten or downplayed that most of the American Founding Fathers believed that voting rights should be restricted to the white male property-owing classes.
17. *TMS*, IV.I.10.
18. The subtitle of Disraeli's *Two Nations* seems to echo that of Smith's *Wealth of Nations*.
19. See *Endymion* by Benjamin Disraeli, Chapter 61.
20. See Revised Report of the Proceedings at the Dinner of May 31, 1876, held in celebration of the hundredth year of the publication of the "Wealth of Nations," Political Economy Club (founded 1821), Right Honorable W.E. Gladstone, M.P., in the chair (Longmans, Green, Reader, & Dyer, 1876), 6.
21. *Ibid.*, 21.
22. Marx first criticized Smith's theories in his *Theories of Surplus Value*, written during the early 1860s, but not published until the 20th century. The first volume of *Das Kapital* appeared in 1867, but it was the second volume, written around 1880 and published in 1885, that disputed Smith's views in detailed length.
23. Carey was voted membership in the prestigious Royal Swedish Academy in 1868.
24. Carey, Henry Charles, *Commerce, Christianity, and Civilization Versus British Free Trade: Letters in Reply to the London Times* (Collins, 1876), 4, 36 (Letters First & Eighth). Carey was also among the first economists to accurately insist that Smith had not in fact been proponent of free trade under all circumstances. "Were Adam Smith an American, would he not be a protectionist?" wrote Carey provocatively. See 24–25 (Letter Fifth).
25. Carey, like Smith, held in low regard quantity of precious metals as a measure of true wealth. This issue would come to the forefront of American politics by the end of the 19th century (see Chapter 9).
26. Forrest was the first white speaker invited by the Order of Independent Pole-Bearers Association. The name of the organization is a reference to voting rights.
27. Forrest forever stands accused of ordering or condoning the massacre of black POWs at Fort Pillow, Tennessee. Given the unusually bitter nature of the war, one in which both sides are alleged to have committed atrocities, I am inclined to take a lenient view towards Forrest on this question. Most likely, he did not either give the fatal orders, or the fury of the moment temporarily overwhelmed the powers of his otherwise firm command.

Chapter 8

1. *TMS*, I.I.1.
2. Mary Paley was the great granddaughter of English philosopher William Paley (1743–1805), a younger contemporary of Smith.
3. The continental African interest of the United States at the time related strictly to Liberia as a potential resettlement ground for former American slaves. In hindsight, the relative insignificance of this minor afterthought in comparison to the major extent of African territories and resources being divvied up by European powers causes the American viewpoint to appear trivial and naïve.
4. Luckily for Grant's family, this net worth was partially restored after his death by the successful publication of his memoirs by Mark Twain.
5. Grover Cleveland, the only Democratic to occupy the White House during the 1880s, won the popular vote in 1889, but lost in the Electoral College to Benjamin Harrison. James Garfield was assassinated in 1881 shortly after being sworn into office. Hoosier-born Benjamin Harrison was the grandson of former President William Henry Harrison (see Chapter 5).
6. See Stewart, Sections I, III.
7. Hutcheson, if nothing else, was well known to have brought a more secular outlook to his students' impressionable sensibilities, often to the chagrin of older, more Calvinist academics of that time and place.
8. Such plays were common practice at the time in Scottish elementary education, despite frequent opposition from Presbyterian Church leaders. See Rae, 5–6.
9. This is not necessarily to say that Garrick admired Smith. Garrick, stunned at Smith's decidedly undramatic conversational style, reportedly quipped to a friend "What say you to this? Eh, flabby, eh?" See Rae, XVII.6.
10. See Stewart, Sections III.
11. *WN*, IV.VII, Part II, 716.
12. *Ibid*.
13. *Ibid*.
14. Religious commentator Karen Armstrong, in her fine recent work *The Great Transformation* (2008), argues persuasively that ancient Greek drama, particularly tragedy, grew out of a spiritual need for colonizing Hellenic culture not only to see their own stories reen-

acted on the public stage, but also a surprisingly deeper need to sympathize or empathize with their adversaries or outcasts.

15. The letter is dated April 24, 1881. See *Letters of Lord Acton to Mary Gladstone*, edited, with a memoir, by Herbert Paul (MacMillan, 1905), 194.

16. *Ibid.*, 194–195.

17. After purchasing Acton's valuable library, Carnegie presented the acquisition to John Morley (see Chapter 10), who in turn appropriately bequeathed it to Cambridge University.

18. Some of Carnegie's libraries, on the other hand, have been unfortunately and inexplicably demolished.

19. The article appeared in the December 1908 issue of *Century Magazine*.

20. Cody had dabbled in show business as early as 1872, when he is first known to have appeared on stage in Chicago.

21. Cody, who had experienced war and combat firsthand, always understood that his show was merely an act; whether the future Kaiser could make the same distinction, it is difficult to say.

22. The Wounded Knee Massacre later inspired the famous poem by Stephen Vincent Benet (1931), as well as a book by the same title (1970) and a Native American Civil Rights protest (1973).

Chapter 9

1. *WN*, I.XI, Part III, 258–259.

2. Melville's family appears to have been of Anglo-Scots ancestry.

3. *Billy Budd* was not published posthumously until 1924.

4. Melville, Herman, *Redburn*, Chapter XVIII.

5. After the Spanish-American conflict, Admiral Dewey helped to sabotage his own political career in part by accurately predicting that America's next war would be with Germany.

6. The 1896 election represented the first of Bryan's three unsuccessful Presidential bids, the other two being in 1900 and 1908.

7. "You shall not crucify…" Thus sermonized Bryan at the 1896 Democratic National Convention in Chicago while gaining his Presidential nomination.

8. See, for example, William Robert Scott, *Francis Hutcheson: His Life, Teaching and Position in the History of Philosophy* (MacMillan, 1900), 238–239.

9. Smith declared that "produce of land and labour" constituted "the real revenue of every society," as opposed to "circulating capital." See *WN*, II.II, 372. Later, as a specific example, Smith cites the American colonies, who "have no gold or silver money," but are nonetheless considered very wealthy. Almost jokingly, Smith rhetorically asks: "How is it possible to draw from them what they have not?" See also *WN*, V.III, 1198.

10. One might easily go even further and say that Smith was interested less in wealth itself than in specifically how that wealth was employed for the advancement of society.

11. Smith wrote: "It [hard currency] is a very valuable part of the capital of a country, which produces nothing to the country." See *WN*, II.II, 409. See also *WN*, II.II, 367–368, in which Smith makes one of his numerous references to "neat revenue" or net revenue, as if it were a style of fine Scotch whiskey not being diluted or diminished by the necessary and unavoidable evils of gold and silver currency. Most recently, the former passage was quoted by Nobel Prize-winning economist Paul Krugman in reference to (and criticism of) the Bitcoin phenomenon in cyberspace. See "Adam Smith Hates Bitcoin" by Paul Krugman, *The New York Times*, April 12, 2013.

12. For example, see *WN*, I.IV, 36.

13. *WN*, I.IV, 35.

14. *WN*, II.II, 409.

15. See http://www.fmcs.gov/internet/itemDetail.asp?categoryID=21&itemID=15810. That same year (1891) Webb authored *The Cooperative Movement in Great Britain*, advocating consumer cooperatives only two years after Germany had legitimized these through legislation (see Chapter 8). Six years later, in 1897, the concept of collective bargaining was elaborated upon by Webb as a feature section of *Industrial Democracy*, coauthored with her husband Sidney Webb.

16. Quoted by Emma Rothschild in *Economic Sentiments* (Harvard University Press, 2001), Chapter 2, Note 85 ("One-Sided Rationalistic Liberalism").

17. Webb's many accomplishments appear more impressive in hindsight, given that most were achieved before women were even allowed the right to vote.

18. Skidelsky, Robert, *John Maynard Keynes (Volume Three): Fighting for Freedom, 1937–1946* (Penguin, 2000), 168. Keynes' comment also possibly represented a dig at Shaw's notorious male ego.

19. A valuable introduction to the 1965 reissue of Rae's work was added by the distinguished Canadian economist Jacob Viner (1892–1970). The "other" John Rae (the Scottish-born econ-

omist) was in fact one of the first major critics of Adam Smith's theories.

20. *WN*, V.II, Part II, 1043. See also Bryan, William Jennings and Mary Baird, *The Life and Speeches of Hon. Wm. Jennings Bryan* (R.H. Woodward Company, 1900), 234, 236.

21. *Ibid.*, 236.

22. Russell, Henry Benajah, *The Lives of William McKinley and Garret A. Hobart, Republican Presidential Candidates of 1896* (A.D. Worthington & Company), 197, 202.

23. After victory against the Spanish, former Philippine U.S. allies immediately rebelled against American dominance and were violently suppressed.

24. McKinley's assassin, Frank Czolgosz, the son of Polish immigrants, was quickly tried, convicted, and executed before the end of October. There is some reason to believe that his mental instability may have been caused or worsened by working for several years in the steel mills, before the Panic of 1893—the same event propelling McKinley into the White House—caused Czolgosz to join the ranks of the permanently unemployed. If true, and causal effects of this tragedy would be truly profound.

25. For example, the Roosevelt family had been wealthy New Yorkers long before Andrew Carnegie had been born, let alone set foot on American soil.

Chapter 10

1. *WN*, IV.VII, Part III, 779.

2. It should be remembered that the Scottish Jacobite Rebellion of Smith's own day had been put down, with full or tacit approval from many pro–Union Scots such as Smith, by British forces fighting for a German-English Hanoverian king.

3. The Sherman Anti-Trust Law was named after its sponsor, Senator John Sherman, brother to Civil War hero General William Tecumseh Sherman.

4. Roosevelt was careful not to give the unions any official recognition, but tacitly did so by forcing everyone to sit together at the same negotiating table. In essence, he recognized their right to collectively bargain.

5. See *WN*, V.II, Part II, Appendix to Article 1st and 2nd, 1086–1094.

6. Stewart, III.9.

7. Rae, III.8.

8. Rae, III.3

9. Rae, III.1 & III.11.

10. Rae, III.7.

11. Rae, III.5 & III.16

12. Rae, III.15.

13. *WN*, V.I, Part III, Article 2nd, 986.

14. *WN*, xiv (Introduction).

15. *WN*, I.VIII, 94–95.

16. *WN*, I.II, 414.

17. *Ibid.*

18. *WN*, I.VI, 74.

19. *WN*, I.VI, 70.

20. La Follette, Sr., was Governor of Wisconsin from 1901 to 1906, a Progressive Party presidential candidate, and a U.S. Senator from 1906 to his death in 1925. His great grandnephew Doug La Follette (b. 1940) is the current Wisconsin Secretary of State.

21. *The Political Philosophy of Robert M. La Follette*, as revealed in his speeches and writings, compiled by Ellen Torelle, assisted by Albert O. Barton and Fred L. Holmes, (Madison: The Robert M. La Follette Co., 1920), 358.

22. Reprinted in *A Cartoon History of Roosevelt's Career* by Albert Shaw (The Review of Reviews Company, 1910), 96–97.

23. Even more unlikely was Roosevelt's being earlier awarded the Nobel Peace Price in 1906 (the first American to be so honored), for helping to negotiate settlement of the Russian-Japanese conflict that same year.

Chapter 11

1. *WN*, V.III, 1157.

2. Using instability of the Austro-Hungarian Hapsburg monarchy combined with ethnic unrest in the Balkans as a pretext, Germany had effectively begun the shooting war by aggressively invading France and the Low Countries in 1914. A similar strategy had worked for Germany during the Franco-Prussian War of 1870–1871, but this time Great Britain decisively came to the aid of France.

3. The late Eliot Asinof has ably chronicled these unhappy events of 1919 in much of his historical work, especially *1919: America's Loss of Innocence* (Donald I. Fine, 1990). See also my previous study, *Eliot Asinof and the Truth of the Game* (McFarland, 2012).

4. Rae, 42.

5. *WN*, V.III, 1183.

6. *WN*, V.III, 1170–1171.

7. *WN*, V.III, 1156.

8. *WN*, V.III, 1171.

9. *WN*, V.III, 1180–1181.

10. *WN*, V.III, 1184.

11. See my earlier study, *Ulysses S. Grant 1861–1864: His Rise from Obscurity to Military Greatness* (McFarland, 2007).

12. Not to be confused with a Juris Doctor or law degree, held by a number of U.S. Presidents. Wilson earned his Ph.D. in History and Political Science from Johns Hopkins University ("The Hopkins") in 1886. He had attended for three years.

13. The regulatory aspect of the Wilson administration seems currently most appropriate as the 2014 Nobel Prize in Economics was awarded to the French economist Jean Tirole of Toulouse, an eloquent champion of government regulation.

14. Reprinted in *An Old Master* and Other Political Essays, by Woodrow Wilson (Charles Scribner's Sons, 1893). The essay had originally appeared five years earlier in the *New Princeton Review* (Sept. 1888, Vol. 6), 210–220.

15. Wilson, 23.
16. Wilson, 27.
17. Wilson, 28.
18. Among Ely's continuing namesake legacies is the Ely (Chicago) Chapter of Lambda Alpha International, an honorary land economics society.

19. Ely spent the greatest part of his academic career (1892–1925) at the University of Wisconsin where, despite Progressive sympathies, he was a sharp critic of Senator Robert M. La Follette (see Chapter 10) for his isolationist anti-war stance. Later still, Ely taught at Northwestern University in Evanston, Illinois.

20. See *Library of the World's Best Literature* by Charles Dudley Warner (Vol. 34, R.S. Peele & J.A. Hill, 1896). Warner was a friend of Mark Twain and sometimes writing collaborator with him. *Library* was very successful and went through several subsequent editions. Twain's public joke about the "classics" (see Introduction) a few years later may have represented a shrewd marketing ploy on his part.

21. *Ibid.*, 13519.
22. *Ibid.*, 13523.
23. *Ibid.*, 15222.
24. See *WN*, V.II, Article I.
25. Churchill later himself repudiated the British Ten Year Rule as the German Nazi threat steadily grew during the early 1930s. By that time, a world Depression had also gripped the U.S. and European economies; renewed military spending proved to be a needed boost for all of these economies as well (see Chapter 13).

26. See *Forty Ways to Look at Winston Churchill: A Brief Account of a Long Life*, by Gretchen Rubin (Random House, 2004), 52.

27. See "The Budget and Property" from *Liberalism and the Social Problem*, Second Edition, by Winston Spencer Churchill, M.P. (Hodder and Stoughton, 1909), 397.

28. Delacroix's masterpiece today hangs in the museum of Louvre-Lens.
29. *WN*, IV.VII, Part III, 768.

Chapter 12

1. *WN*, V.III, 1103–1104.
2. Harding reportedly won 60 percent of the popular vote, the biggest Presidential landslide in American history.

3. On the positive side of the ledger for Harding, he was known to have a soft spot for oppressed minorities and women, but even this desirable trait sometimes served to undermine reform efforts by alienating the powerful interests claiming his first allegiance.

4. The first motion picture with synchronized sound or "talkie" appeared in 1927 with *The Jazz Singer*. After that, there was no going back; moreover, the trend rapidly went worldwide.

5. For example, though hard evidence is lacking, Johnson and Boswell are today still associated with London's landmark pub on Fleet Street, Ye Olde Cheshire Cheese. It is possible that Smith visited the establishment as well. This writer made a memorable visit there in late 1967. As for Smith, he is known to have resided in London at the British Coffee-House in Cockspur Street. See Rae, XVII.5.

6. See *Adam Smith and the Scotland of His Day* by C.F. Fay (Cambridge University Press, 1956), 100.

7. *WN*, IV.III, Part II, 620.
8. *WN*, IV.III, Part II, 621.
9. *WN*, IV.III, Part II, 1130.
10. Like a true connoisseur, Smith remarks that the best French wines come from provinces in which there are fewest restraints on trade. See *WN*, V.II, Article 4th, 1144.

11. *WN*, IV.III, Part II, 619.
12. *Ibid.*
13. *WN*, IV.III, Part II, 620.
14. Going further, we question whether the very idea of strict Prohibition would have ever occurred to Smith, except perhaps in a humorous context.

15. *WN*, IV.III, Part II, 620.
16. *Ibid.*
17. *WN*, IV.III, Part II, 620–621.
18. *WN*, IV.III, Part II, 621.
19. *WN*, V.II, Article 4th, 1120.
20. *WN*, V.II, Article 4th, 1117, 1120–1121.
21. *WN*, V.II, Article 4th, 1119.
22. *WN*, V.II, Article 4th, 1130.
23. *WN*, V.II, Article 4th, 1140.
24. To give a single example, Michigan law

enforcement officials were quickly overwhelmed. Complaints soon followed from Michigan residents (no teetotalers themselves) that Indiana teenagers could not hold their liquor, to which there was probably a grain of truth.

25. For readers interested in such things, both of my parents were extremely light drinkers. My father, not otherwise inclined to healthy living, came of age in Chicago during the Roaring Twenties and had witnessed many horrible things. He instilled in his children a firm mistrust of government's ability or even right to regulate the personal morals of its citizens. My mother, hailing from the rural South, had seen many lives unnecessarily destroyed by alcoholism, and objected to any form of recreational drinking. As for myself, I learned at very early age that my own physical tolerance for spirits was extremely low. Otherwise, I have no objections to any form of moderate indulgence.

26. See *Socialism and Society* by James Ramsay MacDonald, M.P. (Independent Labour Party, 1906), 203. The mostly self-educated MacDonald stayed on the periphery of British politics until his 40th year saw him elected M.P. He went on to become a central and often controversial figure in history of the British Labour Party.

27. See *American Individualism* by Herbert Hoover (Doubleday, 1922), 53.

28. Mellon was the only person to hold the same cabinet post under three consecutive Presidents. Hoover was the only former cabinet member to later become President.

29. See *Taxation: The People's Business* by Andrew Mellon (MacMillan, 1924), 14–15. See also *WN*, V.II, Part II, 1044–1045.

30. As this is being written, it seems fitting that Naste's namesake corporate descendent is leading the move-in to the new World Trade Center in New York City (see Chapter 18). See "World Trade Center Opens for Business" in *USA Today*, November 3, 2014.

Chapter 13

1. *WN*, V.I, Part IV, 1031.
2. O'Rourke, 111–112. Later, O'Rourke perceptively adds that the frequent modern day Libertarian equation of wealth with freedom was another common distortion of Smith's philosophy. See 129.
3. Numerous excellent FDR biographies and accounts of this period have been written in recent years. A personal favorite is Jean Edward Smith's *FDR* (Random House, 2007), in large part due to his unusually detached, objective tone. At the other end of the spectrum, more sentimental yet unvarnished, is the exhaustive 2014 Ken Burns documentary, *The Roosevelts*.
4. The FDIC was a product of the Banking Act of 1933.
5. Today's Public Broadcasting System is a distant descendant of the controversial idea that tax dollars should sometimes support the arts via public media. The concept would have been foreign to Smith, and yet he would have surely classified the idea itself of public broadcasting as commercial infrastructure, and therefore the proper object of tax funding.
6. The rural phrase would have been familiar and understandable to any Depression-era farmer. Interestingly, the first use of the phrase in an economic context reportedly occurred in 1932 during the last year of the Hoover administration.
7. Perkins held a graduate degree in Political Science from Columbia University. FDR, legendary for his deviousness, is said to have deliberately chosen a woman as Labor Secretary to offset that faction's bellicose tendencies.
8. Quesnay and his fellow Physiocrats all used the phrase in opposition to official French mercantilist policies. The most plausible source derived from Quesnay's defense and advocacy of Chinese policies, based on the Taoist principle of *wu wei*, best described as a kind of measured, constructive form of inaction. Quesnay's well-known work, *Le depotisme de la Chine* ("The Despotism of China"), appeared in 1767, the year after Smith returned to Scotland from France.
9. Both Smith and Quesnay had witnessed spectacular banking abuses in their respective homelands, but Quesnay more so. Smith had also seen far more instances of successful banking, especially in Scotland, and wrote extensively of these in *WN*.
10. *WN*, II.II, 378.
11. *WN*, II.II, 387.
12. *WN*, II.II, 405. Smith almost seems to revel in the fact that the greatest then-known economic bubble in history had been prompted by a visionary Scotsman promoter.
13. *WN*, I.V, 45.
14. It is worth noting that the modern appraisal profession in the United States began taking shape as a direct consequence of the Great Depression. The American Institute of Real Estate Appraisers, today the Appraisal Institute, was founded in 1932. The Society of Real Estate Appraisers, which merged into the former in 1991, was founded in 1935.
15. *WN*, V.I, Part III, Article I, 917, 928–929, 981.

16. *WN*, V.I, Part III, Article I, 930.
17. *TMS*, VI.III.48.
18. FDR's seemingly limitless high self-appraisal likely derived from his incredibly pampered, privileged upbringing under the care of Sara Delano Roosevelt, combined with his emotional and spiritual triumph over polio during midlife. The latter tragedy also furnished a needed touch of humility and compassion.
19. *TMS*, VI.III.46.
20. For example, Keynes made the cover of *Time* magazine in 1965 for his economic influence on the U.S. military-industrial complex, almost 20 years after his death (see Chapter 15).
21. The famous interaction between FDR and Keynes had been facilitated by mutual friend and future U.S. Supreme Court Justice Felix Frankfurter.
22. Skidelsky, Robert, *John Maynard Keynes: Hopes Betrayed* 1883–1920 (Penguin 1983), 252.
23. Eccles self-made, immigrant father was born in Scotland. His mother was from Northern Ireland.
24. Eccles, Marriner Stoddard, *Beckoning Frontiers: Public and Personal Recollections*, Edited by Sidney Hyman (Alfred A. Knopf, 1951), 3.
25. *Ibid.*, 4.
26. *Ibid.* See also *WN*, V.I, Part III, Article I, 916.
27. *Ibid.*, 81–82.
28. See http://www.umich.edu/~ac213/student_projects06/sdtber/Detroit%20institute.html
29. Fittingly, Rivera's "Detroit Industry" was designated a National Historic Landmark in 2014.
30. Vidal, Gore, *United States Essays 1952–1992* (Random House, 1993), 738.

Chapter 14

1. *WN*, V.I, Part III, Article 2d, 987–988.
2. Gibbon, Edward, *The Decline and Fall of the Roman Empire*, Vol. I (Modern Library, 1776/1995), 61. Gibbon's controversial pronouncement has been criticized for, among other things, not factoring in lack of contentment for the huge slave population of Imperial Rome. Smith would have probably viewed this simply as an inefficient form of ancient labor, since he lived in a time during which slavery was still legal within the broad confines of the British Empire (see Chapter 4).
3. The Russian Soviet Union, fighting elite elements of the *Werhmacht* more or less alone on the Eastern front until 1943, hosted some of the most massive land battles in history, several of which are likely never to be surpassed in terms of scale or horror. After this, the U.S. and Great Britain successfully opened up a second front against Germany and Italy in the West. For the full duration of the conflict, however, Americans fought in the Pacific mostly unaided against a fanatical and determined opponent.
4. FDR analogized lending a garden hose to a neighbor putting out a fire, lest his own property be consumed by the same conflagration. After the fire was put out, FDR explained, he did not want money, rather "I want my garden hose back." Churchill, with the rhetorical flourish for which he was famous, declared Lend-Lease to be "the most unsordid act in history."
5. It is worthy of note within these pages that my late father was slated for the Invasion of Japan when Hiroshima and Nagasaki were bombed. It was always his firm belief that, had Truman not authorized use of atomic weaponry against Japan, my father would not have survived the war to start a family. Many years later, my esteemed professor at Valparaiso University, the late Dr. Allen Tuttle, having close familiarity with high casualty rate estimates for that thankfully cancelled campaign, assured me that my father was probably correct in his belief.
6. A decade earlier, such attitudes in the isolationist-dominated U.S. were rare.
7. To his eternal credit, it was Eisenhower who probably did more than anyone to strike McCarthy down after a long, painful period of reluctant tolerance. The shift was said to have been sparked by rumors of McCarthy planning a character attack against General Marshall, which Eisenhower found intolerable.
8. Among many similar-themed works, Dewey's *Freedom and Culture* (1939), published on the eve of World War II, had stressed this connection.
9. Symbolically, the Union Jack flag of Great Britain is a combination of the English St. George's cross and the Scottish St. Andrew's cross.
10. *WN*, V.I, Part III, Article 2d, 987.
11. *WN*, V.I, Part III, Article 2d, 990.
12. *WN*, V.I, Part III, Article 2d, 994.
13. Once again, it is difficult in this regard not to draw direct parallels with the modern day United States. After several generations of neglect in our public educational system, are the effects that Smith warned against beginning to catch up with us in the political arena?
14. *WN*, V.I, Part III, Article 2d, 994.
15. Hayek quotes Smith via Dugald Stewart early in the work.
16. Hayek, after his retirement, and much to

his own surprise, was awarded the Nobel Prize in 1974.

17. Keynes wrote to Hayek on June 28, 1944. See Skidelsky, Robert, *John Maynard Keynes: Fighting for Freedom 1937–1946* (Macmillan, 2000), 284–285, 532n66.

18. See http://www.maynardkeynes.org/john-maynard-keynes-world-bank-imf.html.

19. *Ibid.*

20. Quoted in "*The Return of Adam Smith*: Some Thoughts on Collectivism and Democracy" by William McLaren, *ABA Journal*, March, 1950, Vol. 36, 203.

21. In defense of Montgomery's book, it appears to have been one of the first alternative, English-language interpretations of Smith's work in nearly half a century since Francis Wrigley Hirst's published biographical sketch in 1904 (see Chapter 10). It was also possibly the first ever written by an American.

22. Galbraith, *The Affluent* Society (Houghton Mifflin, 1958), 21.

23. For an excellent obituary of Paolozzi, see http://www.theguardian.com/culture/2005/apr/22/obituaries.

24. These images, or their surviving remnants, may be viewed (among other places) at http://www.artgallery.nsw.gov.au/collection/works/?group_accession=139.2002.1–45.

25. In which four monstrously oversized toddlers lord it over their adoring, miniature mothers, along with other toys and prize possessions.

26. *TMS*, VI.III.28.

27. *Ibid.*

Chapter 15

1. *WN*, III.II, 491, 493.

2. Eisenhower's incredible speech is easily accessible on the Internet from multiple sources, either in text or audio-visual. It deserves to be revisited on regular basis. Early drafts reportedly sought to include, in McCarthy-like fashion, academia as a subversive influence on American culture, but Ike wisely ignored the suggestion. "Don't be afraid to go in your library and read every book," he famously quipped.

3. Kennedy was also an Irish Catholic President, both firsts for the White House. Although campaign issues, in retrospect these things had little or nothing to do with his shortcomings as a world leader. JFK was simply a man of his time and place, certainly fearless but too often overreacting, without Eisenhower's profound and patient understanding of world affairs, one based upon the hard school of long experience.

4. The failed Bay of Pigs invasion occurred in April 1961, barely four months after Kennedy took office.

5. The famed March on Washington, D.C., led by Martin Luther King, Jr., occurred on August 28, 1963, roughly three months before JFK's assassination.

6. "There goes the south for a generation" quipped the politically astute LBJ.

7. Both men came to the presidency with good resumes, both were respectable products of the New Deal, albeit from different generations. Both were overwhelmed by changing world affairs.

8. My late father, trained in economics and a World War II veteran with hawkish tendencies, was truly bewildered by public opinion that favored the war. "Is this thing really worth the lives of our children?" he would ask angry neighbors in rural Indiana. My older brother drew a high number in the draft. Many of his schoolmates were less fortunate.

9. The rural Hmong of southeastern Asia had fought with the Americans against the Viet Cong. As result, after the war they were forced to flee for their lives. American religious philanthropy facilitated their immigration, particularly in Wisconsin and Minnesota,

10. Thatcher had first been elected to Parliament in 1959.

11. Interestingly, one of Heath's more influential professors at university had been the British social democratic philosopher A.D. (Sandie) Lindsay (1879–1952). Lindsay held the chair of Moral Philosophy at the University of Glasgow, the same position occupied by Smith during the 1750s. Both Heath and Lindsay had also been at Oxford University, where Smith's experience was far less happy (see Chapter 10).

12. Attorney and future Founding Father John Adams defended at trial the British troops accused of murder, successfully having the conviction reduced to manslaughter for those who pulled the trigger, by emphasizing the uncertain threat they faced in the heat of the moment. The American public, however, more retained sensationalist images of propaganda concocted by Paul Revere.

13. *WN*, V.I, Part III, Article 2nd, 978.
14. *WN*, III.II, 491–492.
15. *WN*, V.I, Part III, Article 2nd, 977.
16. *WN*, V.I, Part III, Article 2nd, 991.
17. *WN*, V.I, Part III, Article 2nd, 987.
18. *WN*, V.I, Part III, Article 2nd, 994.
19. *WN*, I.V, Part II, 174–175.
20. *WN*, IV.I, 553.
21. *WN*, IV.I, 553–554.
22. *WN*, V.III, 1208.
23. Friedman, *Capitalism and Freedom*, Chapter VIII.

24. *Ibid.*, Chapter XIII.
25. More precisely, Smith is said to have replied "There is a great deal of ruin in a nation." Making allowance for several valid interpretations, Smith seemed to be hinting that military defeat abroad was the least of Great Britain's problems at the moment. More pressing internal problems, such as the mercantilist system and the undue influence it exerted over Parliament, had been the great theme of Smith's *WN*, published the previous year in 1776.
26. See http://www.nytimes.com/2006/04/30/obituaries/30galbraith.html?pagewanted=all&_r=0.
27. Galbraith makes reference in this work to the concept of vertical integration, i.e., industries taking over ownership of their suppliers for the sake of efficiency. This method of production had been more or less perfected by Andrew Carnegie during the 19th century (see Chapter 8), and then later adopted by leading captains of industry such as Henry Ford (see Chapter 13).
28. Roosevelt University (named in honor of FDR) sponsored the Walter Heller International Finance Lecture, whose attendees that day included Mayor Richard J. Daley (1902–1976).
29. See http://www.margaretthatcher.org/document/102465.
30. In his *New Industrial State* (Oxford & IBH, 1967), Galbraith unconvincingly wrote that "no traveler of predominantly artistic interest ever visits an industrial city and he visits very few of any kind which owe their distinction to architecture and urban design postdating the publication of Adam Smith's *Wealth of Nations* in 1776" (p. 349). Modern foreign tourists visiting U.S. industrial urban centers such as Chicago specifically to view Mies' modern skyscraper designs would seem to refute that claim.
31. The Chicago Loop Station Post Office was completed in 1973, four years after Mies' death. On paper, he is said to have considered it his favorite building. The finished reality lives up to the inspired conception.
32. Calder's grandfather, the sculptor Alexander Milne Calder, was born in Scotland circa 1846.

Chapter 16

1. *WN*, V.II, Part II, Article 2nd, 1084–1085.
2. Three years later in 1990, *Bonfire* was unfortunately converted into a not-so-critically-acclaimed and a not-so-commercially successful film. "It's morning again in America" was a phrase popularized by President Reagan during a campaign advert lauding economic recovery in 1984.
3. The ITC is a good concept whenever used with surgical discipline and strict regulatory oversight, as opposed to *carte blanch*.
4. Belatedly, Carter was awarded a Nobel Peace Prize in 2002 for this and other numerous accomplishments. In contrast to the dismal economic performance of his administration, Carter's Habitat for Humanity has proven a consistent source of constructive good works over the last four decades.
5. In addition to the cash savings of innocent account holders being wiped out by the 1987 S&L crisis, many prominent politicians had their careers ended with criminal convictions tied to the scandal, perhaps most notoriously, the "Keating Five" of the U.S. Senate.
6. From a Bush Senior speech given on April 10, 1980.
7. Thatcher had defeated in 1979 the Labour Party Prime Minister James Callaghan (1912–2005), whose personal initials, like Jimmy Carter's, curiously were "J.C.".
8. "Whole chapters seem to have been put through the forge afresh" wrote Rae. Smith's later rewrite was attested to by David Hume in a 1776 letter to Smith. See Rae, XVII.2.
9. Rae states that Smith and Franklin had known each other as early as 1759 during Smith's visit to Edinburgh. See Rae, XVII.2.
10. Rae, XVII.3–4. Wedderburn was also a patron to Smith (see Chapter 2), placing his relations with Franklin in a complicated position.
11. *WN*, V.III, 1190.
12. *WN*, V.II, Part II, Article 1st, 1068.
13. Earlier, Smith lays down his four principles or "maxims" of taxation: "equality"; "certainty"; "convenience of payment"; and "economy in collection." See *WN*, V.II, Part II "Of Taxes."
14. *WN*, IV.VIII, 839.
15. *WN*, I.II, 901–902.
16. *WN*, I.II, 902.
17. Galbraith, *Annals of an Abiding Liberal* (Houghton Mifflin, 1979), 89.
18. *Ibid.*, 86, 89–91, 96–98.
19. *Ibid.*, 95.
20. *Ibid.*, 102.
21. Voltaire's *Candide* was published in 1759, the same year as Smith's *The Theory of Moral Sentiments*.
22. Say's supply-side ideas became widely known as "Say's Law." Popularization of the phrase "build it and they will come" is traceable to the 1982 baseball novel by W.P. Kinsella,

Shoeless Joe, in which an inner voice tells the hero, "If you build it, he will come." This was quickly seized upon and bowdlerized by the real estate industry, among others. The novel was subsequently made into a popular film, *Field of Dreams* (1989).

23. For Goodman's obituary, see http://variety.com/2014/tv/people-news/journalist-george-goodman-pbs-adam-smith-dies-at-83-1201025134/.

24. The Adam Smith necktie reportedly first appeared in Scotland during the early 1960s, although it did not achieve widespread prominence before becoming popular in American conservative political circles during the early 1980s.

25. Volcker's controversial term as Fed Chairman was recounted in journalist William Greider's excellent exposé, *Secrets of the Temple: How the Federal Reserve Runs the Country* (Simon & Schuster, 1987).

26. The text of Lawson's address appeared soon afterwards in *Standpoint* (January/February 2011).

27. Ibid.

28. Galbraith, *Economics and the Public Purpose* (Houghton Mifflin, 1973), 61.

Chapter 17

1. *WN*, IV.VII, Part II, 722.

2. Carville made the phrase a top bullet point for Clinton campaign workers in 1992.

3. Bush Senior, no doubt with the hard lesson of Vietnam in the back of his mind, was careful to conduct the first Gulf War in a completely different fashion. In addition to being short and relatively inexpensive, the campaign was conducted in tandem with a strong international coalition of allies, including other Arab states, and only after extreme provocation by Iraqi dictator Saddam Hussein. He also sensibly avoided any pretenses of total conquest or new nation building.

4. Hillary Rodham Clinton would go on to have her own political career as a highly effective U.S. Senator for New York state and globetrotting Secretary of State. She is currently a rumored Democratic Presidential candidate for 2016.

5. On a state level, however, the Republicans scored an important triumph when Bush Senior's son George W. defeated incumbent Anne Richards for Governor of Texas in 1994. Eight years later, Bush Junior would move into the White House, though not without considerable electoral controversy.

6. Ireland's prosperity turned, almost as quickly, into hardship during the economic downturn of 2007–2008 (see Chapter 18); nevertheless, its membership in the German-dominated E.U. certainly helped to blunt the impact of this downturn on the Irish economy.

7. Traditionally, the four economic "Asian Tigers" have referred to Hong Kong, Singapore, Taiwan, and South Korea.

8. Currie's most famous work was the first biography of Robert Burns, published in 1800.

9. Rae, XIV.25.

10. *TMS*, III.I.56.

11. *WN*, IV.IX, 864.

12. Smith also criticizes prevailing interest rates of 12 percent then prevalent in China as being unnecessarily too high and counterproductive to growth. See *WN*, I.IX, 133.

13. *WN*, IV.III, Part II, 615.

14. Smith wrote: "According to the natural course of things, therefore, the greater part of the capital of every growing society is, first, directed to agriculture, afterwards to manufacturing, and last of all to foreign commerce. This order of things is so very natural, that in every society that had any territory, it has always, I believe, been in some degree observed." See *WN*, III.I, 486.

15. *TMS*, VI.II.30.

16. *WN*, IV.VIII, Part III 779–780. See also *WN*, IV.VII, 739, 741.

17. *WN*, I.XI, Part II, 339.

18. Ibid.

19. Galbraith, John Kenneth, *Culture of Contentment* (Houghton Mifflin, 1992), 99.

20. Friedman, Milton, *Two Lucky People* (University of Chicago Press, 1998), 262–263.

21. *WN*, Introduction by Robert Reich (Modern Library, 2000), xv.

22. Ibid., xx.

23. See http://www.johnmajor.co.uk/page1179.html.

24. Major's use of public education as an example is especially misleading, since education was specifically cited by Smith as a service that should be publicly supported rather than completely privatized.

25. Rae, VII.17.

26. The Getty is often cited as America's richest museum—by far, in fact. See http://online.barrons.com/articles/billionaire-art-museums-1417230557. LACMA is frequently listed as the largest museum in the western United States. It recently received a whopping $500 million private donation. See http://www.latimes.com/entertainment/arts/museums/la-et-cm-lacma-donate-20141105-story.html#page=1.

27. According to Rae, Smith researched the

history of Roman colonial rebellions for comparison to events then transpiring in the British American colonies. See Rae, XV.5–6.

28. See *Essays*, 176–213.

29. In the landmark decision of *Bush v. Gore* (2000), the U.S. Supreme Court halted highly disputed voter recounts in Florida, upon which Presidential victory in the Electoral College depended.

30. The Japanese attack on Pearl Harbor in 1941, often cited in comparison to the 9-11 attacks, was a one-time affair not applicable to North America, although many residents of the western U.S. coast afterwards lived in fear of Japanese invasion.

Chapter 18

1. Smith, Adam, *Essays*, 49.

2. Thatcher, Margaret, *Statecraft: Strategies for a Changing World* (Harper Collins, 2002), 412.

3. *Ibid.*, 415.

4. In contrast to widespread criticism of France, American reaction to German skepticism towards U.S. military operations in the Middle East was curiously muted. By this time, Germany had far superseded France on the world economic stage, and possibly Great Britain as well. The shift had prompted one prominent economist, Richard Wolff, to assert that Germany had achieved through international trade what Hitler had earlier attempted and failed to accomplish through military force, namely, dominance of Europe and beyond. See Chomsky, Noam, *Power Systems* (Metropolitan Books, 2013), 88.

5. See http://www.nytimes.com/2004/04/03/news/03iht-globalist_ed3_.html.

6. See http://www.washingtonpost.com/blogs/monkey-cage/wp/2014/09/13/what-would-adam-smith-say-about-scottish-independence/. See also http://www.npr.org/blogs/parallels/2014/09/16/348782242/will-scotland-vote-to-cut-the-cord.

7. There is no indication that Smith was a golfer or even much of a sportsman; nevertheless, he would have surely been aware of the game. The ubiquitous St. Andrews Golf Club was officially founded in 1754 while Smith was a professor in Glasgow. The historic Musselburgh Links had been in recorded usage since the 17th century. Both locations are not far from Edinburgh.

8. *TMS*, VI.II.45.

9. In a very similar passage from *TMS* (III.I.40), Smith expounds at length on the afterlife,

acknowledging its many attractions without giving the concept any express endorsement or dismissal. He merely acknowledges that belief in the afterlife makes us happier than we would otherwise be.

10. Coincidentally, Newton was buried at Westminster Abbey in 1727, around the same time that the approximately three-year-old Smith was temporarily abducted by gypsies near Kirkcaldy.

11. Newton was himself viewed as having unorthodox religious beliefs, for which he was probably admired all the more by Smith.

12. Smith, Adam, *Essays*, 92.

13. Rae, XXIV.4.

14. With respect to the pending murder of Banquo, Macbeth sinisterly hopes that the "invisible hand" of nighttime will conceal his anticipated deed. Rothschild underscores that prior usage of the phrase in English rarely or never had a reverential or benevolent connotation, and that Smith would mostly likely be following suit in this regard. All three recorded instances of his usage present strong arguments against any one-dimensional interpretations, which unfortunately later became the norm.

15. See http://www.theguardian.com/education/2002/dec/20/highereducation.uk1.

16. In 2005, one of Bush's former professors at Harvard alleged that the future President held extreme economic views very early on. See http://billtotten.blogspot.com/2005/03/adam-smith-would-decry-president-bushs.html.

17. See http://www.nytimes.com/2010/01/31/opinion/31volcker.html?pagewanted=all&_r=0.

18. No one within the banking industry was even prosecuted. Only a few over-compensated middle men in the stock market (such as Bernard Madoff) went to jail, possibly not so much for their heinous acts as for overcharging their illicit services. They also made convenient media symbols.

19. See http://opinionator.blogs.nytimes.com/2012/10/21/sleight-of-the-invisible-hand/.

20. See http://ipr.cua.edu/blogs/post.cfm/paul-ryan-s-adam-smith-problem.

21. Blair, despite being on the opposite side of the political aisle from his predecessor John Major, was frequently praised by the political opposition for his frequent borrowings of Conservative Party policies. Like Major and Thatcher before him, Blair was known to turn occasionally towards the Libertarian Adam Smith Institute (see Chapter 17) for economic policy input.

22. See http://www.thecourier.co.uk/news/politics/how-kirkcaldy-helped-gordon-brown-on-path-to-downing-street-1.99782.

23. See http://www.dailyrecord.co.uk/news/politics/independence-referendum-alex-salmond-accuses-4263058. Salmond was paraphrasing Smith's from *WN*, I.VIII, 110–111 (see Chapter 7).

24. One World Trade Center is also currently ranked as the fourth tallest building in the world.

25. For various criticisms of the entire project and process, see http://www.theguardian.com/cities/2014/sep/08/-sp-one-world-trade-center-new-york-rebuild-ground-zero-twin-towers; see also http://www.nytimes.com/2014/11/30/nyregion/is-one-world-trade-center-rises-in-lower-manhattan-a-design-success.html. Before 9-11, most New Yorkers had been even more aesthetically critical of the old twin towers.

26. By way of contrast, this writer flew into Reagan International Airport near Washington, D.C., on a clear day in October 2001, observing from the air that recent damage repair to the Pentagon was rapidly nearing completion. This was approximately one month after the 9-11 terrorist attacks.

Summary

1. *WN*, I.XI, Part III, 338.
2. O'Rourke, 133.
3. By way of contrast, Smith in *WN* marvels at the size, prosperity, and resilience of Portuguese Brazil in South America. See *WN*, IV.VII, Part II, 720–721.
4. Benjamin Franklin, the Founding Father who may well have introduced the American Revolution to Smith (see Chapter 1), is a case in point. Franklin's own family was permanently split over independence, and Franklin himself is known to have favored continued union with Great Britain as late as 1774. Moreover, even highly committed revolutionaries such as Thomas Jefferson were known to later acknowledge that early on, the struggle could have easily gone either way.
5. Smith, it clearly appears from *WN*, also favored representative union as a solution to political discord, though not to be militarily enforced without a serious cost-benefit analysis.

6. Noam Chomsky characterized Smith, perhaps most accurately of all, as "an old-fashioned conservative" with "moral values," as opposed to "what's called conservativism now." See Chomsky, Noam, *Power Systems* (Metropolitan Books, 2013), 9.

7. To be more precise, Smith states that there appears to be a far greater spread of difference between various dog breeds versus different classes of humankind. See *WN*, I.II, 22, 26.

8. *WN*, I.II, 25–26.

9. This is not a new problem, though one that seems to be getting worse as time goes along. One is reminded of the anecdote from the Roman historian Suetonius, in which the emperor Vespasian was presented with a brilliant engineering scheme to save labor costs on public works. Vespasian declined the offer, gave the engineer a small reward, and explained that the common people must be kept employed, even sometimes at the price of inefficiency, for the sake of continued, overall social stability.

10. *WN*, I.VIII, 94. This same passage was quoted by J.K. Galbraith in *The Affluent Society* (Houghton Mifflin, 1958), 21.

11. *WN*, V.I, Part II, 907.

12. Not counting footnotes, Piketty mentions Smith once; Moretti, not at all.

13. In *TMS*, Smith memorably portrays a similar phenomenon, probably making allusion to the Jacobite uprising recently suppressed in his homeland during the previous decade. Chosen representatives, after repeatedly pandering to the prejudices and misconceptions of their constituents, begin to believe these fallacies themselves or become, as Smith phrases it, "dupes of their own sophistry" (VI.II.40); by way of contrast, the "good citizen" for Smith is respectful of government institutions and seeks "to promote, by every means in his power, the welfare of the whole society of his fellow-citizens" (VI.II.36).

14. See http://www.neh.gov/about/awards/jefferson-lecture/david-mccullough-interview. McCullough's next work was the award-winning *1776* (2005). *John Adams* was subsequently made into an award-winning television series by HBO in 2008.

15. Generally attributed to George Santayana (1863–1952).

Selected Bibliography

Buchan, James. *The Authentic Adam Smith: His Life and Ideas*. W.W. Norton, 2006.
Kennedy, Gavin. *Adam Smith's Lost Legacy*. Palgrave Macmillan, 2005.
O'Rourke, P.J. *On The Wealth of Nations*. Atlantic Monthly Press, 2007.
Phillipson, Nicholas. *Adam Smith: An Enlightened Life*. Yale University Press, 2012.
Rae, John. *Life of Adam Smith*, with Introduction by Jacob Vinver. Augustus M. Kelly, 1895/1965.
    Also available at http://www.econlib.org/library/YPDBooks/Rae/raeLS.html.
Ross, Ian Simpson. *Life of Adam Smith*, 2nd ed. Oxford University Press, 2010.
Skinner, A.S., and T. Wilson, eds. *Essays on Adam Smith*. Oxford University Press, 1976.
Smith, Adam. *The Correspondence of Adam Smith*. E.C. Mossner, and I.R. Simpson, eds. Clarendon Press, 1977.
_____. *Essays on Philosophical Subjects*. W.P.D. Wightman, and J.C. Bryce, eds. With Dugald Stewart's "Account of the Life and Writings of Adam Smith." I.S. Ross, ed. D.D. Raphael, and A.S. Skinner, general editors. Clarendon Press, 1980.
_____. *An Inquiry into the Nature and Causes of the Wealth of Nations*. R.H. Campbell, and A.S. Skinner, eds. W.B. Todd, textual editor. Liberty Fund, 1981.
_____. *Lectures on Jurisprudence*. D.D. Raphael and P.G. Stein, eds. Oxford University Press, 2007.
_____. *Lectures on Rhetoric and Belles Lettres*. J.C. Bryce, ed. Liberty Fund, 2009.
_____. *The Theory of Moral Sentiments*. D.D. Raphael, and A.S. Skinner, eds. Liberty Fund, 2009.
_____. *The Wealth of Nations*. Introduction by Alan B. Krueger. Bantam Classic, 2003.

Index

Adams, Abagail 34, 216
Adams, Charles Francis 68, 74
Adams, John 3, 17, 35, 41, 68, 74, 226
Adams, John Quincy 50, 74
Adams, Samuel 17
Addington, Henry 216
Akins, Charmian 213
Alexander the Great 3, 84
Alexander II, Czar 68, 70, 219
Andropov, Yuri 179
Armstrong, Karen 220
Arnold, Benedict 14
Arthur, Chester 92
Asante, Amma 217
Asinof, Eliot 222
Asquith, H.H. 127
Attlee, Clement 156
Atwater, Catherine 161
Atwater, Lee 184

Baldwin, Stanley 133, 144
Ballou, Adin 66
Bascom, John 119
Baum, Lyman Frank 92
Belle, Elizabeth Dido 217
Bellew, Frank 87
Benet, Stephen Vincent 221
Bentham, Jeremy 43, 116
Berlin, Ira 69
Biddle, Nicholas 50, 54
Billings, Hammatt 76
Bismarck, Otto von 80, 86, 91
Black, Joseph 49
Blair, Tony 187, 203, 229
Bland, Richard 215
Boesky, Ivan 183
Bonaparte, Napoleon 33, 36, 44
Boswell, James 27–29, 116, 134, 169, 199, 215, 213
Brenner, Yul 216
Brezhnev, Leonid 179
Brougham, Henry Peter 52–53, 106, 118, 217

Brown, Gordon 203
Brown, John 70
Bryan, William Jennings 104, 107, 109, 138, 221
Buchan, James 2, 5, 202
Buchanan, James 67, 155
Buckle, Henry Thomas 4
Buckley, Daniel 155
Burke, Edmund 18, 30, 34
Burns, Ken 224
Burns, Robert 42, 217, 228
Burr, Aaron 25, 35, 46, 217
Bush, George H.W. 177, 184–185, 195, 227–228
Bush, George W. 184, 195, 197, 202, 228–229

Cairncross, Frances 218
Calder, Alexander 227
Calhoun, John C. 46, 217
Callaghan, James 227
Cameron, David 204
Carey, Henry Charles 75, 8687, 91, 97, 108, 115, 132, 219–220
Carlyle, Thomas 213
Carnegie, Andrew 93, 95–97, 103, 105, 221–222, 227
Carroll, Lewis 213
Carter, Jimmy 177, 179, 185, 227
Carville, James 185, 228
Chamberlain, Neville 144
Chase, Salmon P. 74–75
Chernenko, Konstantin 179
Childs, David 204
Chomsky, Noam 4, 213, 230
Christy, Howard Chandler 128–129
Chrysippus 190
Churchill, Winston 102, 128, 133, 137, 144, 148, 155, 167, 223, 225
Clay, Henry (academic) 159–160
Clay, Henry (senator) 51–52, 54, 58–59, 66, 217–218
Cleveland, Grover 92, 103, 107, 220

233

234 Index

Clinton, Bill 185–187, 191–192, 194, 228
Clinton, Hillary Rodham 180, 228
Cobden, Richard 64–65, 218
Cody, William "Buffalo Bill" 97–99, 221
Coffin, Frederick M. 76
Commodus 152
Condorcet, Marquis de 201
Coolidge, Calvin 131, 140
Cooper, Grey 26
Cornwallis, Charles 23
Crockett, Davy 217
Cumberland, Duke of 38
Currie, James 189, 228
Custer, George Armstrong 80, 98
Czolgosz, Frank 222

Dahlberg-Acton, John Edward 95–96, 161, 221
Daley, Richard J. 227
Dalrymple, Louis 109
Darwin, Charles 183
Davila, Enrico Caterino 216
Dawe, Philip 20
Defoe, Daniel 5
Delacroix, Eugène 129, 223
DeMille, Cecil B. 37, 216
Dew, Thomas Roderick 52, 217
Dewey, George 102, 109, 221
Dewey, John 155
Dickens, Charles 7, 58–59, 65–66, 68–70, 81, 84, 91, 207
Diogenes of Sinope 3, 84
Disraeli, Benjamin 80, 84–86, 128
Dixon, Jeremiah 217
Domitian 152
Douglas, David 215
Douglas, Michael 183–184
Douglas, Stephen 66, 70
Douglass, Frederick 75–77
Drew, Mary Gladstone 95
Dryden, John 213
Dukakis, Michael 184

Eccles, Marriner Stoddard 148–149, 225
Edward VII, King 109, 111–112
Edward VIII, King 155
Ehrhardt, S.D. 109
Eisenhower, Dwight 154, 163, 165–166, 173, 178, 225–226
Elizabeth II, Queen 155
Elwes, John 65
Ely, Richard T. 127, 223
Epictetus 190
Euripides 3, 95, 98

Fall, Albert 131
Fillmore, Millard 67, 219
Fish, Anne Harriet 138–139

Fitzgerald, F. Scott 138
Ford, Edsel 150
Ford, Gerald 166
Ford, Henry 150, 227
Ford, John 97
Forrest, Nathan Bedford 79, 87–88, 220
Fox, James 27
Frankfurter, Felix 225
Franklin, Benjamin 2, 14, 17–18, 20, 25–26, 31–32, 179–180, 214–215, 227, 230
Friedman, David 171
Friedman, Milton 170, 172, 181–182, 191–192, 201–202
Friedman, Rose Director 171

Galbraith, James K. 161
Galbraith, John Kenneth 161, 171–172, 181, 184, 191–192, 196, 201–202, 227
Gandhi, Mahatma 155
Garfield, James 92, 220
Garrick, David 93, 220
Gates, Horatio 14
George, David Lloyd 127
George, Henry 108, 127
George II, King 156, 194
George III, King 13
George V, King 112
George VI, King 155
Gibbon, Edward 18, 116, 152–153, 188, 225
Gladstone, William Ewart 80, 84–86, 95, 101
Goodman, George 182, 228
Gorbachev, Mikhail 179
Gore, Al 195
Grant, Ulysses S. 54, 64, 71, 80, 86, 92, 191, 218–220
Greene, Catherine 217
Greene, Nathaniel 217
Griffith, D.W. 219

Hamilton, Alexander 17, 25–26, 31–32, 34–36, 40–43, 46, 50, 65, 67, 97, 216–217
Hammond, James Henry 219
Harding, Warren G. 122, 130–132, 140–141, 164, 223
Harrison, Benjamin 92, 220
Harrison, William Henry 51, 58–59, 216, 218, 220
Hay, John 102
Hayek, Friedrich 159–160, 172, 225–226
Hayes, Rutherford B. 92
Heath, Edward 167, 226
Henry IV, King 15
Herndon, Billy 74
Hindenburg, Paul von 133
Hirohito 133
Hirst, Francis Wrigley 118–119, 225
Hitler, Adolf 155, 173, 229

Index

Hobart, Garret 109
Hogarth, William 20
Hoover, Herbert 132, 137–138, 140, 224
Hopkins, Harry 149
Horne, George 28
Horton, Willie 184
Houston, Sam 55
Hume, David 2, 17–19, 27–29, 72, 116, 179, 189, 199–201, 213, 215, 227
Hussein, Saddam 228
Hutcheson, Francis 62, 92, 104–105, 116, 134, 156, 161, 215, 220

Jackson, Andrew 34, 37–38, 46, 49–52, 54–55, 59, 61, 74, 217
Jay, John 217
Jefferson, Thomas 17, 20, 24–25, 30–31, 34–37, 41, 43, 50, 215–216, 230
Johnson, Andrew 80
Johnson, Lyndon B. 165, 172, 178, 226
Johnson, Samuel 27–29, 41, 118, 134, 169, 215, 223
Jones, John Paul 29, 215

Kay, John 30
Kennedy, Gavin 202
Kennedy, John F. 164–165, 171, 175, 186, 226
Kennedy, Robert F. 165
Kent, James 216
Kerry, John 197
Key, Francis Scott 216
Keynes, John Maynard 90, 106, 122, 133, 147–148, 155–156, 159–162, 170, 172, 183, 221, 225
King, Martin Luther, Jr. 165, 226
Kinsella, W.P. 227
Kornbluth, Jacob 192
Krueger, Alan 116
Krugman, Paul 221

Lafayette, Marquise de 214
Lafitte, Jean 37–38, 43, 216
La Follette, Doug 222
La Follette, Robert "Fighting Bob" 118–119, 222–223
Lamb, William 150
Lang, Fritz 151
Lange, Dorothea 150
Law, John 145, 178, 203, 224
Lawson, Nigel 183, 228
Lebeskind, Daniel 204
Lee, Arthur 48
Lee, Robert E. 64
Leech, John 65
LeHand, Missy 143
Lincoln, Abraham 53–54, 65, 70, 75, 78, 112, 175, 217, 219

Lindsay, A.D. (Sandie) 226
List, Friedrich 86, 91
Louis Napoleon 80
Louis XV, King 144
Louis XVI, King 33

MacArthur, Douglas 141
MacDonald, James Ramsay 137, 144, 224
Madison, Dolly 217
Madison, James 17, 24–25, 31, 36–37, 50, 58, 217
Madoff, Bernard 229
Major, John 187, 193, 228–229
Malcolm, John 20
Malthus, Thomas Robert 52, 65
March, Fredric 216
Margolyes, Miriam 58
Marie Antoinette, Queen 33
Marshall, Alfred 90–91, 105, 122, 148
Marshall, George C. 154, 225
Marshall, Mary Paley 90, 220
Marx, Karl 81, 84–86, 91, 96, 181, 207, 220
Mason, Charles 217
Maurivaux, Pierre de 190
McCarthy, Joseph 160, 225–226
McCullough, David 211, 230
McKinley, William 51, 104, 107–109, 222
McLaren, William Gardner 160
M'Clung, Alexander K. 51
McQueen, Steve 69, 77
Mellon, Andrew 138, 140
Melville, Herman 7, 100–101, 221
Mercer, Lucy 143
Mies van der Rohe, Ludwig 173, 227
Mill, John Stuart 52
Millar, David 92
Milne, Alexander 227
Monroe, James 50
Montgomery, George 160, 226
More, Thomas 175, 180
Moretti, Enrico 209, 230
Morgan, J.P. 114
Morgenthau, Henry 143, 149
Morley, John 118, 221
Murray, William 217
Mussolini, Benito 161

Napoleon Bonaparte 33, 36, 44
Nast, Thomas 55, 87
Nast, Condé 138–139
Newton, Isaac 200, 229
Nicholas I, Czar 69–70
Nixon, Richard 63, 165–167, 188
North, Frederick 12, 26, 214
Northrup, Solomon 69, 75–76

Oakley, Annie 97
Obama, Barak 197, 202

O'Donnel, Bridget 66
O'Rourke, P.J. 3–4, 140, 202, 207, 224
Orr, Nathaniel 76
O'Sullivan, John L. 61
Otway, Thomas 95

Paine, Thomas 33–34, 215
Paley, William 220
Paolozzi, Eduardo 161–162, 226
Peel, Robert 63–65
Perkins, Francis 143, 224
Petty, William 27, 215
Phillipson, Nicholas 202
Pierce, Franklin 67, 218
Piketty, Thomas 209, 230
Pitt the Elder, William 22
Pitt the Younger, William 27, 42, 52, 160, 216
Plutarch 3, 60
Polk, James K. 61, 64, 74
Pope, Alexander 41
Pullman, George 103

Quesnay, Françoise 2, 13, 15, 144–145, 224
Quinn, Anthony 216

Racine, Jean 95, 190
Rae, John (biographer) 7, 106–107, 116, 118, 179, 189, 217, 221, 227–228
Rae, John (economist) 221–222
Randolph, Thomas Mann 215
Reagan, Ronald 175–179, 181–186, 196, 227
Reich, Robert 192
Revere, Paul 226
Ricardo, David 43
Riccoboni, Marie-Jean 189–190
Richards, Anne 228
Richardson, Samuel 189–190
Rivera, Diego 150–151
Robinson, H.R. 55
Rochambeau, Comte de 23
Rockefeller, John D. 114
Rodgers & Hammerstein 68
Romney, Mitt 203
Rongji, Zhu 188
Roosevelt, Eleanor 113, 121, 143, 151, 154
Roosevelt, Franklin Delano 113–114, 121–122, 141, 143–144, 146–147, 153, 155, 178, 198, 225, 227
Roosevelt, Sara Delano 142–143, 225
Roosevelt, Theodore 8, 102, 109–115, 118–121, 130–132, 140–141, 146–147, 165, 222
Ross, Ian Simpson 202
Rothschild, Emma Georgina 201, 229
Ruth, Babe 132
Ryan, Paul 203

Salmond, Alex 204
Santayana, George 211, 230
Say, Jean Baptiste 182, 227
Schwartz, Anna J. 170
Scott, Henry 13, 214
Scott, Walter 29, 215
Scott, Winfield 71
Scroggie, Ebenezer 59, 65, 218
Selkirk, Earl of 215
Shakespeare, William 5, 41, 86, 95, 109, 201, 213, 215, 229
Shaw, George Bernard 106, 221
Shays, Daniel 23–24
Sherman, John 222
Sherman, William Tecumseh 54, 218, 222
Sitting Bull, Chief 97, 99
Sloane, Hans 194
Smith, Adam agriculture and manufacturing 71–72; alcoholic beverages 134–136; Battle of Culloden 38–39; Benjamin Franklin 17–18, 179; childhood abduction 46–47; François Quesnay 144–145; French travels 2, 14–15; Glasgow student days 156; Irish influences 14–15; London literary circles 27–29; Oxford University 115–116; precious metals 104–105; religious beliefs 198–200; return to Kirkaldy 167–168; romantic interests 188–189; Seven Years War 123; as a teacher 208; theatrical interests 93
Smith, Jean Edward 224
Smith, Margaret Douglas 30, 93
Socrates 27
Solon 60
Sophocles 3, 95, 98
Stewart, Dugald 43, 52, 73–74, 93, 106, 115, 118, 189, 213, 215–217, 225
Stiglitz, Joseph 201
Stone, Oliver 183
Stowe, Harriet Beecher 68–69, 75–77
Strahan, William 27
Stuart, Charles Edward 38, 41
Suckley, Daisy 143
Suetonius 230
Swift, Jonathan 5, 62, 69, 134, 213

Taft, William 113, 119–120
Taney, Roger B. 75
Tassie, James 30
Taylor, Zachary 67, 218
Tecumseh, Chief 216
Temple, John Henry 70, 73–74
Thatcher, Margaret 167, 172–173, 178, 183, 191, 196, 198, 210, 226–227, 229
Tirole, Jean 223
Tocqueville, Alexis de 53–54, 58, 69–70, 217
Tomasi di Lampedusa, Giuseppe 214

Townsend, Charles 13–14
Truman, Harry 153–155, 225
Tuttle, Allen 225
Twain, Mark 1, 9, 97, 119, 213, 220, 223
Tyler, John 51, 58

Valentiner, William 150
Van Buren, Martin 51, 55, 74, 217
Vespasian 230
Victoria, Queen 55, 73, 85, 90, 98, 109
Viner, Jacob 221
Volcker, Paul 177, 182, 202, 228
Voltaire 41, 95, 182, 190, 208

Walker, Robert J. 64–65, 218
Walpole, Robert 156
Warhol, Andy 162
Warner, Charles Dudley 127, 223
Washington, George 2, 14, 17, 20, 23–26, 31, 34–35, 41, 123, 214–216
Watkins, Sam 71, 219
Watt, James 49, 88, 193

Wayland, Francis 75
Webb, Martha Beatrice Potter 105–106, 108, 118, 201, 221
Webb, Sidney 221
Webster, Daniel 51–52, 54, 218
Wedderburn, Alexander 26, 179
Whitney, Eli 45, 216–217
Wilberforce, William 52
Wilhelm II, Kaiser 91, 98, 221
Wilson, Harold 167
Wilson, Woodrow 52, 113–115, 122–123, 126–127, 142, 153, 223
Wolfe, Tom 175, 184
Wolff, Richard 229

Xiaoping, Deng 188

Yellow Hair 98
Young, Brigham 66

Zemin, Jiang 188
Zeno 190